Revitalizing Congregational Life:
A Synagogue 2000 Series

Becoming a Congregation of Learners

Learning as a Key to Revitalizing
Congregational Life

Isa Aron, Ph.D.

Director, the Experiment in Congregational Education (ECE),
a project of the Rhea Hirsch School of Education,
Hebrew Union College–Jewish Institute of Religion

Foreword by

Rabbi Lawrence A. Hoffman

Co-Developer, Synagogue 2000

JEWISH LIGHTS P[...]

WOODSTOCK, V[...]

D1057564

Becoming a Congregation of Learners: Learning as a Key to Revitalizing Congregational Life

Grateful acknowledgment is given for permission to use the following material:

Excerpts from *The Dance of Change: The Challenges to Sustaining Momentum in Learning Organizations* by Peter Senge, et al. and *The Fifth Discipline: The Art and Practice of the Learning Organization* by Peter Senge are reprinted by permission of Doubleday, a division of Random House, Inc.

Excerpt from *Finding a Spiritual Home: How a New Generation of Jews Can Transform the American Synagogue* by Sidney Schwarz, copyright ©2000 by Sidney Schwarz is reprinted by permission of Jossey-Bass, Inc., a subsidiary of John Wiley & Sons, Inc.

Library of Congress Cataloging-in-Publication Data
Aron, Isa.
   Becoming a congregation of learners : learning as a key to revitalizing congre-
      gational life / Isa Aron ; foreword by Lawrence A. Hoffman.
        p.   cm. — (Revitalizing congregational life)
      ISBN 1-58023-089-X
      1. Jewish religious education—United States. 2. Synagogues—United
   States. I. Hoffman, Lawrence A., 1942– . II. Title. III. Series.
   BM75 .A76 2000
   296.6'8—dc21   00-010988

10 9 8 7 6 5 4 3 2 1

Manufactured in the United States of America

Cover design: Lisa Buckley
Text design: Chelsea Cloeter

Published by Jewish Lights Publishing
A Division of LongHill Partners, Inc.
Sunset Farm Offices, Route 4, P.O. Box 237
Woodstock, Vermont 05091
Tel: (802) 457-4000   Fax: (802) 457-4004
www.jewishlights.com

To my parents,
Moshe *(z"l)* and Sylvia Ettenberg,
exemplary Jewish teachers
who shaped my earliest experiences of Jewish learning

This book is the product of the work done by the Experiment in Congregational Education (ECE), a project of the Rhea Hirsch School of Education, Hebrew Union College–Jewish Institute of Religion, Los Angeles.

The ECE's goal is to assist congregations to become both *congregations of learners,* in which congregants of all ages are actively engaged in learning, and *learning congregations,* incorporating reflection and deliberation into all of their activities.

CONTENTS

KEY TO SYMBOLS USED IN THIS BOOK

 Exercise

 Handout

 Text Study

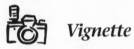 *Vignette*

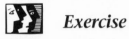 *Vision Statement*

FOREWORD

by Lawrence A. Hoffman, Co-Developer, Synagogue 2000

We take synagogues for granted, here in America. But in truth, the American neighborhood synagogue is an historical anomaly. Though synagogues abound world-wide, only here have they become such a fixture of civic life. Their ubiquitous centrality is a by-product of an eighteenth-century religious awakening that planted churches on every New England village green, and, thereafter, on every street corner, so to speak, of every American city. Still today, more than two centuries after that awakening, it is impossible to imagine America without religion at its core, or American Judaism without the synagogue at its center. To study American Judaism without noticing synagogues would be like studying American geography and missing the Rockies.

There are other Jewish institutions, to be sure: Jewish community centers, Hillel Houses on campuses, day schools, and a bewildering array of social service and Israel-oriented agencies. But none of these are essentially religious, and North American Jews are becoming more, not less, religious. If the synagogue arose because of that early religious awakening, it has the opportunity to flourish now because of another such awakening going on all around us.

The opportunity to flourish, however, is not the same as actually flourishing. Unlike business where profit is the bottom line, synagogues, as non-profit institutions, have been notoriously slow in adjusting to new conditions. If they changed at all, it was through additive change—piling new programs onto old ones with no overall synagogue vision to govern the emerging whole. By contrast, institutions that prosper in new times foster zero-based visioning, develop a mission, measure what they do by what they believe, and engage all their stakeholders in common labor toward a common goal. This approach is what we mean by transformative change, and the big news for synagogues as we move into the twenty-first century is that transformative thinking has arrived.

Synagogue 2000, the best-known champion of synagogue transformation, calls on synagogues to become moral and spiritual centers responsive to the exciting new demographic and religious realities of Jewish life. Toward that end, we present this Synagogue 2000 series: a collaborative venture by Jewish Lights Publishing and Synagogue 2000 to highlight the best practices, deepest thinking, and newest discoveries in the field of synagogue transformation. This, our first publication in the series, showcases the Experiment in Congregational Education (ECE), the first wide-scale instance of transformational thinking, and a leader still in the emerging field of synagogue change.

The ECE was born in 1992, with author Isa Aron as its director. She and her colleagues at the Rhea Hirsch School of Education, an arm of Hebrew Union College–Jewish Institute of Religion in Los Angeles that is directed by Professor Sara Lee, began work that year with two congregations who approached them for consultative help in re-imagining synagogues. A two-fold goal emerged: first, to make synagogues into congregations of learners; and second, to make them learning congregations. The second goal, to make synagogues more consciously deliberative and develop shared leadership within them, is the topic of a forthcoming volume in this series. The first goal is the topic of *Becoming a Congregation of Learners*.

The ECE modeled its own value of being a learning organization. After working first with the initial two synagogues, it then took on five more, and after that, yet a third cohort of seven congregations. At each step along the way, it adapted its program to what it was learning. *Becoming a Congregation of Learners* presents the latest stage of what is currently known about developing a congregation where learning of all sorts (formal and informal) abounds among people of all sorts (children and adults), and where learning in one way or another is woven into the very fabric of synagogue life. Dr. Aron not only explains the ECE process, but reflects on what it has taught us, and provides a hands-on guide for congregations which, on their own, want to replicate what the fourteen sample congregations have done. This is a book on theory and practice, born from eight years of experiment and discovery.

The time is especially ripe for synagogues to evolve alongside current changes in the way Americans of all faiths "do religion." Indeed, synagogue transformation is applicable to churches as well, since churches and synagogues alike are impacted by social forces rippling through the larger American landscape.

- The baby boom of the fifties and sixties, when most of our current synagogues came into being, made synagogues child-centered havens for struggling mothers in suburbs. Even if there was a "typical" family structure back then, there certainly isn't anymore. Successful synagogues now will have to reach out to single parents, Jews without children, Jews who are not married, gays and lesbians, and Jews by choice, to name but several obvious categories.

- Jews in the fifties and sixties still cared about ethnicity. Indeed, just moving into suburbs where no Jews had lived before, and where the newcomers were not always welcome, reinforced common memories of Yiddish jokes, "Jewish" food, and, as Philip Roth once put it, an "us against them" mentality. Successful synagogues now will have to speak convincingly to Jews who can just as easily leave Judaism as stay, and who have no interest whatever in the folk memories of a former generation.

● Synagogues of the fifties and sixties appealed to people for whom Jewish identity was a given. Successful synagogues now must work with a population seeking spiritual meaning and personally transformative insight from the wisdom of Jewish tradition. Ultimately, synagogue transformation depends on, and leads to, personal transformation of individuals.

This Synagogue 2000 series will explore these and other issues pertinent to the synagogue of tomorrow, in the firm belief that synagogues matter profoundly. Especially in America, Jewish continuity will stand or fall on the synagogue's ability to reinvent itself, taking from its past all that serves its present and then, thoughtfully and deliberatively, deepening the present to arrive at a yet unimagined future. Synagogue 2000 joins Jewish Lights—and in this, our first volume, the Experiment in Congregational Education—as a service to synagogues who dare to think differently; who have faith enough to face the future; who see the synagogue as the institutionalization of the covenant between God and Israel; and who believe that synagogues are poised at an historic moment in time to play out the next and finest chapter in the saga of Jewish destiny.

ACKNOWLEDGMENTS

The ideas embedded in this book were germinated, incubated, nurtured, and pruned through conversation and collaboration. Though the final formulation is my own, it is no exaggeration to say that neither the theoretical nor the practical aspects of the book could have been developed without the assistance of the following people and organizations, to whom I owe many, many thanks.

First and foremost, to my colleagues at the Rhea Hirsch School of Education (RHSOE), with whom the Experiment in Congregational Education was first conceived: Professor Sara Lee, director of the RHSOE, my mentor and colleague, who first articulated the need to work with the congregation as a whole unit, and who spent untold hours brainstorming with me; Dr. Michael Zeldin, my very close colleague at the RHSOE, whose own work on a parallel project, Jewish Day Schools for the 21st Century, served as a catalyst for many fruitful conversations; and Dr. William Cutter, who has been so generous with his time, reading my early drafts and responding with interesting and challenging comments.

I began working on this book while I was on sabbatical from teaching at the Hebrew Union College–Jewish Institute of Religion, and I would like to thank the College-Institute for affording me the luxury of a semester off from teaching. Concurrent with my writing, a tidal wave of change swept over the College-Institute itself, and I am eternally grateful to the new administration for creating the hopeful conditions that enabled me to be so optimistic about change. To Rabbi Sheldon Zimmerman, the Rosh Yeshiva; Provost Norman Cohen; Vice President Arthur Grant; and Dean of the Los Angeles campus, Dr. Lewis Barth—many, many thanks for making HUC–JIR such an interesting and supportive place to work.

Second, my gratitude to the foundations whose generous support encouraged us to imagine, plan, and implement the ECE. To the Nathan Cummings Foundation, which has been the primary funder of the project from its inception, at a conference on congregational education; to the Mandel Associated Foundations, whose original planning grant enabled us to dream, and whose subsequent gift enabled us to make that dream a reality; to the Covenant Foundation, whose early grant to the first seven ECE congregations made it possible for them to embark on a wholly untested exploration; and to the Gimprich Family Foundation, whose funding strengthened our research capability.

Though many staff and board members of these foundations were instrumental in the founding and continuation of the ECE, particular thanks are due to: Rabbi Rachel Cowan of the Cummings Foundation, who never wavered in her encouragement and support, and whose championship of groundbreaking initiatives has become legendary; Mort Mandel, whose own vision of Jewish education continues to inspire; Dr. Judith Ginsberg, Eli Evans, Dr. Jonathan Woocher, and Susan Crown, of the Covenant Foundation, who overcame their skepticism to gamble on what looked, at first, like a risky venture; and David Fishman, who shepherded our proposal through the Gimprich Family Foundation with concern and care.

The most rewarding part of the ECE has been the luxury of learning from an extraordinary staff, colleagues who have taught me most of what I know about congregational life and organizational change: consultants Rabbi Sheldon Marder, Edward Reynolds, Linda Thal, Dr. Jack Ukeles, and Dr. John Watkins; advisers Marci Dickman, Susan Huntting, Dr. Cecile

Jordan, Dr. Sam Joseph, Rabbi Amy Katz, Rabbi Randi Sheinberg, and Dr. Susan Shevitz; and researchers Dr. Laura Samuels and Dr. Diane Schuster. Roslyn Roucher, the first ECE coordinator, shared many traumas and triumphs with me. In the past three years I relied most heavily on Joy Wasserman, the ECE Coordinator, and Dr. Robert Weinberg, our senior consultant; together we perfected the art of being connected by phone, fax, and e-mail concurrently. I am happy to report that their marriage survived the many days on which each of them spent more time with me than with the other. I may not always have been the most responsive student, but they were, and are, truly master teachers.

The outcome of any human experiment depends on the quality of its "subjects," and the ECE is no exception. We had the good fortune to work with a remarkable group of congregations, led by a remarkable group of lay and professional leaders, who brought great courage and commitment to this journey into uncharted territory. That the journey was so rewarding is a testament to their wisdom and resourcefulness. The list of active ECE participants at these congregations is too long to enumerate, so I will simply thank the educators, rabbis, and many committed lay leaders at the following congregations: Congregation Beth Am, Los Altos Hills, California; Congregation Har Sinai, Baltimore; Congregation Shaare Emeth, St. Louis; Congregation Sinai, Milwaukee; Isaac M. Wise Temple, Cincinnati; Leo Baeck Temple, Los Angeles; Temple Beth Torah, Kansas City; Temple Emanuel, Beverly Hills; Temple Emanu-El, San Diego; Temple Emanu-El, Dallas; Temple Shalom of Newton in Massachusetts; Temple Sinai, Stamford, Connecticut; The Temple, Atlanta; and Westchester Reform Temple, Scarsdale, New York.

This book has been greatly enriched by first-hand accounts from the field—vignettes, personal narratives, and reports from congregants, rabbis, educators, and researchers. Though their work is acknowledged in the body of the text, I would like to especially thank them for their willingness to write with insight, passion, and grace in response to a simple phone call from a person far away that (in many cases) they had never met. Thanks to: Lisa Engel, Rabbi Laura Geller, Lee Hendler, Rabbi Richard Jacobs, Stacia Kopeikin, Rabbi Neil Kurshan, Lisa Langer, Dr. Lisa Malik, Perry Oretsky, Marleen Pugach, Roslyn Roucher, Dr. Jeffrey Schein, Rabbi Sidney Schwarz, Dr. Simone Schweber, Rabbi Gordon Tucker, Julie Vanek, Susan Wolfe, and Rabbi Josh Zweiback. Thanks also to Congregation B'nai Jeshurun of Manhattan, Temple Emanu-El of Dallas, and Temple Shalom of Newton for allowing me to use portions of their vision statements.

The people directly responsible for the creation of this book deserve thanks as well. To Stuart Matlins, publisher of Jewish Lights Publishing, and Dr. Lawrence Hoffman, the editor of the series, my thanks for believing that there was an audience for a book like this. Dr. Bill Aron, Dr. Sandy Dashefsky, Rabbi Laura Geller, Susan Huntting, Dr. Riv-Ellen Prell, Joy Wasserman, and Roy Young read drafts of the manuscript at different stages and gave the kind of honest feedback that every author needs. Suzanne Singer, editor extraordinaire, asked all the hard questions, and did not shirk from suggesting major revisions. To Elisheva Urbas, my editor at Jewish Lights, my eternal thanks for all the encouragement and all the feedback. Jewish Lights editors Sandra Korinchak and Emily Wichland, who oversaw all the details of production, took such great care of both me and the manuscript that I never worried about anything other than the actual writing.

Finally, I wish to thank the members of my family, who tolerated me when I was stressed and distracted, and who served as great cheerleaders throughout the process of writing: my sons, Hillel and Jesse, and especially my husband, Bill, who took over when I got overwhelmed, provided a sounding board for my ideas and a sympathetic ear for my kvetching, and whose pride in my work was always a source of deep satisfaction. This book is dedicated to my parents, Moshe *(z"l)* and Sylvia Ettenberg, innovative and formidable Jewish educators in their own right, who set me on the path that led to this vocation.

INTRODUCTION

This book is the product of eight years of work as director of the Experiment in Congregational Education (ECE), a project of the Rhea Hirsch School of Education (RHSOE), Hebrew Union College–Jewish Institute of Religion (HUC–JIR), Los Angeles. The book draws on the experiences of the fourteen congregations that participated in the ECE, and it is informed throughout by the ideas and insights of the leadership team members at these congregations and my colleagues on the ECE staff.

In its first eight years the ECE had two primary goals: 1) To create *congregations of learners* in which congregants of all ages are actively engaged in learning throughout their lives; 2) To evolve *learning congregations* that practice shared leadership and have incorporated deliberation, reflection, and ongoing assessment into all of their activities. This volume focuses on the first of these goals; a future volume in this series will be devoted to the second goal.

The ECE began with the premise that synagogue revitalization requires more than new programming; it requires a change in the congregation's culture and expectations. A number of problematic assumptions must be challenged—that Jewish learning is primarily for children; that the education of children should focus, in large part, on bar/bat mitzvah preparation;

and that adults can only learn from rabbis and scholars. Congregants must realize the importance of learning for all ages, and they must experience first hand the power of learning to enrich their lives, ground their ethical decisions, and connect them in deep ways to their fellow learners. Though a lasting transformation of the congregation requires that each one of its three traditional components (prayer, assembly, and learning) be rethought and reconfigured, our hunch in initiating the ECE was that learning might be the most accessible and effective place to start.

The five-stage change process described in this book is based on the process undergone by the ECE congregations and refined by feedback from the participants and our own observations of what worked and didn't work. This process was designed by a team of two dozen people, each of whom contributed his or her talents and expertise. Over a period of eight years the planners included organizational consultants, a specialist in public school change, researchers in the areas of educational change and adult learning, and Jewish educators whose experience spanned a wide range of settings. In designing this process, we borrowed liberally, but cautiously, from work done in corporations and public schools, bearing in mind the many differences between synagogues and these other organizations. We generated our own hypotheses about the factors that contribute to successful change and tested these hypotheses in a variety of ways. As new congregations joined the project, and as congregations who were not officially part of the project began to utilize the same model, our ideas and activities were continually refined. Of course, the process delineated in this book is far from the final word on this matter, but it represents our best knowledge at this point in time. Our own research is ongoing. Every congregation embarking on this journey can help deepen our collective understanding of how synagogue life can become more vibrant and dynamic.

The fourteen ECE congregations have, indeed, become congregations of learners. Adults in these synagogues are learning in a variety of new and exciting ways: through the arts; in mentoring relationships; at intensive retreats and workshops; and in more conventional classes and lectures.

The excitement of the adults has led to changes in the formats of education for children and adolescents. More adults are studying along with their children. More options for children's learning are being offered to accommodate different interests and needs. More congregants are taking on the responsibility of teaching the next generation. In addition, the culture of ECE congregations has changed in ways that reflect the importance of learning. Meetings now include interactive text study led by congregants. Learning has become a component of worship, social action, new member orientation—indeed of all synagogue activities.

Over time, the impact of the ECE has gone beyond its core group of fourteen congregations. As descriptions of the ECE change process were published, a number of congregations set out to duplicate the process. At least two projects (the Hartford Jewish community's L'Atid program and the Union of American Hebrew Congregations' Creating Learning Congregations) worked with multiple congregations, following the model devised by the ECE. And the term *congregation of learners* has become a Jewish communal buzzword. As interest in synagogue transformation continues unabated, this book, which attempts to distill both the theory and the practice of the ECE, should prove useful to congregational leaders throughout North America.

As I write this introduction, the ECE is poised to enter a new phase, expanding its scope to reach hundreds of congregations and thousands of congregants through a combination of web-based distance learning, coaching and facilitation from an adviser, and large-scale change methodologies. This book summarizes the accomplishments of the ECE in its first phase and can serve as an introduction to the ECE's future.

1

Why a Book on Synagogue Revitalization?

Imagine two synagogues, located at opposite ends of a metropolitan area somewhere in North America. At first glance, the two look very similar. Both have impressive buildings with sanctuaries, social halls, classrooms, and offices. Both hold services on Shabbat and on holidays. Both offer religious school on Sunday mornings and weekday afternoons. But, looking more closely, one begins to notice significant differences.

The atmosphere at the first congregation is quiet and businesslike. Its schedule is regular and predictable. In the mornings the nursery school children arrive; in mid-afternoon they leave, and the religious school students begin streaming in, causing a momentary commotion until the they go into their classrooms. On most evenings small clusters of adults come in for meetings and classes; they sort themselves quickly, and rarely linger in the hallways. On Friday nights and Saturday mornings hushed murmurs can be heard in the sanctuary, where a group of 100 or so congregants assembles. Afterwards, in the social hall, there is polite conversation.

At first glance, this synagogue seems like any other—not particularly exciting, but certainly "good enough." But a closer look reveals the problem that lurks beneath the surface: Most of the adult activities are attended by the same small group of people, week in and week out. These are the synagogue "regulars." They are proud of the congregation, but, in truth, they feel a bit beleaguered. They wonder why most of their fellow congregants don't participate more often, and why these others don't seem to value the institution in which they have invested so much of themselves.

The second congregation, on the other hand, resembles a beehive. Everywhere there is a flurry of activity. All day long adults trickle in, sometimes with small children in tow. They head for the library, the resource room, the classrooms, and even the social hall, where art, music, and dance are scheduled. In the late afternoons and on weekends, schoolchildren arrive, joined by more adults. Though the children start out in classrooms, they don't stay put very long, spilling out into the rest of the building and, weather permitting, onto the grounds. On Shabbat the sanctuary is nearly filled; boisterous singing can be heard, and the laughter and chatter of children echo through the corridors. After services, people linger in the social hall and continue their conversations in the parking lot.

This congregation, like the first, has its own "regulars," but they are a larger and more diverse group. Though they too spend hours volunteering, they are hardly beleaguered, for they can feel their efforts bearing fruit. Together with the professional staff, they have created a vibrant community whose members are connected in multiple and overlapping ways. The parent with children in the religious school is in a study group with the senior citizen who works as a teachers' aide. The teenager who volunteers in the social action program sings in the choir with her friend's parents. People join this synagogue with the expectation that they will become active participants in some aspect of the community. They expect to volunteer in a variety of ways, and the synagogue is able to rely on their help. Although the membership is spread over a large area and many people see one another only at the synagogue, they feel connected. They know they will be there for one another when the need arises, whether it is organizing a blood drive or celebrating a *simcha* (a joyous event).

What enables the second congregation to flourish in this way? How might the first congregation become more lively, and more central in the lives of its members? The purpose of this book, and of the entire *Revitalizing the Synagogue* series, is to answer these questions. Both the book and the series are based on two assumptions: First, the American Jewish community needs many more synagogues like the second one I've described, places that are bursting with activity and in which members feel closely interconnected. Second, we already know a great deal about how all synagogues might rethink and reconfigure themselves to encourage greater participation and create a sense of community.

For the last decade, leaders of the American Jewish community have been wringing their hands over the "continuity crisis," whose most obvious symptom is the rising rate of intermarriage, but whose ancillary symptoms include lower rates of affiliation and observance. In this discussion, synagogues have tended to be seen as part of the problem rather than as part of the solution. In the Jewish press and in community forums there is much talk of the promise of day schools, Israel trips, camps, and Jewish community centers, but very little said about synagogues. Of course, a vibrant Jewish community requires a panoply of institutions. We know that Jewish community centers bring in the unaffiliated and that day schools and trips to Israel can have a profound effect on many of their participants. But important as these are, it would be a mistake to dismiss the potential of a vibrant synagogue for enriching Jewish life.

Synagogues have an important role to play in linking Jews to their heritage and to one another. The synagogue is often the first point of entry into the Jewish community; approximately two-thirds of American Jews belong to synagogues at some point in their lives,[1] many more than will travel to Israel on a teen tour, attend a day school, or join a Jewish community center.[2] Synagogues have the potential for reaching people on a continuous basis throughout their lives and in the context of their families.

Unfortunately, much of this potential is not actualized for two reasons. First, the participation of many Jews in synagogue life is episodic rather than continuous. Jewish children typically begin attending synagogue when they enroll in religious school, where they remain through their bar or bat mitzvah and, perhaps, through confirmation at the age of sixteen or seventeen. Relatively few young adults participate in congregational life, but when they marry and have children of their own, many find their way back, if only to enable their own children to have a bar or bat mitzvah. Having reached this milestone, about a third of these families will drop out.[3]

More problematic is the fact that even those who remain members on a continuous basis rarely participate fully in a congregation's activities. Most synagogues attract members because of the programs they offer and amenities they provide, such as religious school, High Holiday worship, and rabbinic officiation at various life-cycle events. Members pick and choose from the synagogue's offerings, but few see the congregation as important in their lives or as a locus of community.

It wasn't always this way. The traditional *kehilah kedoshah* (holy congregation) was a *bet tfilah* (house of prayer), a *bet midrash* (house of study), and a *bet kneset* (house of assembly) all rolled into one. But as Jews became more assimilated into American society, two of these functions dwindled and were supplanted by other institutions. Jewish learning for everyone devolved into secular learning for children, and became the province of the public school. A variety of social outlets developed: One kind of community could be found in the neighborhood, another in social halls and country clubs, a third in organizations like Hadassah and B'nai Brith. With learning and assembly taken care of elsewhere, the synagogue became, primarily, a house of worship. But in an era in which people questioned God's existence, more and more Jews grew ambivalent about prayer, showing up for state occasions, but feeling too uncomfortable to participate in prayer services on a regular basis.

But times have changed, and the pendulum has begun to swing back. Full participation in American society turned out to be less satisfying than it seemed when Jews were excluded from it. The fabric of American life has become frayed by economic and social upheavals. Along with their relative prosperity and high level of education, Jews, like other affluent Americans, feel increasingly fragmented and isolated. Like their Christian counterparts, they seek nurturing, spiritual, face-to-face communities, and have turned to religion and to religious institutions. In his book *A Generation of Seekers,* sociologist Wade Clark Roof describes the spiritual search of contemporary middle-aged adults:

> Members of [the baby boom] generation are asking questions about the meaning of their lives, about what they want for themselves and their children. They are still exploring, as they did in their years of growing up; but now they are exploring in new and, we think, more profound ways. Religious and spiritual themes are surfacing in a rich variety of ways—in Eastern religions, in evangelical and fundamentalist teachings, in mysticism and New Age movements, in Goddess worship and other ancient religious rituals, in the mainline churches and synagogues, in Twelve-Step recovery groups, in concern about the environment, in holistic health, and in personal and social transformation. Many within this generation who dropped out of churches and synagogues years ago are now shopping around for a congregation.[4]

Another sociologist, Donald Miller, has written perceptively about the "new paradigm" churches, whose success, he believes, is based on their ability to respond to some of the basic needs of contemporary Americans.

> First, human community is in short supply in American society. . . . Second, many people perceive America as a frightening place to live and raise children, and it is not surprising that they turn to the church as a safe haven for taking care of their social as well as spiritual needs. . . . Third, many people seek support for specific needs: They are recently divorced with several small children to raise, they have an addiction problem, they are facing failure at work, they are having problems with their children, their marriage is in trouble. . . . Fourth, for many people in this country there is a "hope deficit," to which

new paradigm churches are responding. . . . Many self-help and community groups attempt to address some of these needs: One can join an Alcoholics Anonymous group or be part of a Neighborhood Watch program. But new paradigm churches are unique in offering a full menu of programs, projects, and groups to address all these needs. In this regard they re-create some of the characteristics of small town life, not in the sense of removing people from their urban environment, but as an enclave within mass society where many fundamental needs can be addressed comprehensively.[5]

Like the "mainline" churches that are losing ground to these new paradigm churches, many synagogues have failed to keep up with the changing needs of their members. As the saying goes, they are "playing broken records" while their constituency is yearning for new tunes. Staid and decorous service in a cathedral-like environment doesn't necessarily satisfy people's spiritual yearnings. Adult-education classes, as traditionally scheduled and taught, don't meet everyone's needs. Committee meetings, Purim carnivals, and fundraising events are pale substitutes for face-to-face, supportive communities.

To recapture their traditional place in the hearts and minds of their members, synagogues need to be rethought and reconfigured. Like the Christians described by Donald Miller, Jews need spiritual fulfillment, social support, hope, joy, and a sense of purpose. The role of the synagogue is to utilize the spiritual resources of the Jewish tradition to meet these needs, and, in the process, to forge cohesive and supportive communities among the disparate individuals who are searching in isolation. Those congregations that have succeeded in meeting this challenge have flourished (first-hand accounts from some of these congregations appear in chapter 3). Some of these congregations are relatively new and were configured differently from their inception; others have forged a new direction in an unplanned, serendipitous fashion. But the majority of congregations that have succeeded in re-visioning and revitalizing themselves have done so as part of an organized change effort. During the past decade approximately twenty projects have been initiated with the goal of transforming synagogue life; each project has worked with multiple congregations. These projects span all four movements—Orthodox, Conservative, Reform, and Reconstructionist—and include synagogues of varying sizes located throughout North America.[6] None of the projects have been completely successful; all have had more success with some congregations than with others. Yet even at this relatively early stage, these projects have much to teach us.

This volume, the first in a series, focuses on learning as a vehicle for revitalizing congregational life. It draws on my experience as director of the Experiment in Congregational Education (ECE), a project that has worked with fourteen congregations since its inception in 1992. Jewish *learning* is critical to synagogue revitalization because learning is at the core of our identities as Jews. For Jews, learning is more than an intellectual exercise; it engages our emotions and influences our actions. It is, by definition, communal; even when one learns alone, one is inextricably linked to Jews in other times and places.

A congregation of learners is much more than a collection of individuals that happens to learn. Learning will, inevitably, spill over into every other aspect of congregational life, changing people's approach to prayer, to ethics, and to social justice. Learning brings people together, creating the sense of community so many are seeking. When members of a congregation have a common understanding that Jewish learning is for everyone, and when they are provided with a range of engaging and stimulating opportunities for learning, that congregation will have become a congregation of learners.

The nature of Jewish learning and of a congregation of learners will be discussed in greater depth in chapter 2. Chapter 3 presents a series of images of synagogues that are on their way to becoming congregations of learners. The remaining chapters are devoted to the process of becoming a congregation of learners. Chapter 4 outlines the steps that a congregation might take over a period of two to three years. Subsequent chapters focus on different parts of the process: assessing the congregation's readiness for change (chapter 5); convening a group to spearhead the change (chapter 6); arriving at a collective vision of a congregation of learners (chapter 7); incorporating Jewish text study into the process of change (chapter 8); experimenting with change (chapter 9); listening to members of the congregation (chapter 10); and planning for the future (chapter 11). The final two chapters deal with how a congregation can sustain itself on its long journey.

Reimagining and reconfiguring a congregation is a difficult job, requiring the concerted effort of many people, and with no guarantee of success. This book can be used as a resource for anyone who is curious about the process and is considering embarking on this sort of effort. It can be used by professional and lay leaders as the springboard for discussion at the congregational level. It can also serve as a sourcebook of ideas for the process of change itself. It would be a mistake, however, to use this book as a how-to manual, to be followed unthinkingly. The creation of a congregation of learners requires much more than a batch of new programs and classes. It requires a change of attitude and a change of culture.

While this book can help congregational leaders think about how to explore and articulate their vision of congregation-wide learning, and can suggest some exercises and text study materials that will facilitate the process, the nature of the change will be different at each site—unfolding in its own unique way, in keeping with a congregation's history, location, ideology, size, culture, and demography. "Congregations have a corporate personality," each with its own "mental image and momentum."[7] The educational vision of a large, urban synagogue with diverse members may differ radically from that of a small, homogeneous synagogue in a small town. Thus, even if the vision statement created at one synagogue were appealing to the leadership of another, it would be a mistake to simply adopt that statement. To do so would be to lose the opportunity for reflection, discussion, and debate that the process of visioning affords. Likewise, exercises that work well in some settings may not work in others. The advice this book offers on both goals and procedures should be filtered through the sensibilities and practical wisdom of the lay and professional leadership.

The current interest in synagogue change is barely a decade old. Even the most successful projects consider their accomplishments modest and hard earned. However inspiring and compelling the ideas presented in this book are (and I hope they will be very inspiring and very compelling), it is important to bear in mind that they should be seen more as hypotheses for discussion than as truths to be honored unquestioningly. The vision offered in this book, appealing though it might be, must be tested against people's own experiences and realities. The best use of this book is for a small group of leaders to read and discuss it; to note their areas of agreement and disagreement, both with the book, and with one another; to experiment with some of the exercises contained in the book and to evaluate the results; and to create their own exercises and processes that will enable a broader range of congregants to explore these ideas. One thing we do know about change, in any sphere, is that the investment and energies of those who participate in a change process are key to its success.

2

What Is a
Congregation of Learners?

Jewish learning can be very powerful. When learning is active and engaging, when it is offered in an environment that is welcoming and supportive, it can enrich people's lives and ignite their interest in Judaism. In the context of a synagogue, it can serve as a catalyst for change.

Unfortunately, this potential is not always achieved. Though the typical American synagogue aspires to live up to its traditional place as a *bet midrash,* a house of learning, it tries to fit Jewish learning into the mold of secular education. Learning, by this model, is reduced to religious school for children and a series of courses and lectures for adults, both of which are problematic. Held at inconvenient hours and plagued by a shortage of good teachers, religious schools are too often boring and irrelevant. And though the classes offered to adults may be excellent, they rarely attract more than ten percent of a congregation's membership.

Some synagogues, however, have succeeded in changing the equation by refashioning learning into a central activity that is vital and stimulating. By adopting a different approach to Jewish learning, they have transformed ordinary members with busy lives into avid learners and active participants in congregational life. In the process, these congregations have also transformed themselves, becoming congregations of learners.

This chapter begins with the stories of two Jews whose lives have been deeply touched by Jewish learning. It continues with a discussion of the ways in which authentic Jewish learning differs from secular education, the reason it is essential to Jewish life, and how it can provide contemporary Jews with an element that is missing from their lives. It examines the barriers that prevent people from becoming involved in learning, and the ways in which a congregation might overcome these barriers. Finally, it describes what a congregation of learners might look like. It concludes with a coda, the stories of two congregants who, having been enriched by Jewish learning, went on to enrich the lives of others.

The Tales of Two Learners

When Lisa Engel joined the Birmingham (Alabama) Institute for Jewish Community Leadership, she had been an adult synagogue member and Jewish community leader for twenty years without feeling a sense of confidence or ownership in her connection to tradition, her community, and especially the prayer services themselves. By the end of her year of learning, she had become a regular synagogue participant and a confident presenter of *divrei torah* (Torah teachings) at Jewish community meetings and events. She describes the change in her Jewish life that came about through her participation in the Institute:

> I was a Jewish novice, standing on the sidelines, watching a beautifully choreographed dance and overwhelmed by its seeming complexity. To outsiders, such as I was (and still am at times), Jewish rituals, while rich with meaning, can make us feel ignorant and lost. The intricate and time-honored "dance" of Jewish observance, passed down from generation to generation, had passed me by. With its own language, its own movements, its precise ordering of events and even its apparent speed, communal Jewish worship seemed impenetrable.

A yearlong opportunity to study Torah and Jewish texts seemed like a lifeline. The Birmingham Institute for Jewish Community Leadership, led by Rabbi Elana Kanter, was marketed toward Birmingham's entire Jewish adult community, from beginner to learned, the only prerequisites being a desire to study and a commitment to attend. With encouragement from friends, family, and Rabbi Kanter, I took the plunge, determined to learn the steps of the dance! Despite the knot in my stomach, I reassured myself that any step forward, no matter how small, was a step worth taking.

There was much to learn and we plunged right in. With only one year, we moved quickly through the Torah and accompanying texts, highlighting the basis for many Jewish rituals and *halakhah* (laws). Sparks of understanding lit up my brain every time one of the "mysterious" rituals was explained. Suddenly lights flashed! I was studying the text basis for Jewish practices, the master choreography written in the Torah.

Events, both life-cycle and everyday, took on additional meaning and clarity when seen through my new knowledge of Torah. There was a *halakhah* for everything: from arising in the morning to going to bed at night, from birth to death, from the important to the mundane. And yes, there was a reason for it all. It wasn't just a hidden code set to deter all but the learned. I quickly realized the steps of the dance are not random. The choreography is really not so difficult.

Studying in a mixed-medium, structured, and hands-on format, we examined the full gamut of Jewish life: birth and circumcision, weddings and covenants, blessings around meals, Shabbat and *Havdalah* (the ceremony for the ending of Shabbat), Torah study, the worship services, relationships with other people, relationships with God, repentance and forgiveness, charity and giving, death and burial. Not only was I exposed to ritual practices and meanings, but I also learned where to look when I needed further insight and explanation.

The more I studied, the more questions I had. If rituals are all based in text, then why are there so many different practices? The text remained the same, and will always remain a constant. But rabbinic scholars in future generations fleshed out the choreography in different ways, adding timing, rhythm, and sequence.

Additional thoughts and questions about *halakhah* popped into my mind rapid-fire. Now I could appreciate the beauty of the intricately woven steps. But why was the dance itself so important? I knew there must be more to learn than the steps themselves.

According to some, all Torah, both written and oral, is holy and by following the laws in a literal way we are acting as a divine light unto the nations. Others propose that Jewish traditions bind us to who we are as a people, and to God, regardless of the specific time and space that we inhabit. Still others think that rituals spark the divine presence in each of us, connecting us to our inner holiness. And even those Jews who don't think that literal ritual practice is relevant encourage the study of text to learn about who we are and to make educated personal decisions.

Reflecting on the year-long Institute for Jewish Community Leadership, I discovered the essential importance and meaning of *halakhah.* By creating our own hands-on rituals, under the guidance of Rabbi Kanter, we understood their relevance to our lives. We created bonds within ourselves, with our Institute group, with the larger Jewish community, and with God. As certain memories and experiences of the Institute fade, the rituals remain vivid, an ever-present connection to Judaism within our rushed and fragmented lives.

For me personally, the Institute was a life-changing experience. Two years later, I carry a proud and confident feeling of belonging to the Jewish people. I know and understand many of the ritual steps, even if my own versions of these steps are not always up to speed. More important, I have taken many small steps forward in every facet of my life. I continue to study Torah with my Institute group on a weekly basis; my family and I say *hamotzi* (the blessing over bread) at our dinner table; I chant the *Shma* with my daughters at bedtime. Prayers of healing for sick friends and relatives are woven into my everyday life, and I say daily personal prayers for guidance and inspiration.

Through the Institute, I realized that it was not enough the be a Jewish communal leader. Now I'm also a beginning dancer in Jewish worship and *halakhah,* no longer a wallflower of the past.

While Lisa Engel's journey from the periphery to the center of Jewish life was the result of a class offered for adults, Susan Wolfe's journey began with an opportunity to learn alongside her children in the Shabbaton program at Temple Beth Am, in Los Altos Hills, California. This program offers families an alternative to religious school, in which parents and children learn together on Shabbat afternoons.

My own Sunday school experience at a large congregation in Seattle was not entirely negative; it was there that I formed a strong sense of Jewish identity, made my best friends, and learned to be a leader among my peers. But the knowledge piece never quite took hold. As an adult, I felt ignorant of our people's tradition. My husband was not Jewish; although he enthusiastically supported a Jewish direction for our family, he had no knowledge of the tradition, either. So, the opportunity to learn alongside our children, rather than drop them off each week for two hours, had high appeal.

We were members of the inaugural Shabbaton class in the fall of 1994, meeting, along with some sixty other families, on Saturday afternoons from 4 P.M. to 6 P.M. That first year we were part of a pilot experiment from which emerged a solid and sensible program structure: We convene at 4 P.M. to sing a bit and to be briefed on the topic of the day. The first year, our overall theme was Jewish heroes; other overarching themes have included the weekly *parashah*, Our Jewish Home, Mitzvah and *Minhag* (custom), and *tfilah* (prayer) and Life Cycle. We say the *brakha* (blessing) for study, and we then move to smaller groups of eight to ten families, facilitated by a religious school teacher. There, one of the families offers a short presentation on the topic of the day, and the educator leads a family activity. Some of our projects have included creating ritual objects and reenacting a Jewish funeral service and *shiva* (seven days of mourning) call. A scavenger hunt, in which scriptural citations were given as clues, taught us how to look up passages in the *chumash* (Five Books of Moses).

At 5 P.M., the children attend grade-level classes, and the adults study with a member of the rabbinic or cantorial staff. Sometimes these study sessions are text-driven; other times, we have focused on the December dilemma, the meaning of prayer, and the hierarchy of *tsedakah* (both justice and charity) as conceived by Maimonides. Occasionally, parents have led the sessions, on creating ethical wills, for example, or on caring for the aged. The parents exhibit a wide range of Judaic knowledge, from virtually none, to day school-educated parents, to those who are finding Jewish study to be a lifelong pursuit. At 5:50 P.M., we reconvene with our children for *Havdalah*.

After five years, how has Shabbaton affected our family? For one thing, it has demonstrated to our children that Jewish learning is not only for children; we are involved in their learning, and in our own. When they go to religious school, we go to religious school. When we come back together, we each have an experience to share on a common Jewish topic. Additionally, we are practicing what we preach: We tell our children that Shabbat is a time for relaxation and study; each Shabbat, we relax and study with other Jewish families at our synagogue. Very often, we complete our evening by going out to dinner with another Shabbaton family and continuing our discussions. Thus, social ties are built into the program.

Our vocabulary of *brakhot* (blessings) has increased dramatically. The prayer before study, the prayer before a snack, and all of the *Havdalah* blessings are now ours. Similarly, our Hebrew word-stock is far more extensive than it would be without attending an education program with our children: Each year family group names are selected based on the year's education theme. One year the groups were named for books of the Torah. Now *Bereshit* (Genesis), *Shmot* (Exodus), *Vayikra* (Leviticus), *Bamidbar* (Numbers), and *Devarim* (Deuteronomy) are familiar to us. This last year, when we focused on prayer and life cycle, our family group name was *gila* (joy). *Shirah* (singing), *mishpachot* (families), *hafsakah* (break), *kitot* (classes), and more all roll off our tongues easily.

But perhaps the most meaningful outcomes have been personal. As much as anything I have learned at Shabbaton, I have learned how very much I have yet to learn. I discovered the depth of my hunger to further my understanding and appreciation of our Jewish heritage. So when I was offered the opportunity to study with the nationally acclaimed Wexner

Heritage Foundation, I jumped at it. It was just after our first Wexner retreat that my husband articulated how much he cherished our membership in a covenantal community, and how he no longer was satisfied to "pass" for Jewish. He wanted to make a full commitment to Judaism.

A year of study, a *bet din,* and a *mikvah* dip later, we are no longer an interfaith family. I attribute much of his decision to convert to our family experience, week after week, year after year, with Shabbaton. A year after conversion, Bob celebrated his bar mitzvah. The ceremony was moving and meaningful, and a beautiful display of commitment for our two boys.

Shabbaton requires a commitment to attend on the part of the parents. That the commitment extends to the pursuit of further adult education, and leadership, both within the congregation at large and the greater Jewish community, may not have been program objectives. But they are both outcomes and blessings. Since embarking on this Jewish journey, I have been privileged to serve on the congregation's board of directors. When I look at my colleagues around the board table, it is striking to see that, of those with children in grades K–6, almost all are Shabbaton parents.

Although the Shabbaton program began as an education program, in part to accommodate an increasing number of religious school students who could not all fit into Sunday school classrooms, it has emerged as a program that offers learning opportunities, praying opportunities, and a sense of community.

In my view, the oft-cited crisis of continuity is largely the result of missed connections between individuals, families, institutions, and the Jewish community at large. If we want to attract those who are less involved into the fold of Jewish community, we must innovate. The family education model offers a multifaceted, far-reaching approach, including both formal and informal avenues that appeal, invite, build identity, and impart knowledge. Offering formal programming in a relaxed and familiar setting presents an opportunity to create, and to demonstrate networks for lifelong Jewish learning and growth.

Authentic Jewish Learning

The program that so engaged Susan Wolfe and her family was different from that which moved Lisa Engel. Beth Am's Shabbaton program was informal, experiential, and multigenerational, while Birmingham's Institute for Jewish Community Leadership was more formal, intellectual, and limited to adults. Despite their differences, these two learning situations had a great deal in common—both were based on a Jewish concept of learning, which is called in Hebrew *torah lishmah,* study for its own sake. Though each of the programs aimed to transmit information, this was not the main goal. Rather, the overarching goal was to bring learners into contact with the richness and depth of the Jewish tradition, and to have them embark on a lifetime of Jewish learning.

In the Jewish tradition, learning is considered an end in itself, an essential part of being Jewish. A famous saying in *Pirke Avot* (Ethics of the Fathers) tells us that "the universe is supported by three things—by study, by prayer, and by good deeds." Just as Jews are expected to pray and to strive to make the world a better place, so are they expected to continue learning throughout their lives.

This notion of learning is very different from the American view of education. In Western societies, education is a means to an end, meant to achieve a larger goal. Parents send their children to school so that they can be properly socialized into society's norms and expectations. Young adults attend college and graduate school so they can prepare for entry into a variety of careers and professions.

In the past two decades, as the term "lifelong learning" has gained greater currency, the American concept of education has moved a bit closer to the Jewish one. A changing economy and a growing sense of social isolation have combined to motivate ever-increasing numbers of adults to enroll in a wide variety of "continuing education" courses and workshops. While some of these courses are prerequisites for career advancement, many endeavor to broaden the students' horizons and enrich their lives.

Americans have begun to discover what Jews have known for centuries—that learning is its own reward.

In traditional Jewish societies learning was an integral part of Jewish living. Children learned about Shabbat and about holidays at home. They learned prayers and the rudiments of the Bible by going to synagogue with their parents. Men continued their learning at the synagogue, where study was woven into the prayer service; many of them belonged to a *chevre shas,* a Talmud study group.[1] Women, in keeping a kosher home and through their participation in communal activities such as *bikur cholim* (visiting the sick) and the *chevrah kadishah* (society for the burial of the dead), were immersed in the fine points of Jewish tradition and ritual practice. This type of learning, which educational theorists term "enculturation," is the most natural and organic; it is also the most effective. Unfortunately, as Jews began to participate more fully in Western society, the resources that supported this all-encompassing and unselfconscious form of learning were depleted. With every passing generation, fewer and fewer families lived this kind of rich Jewish life.

Jews had not been in America very long before Western assumptions about education began to color their conception of *Jewish* learning. Immigrants who were struggling to make ends meet had neither the time nor the inclination to engage in study. Within a few decades, the Jewish ideal of lifelong learning was reduced to religious schooling for children. Through formal instruction rather than informal and holistic enculturation, imparted by paid teachers rather than family members and neighbors, information about how to live a Jewish life became detached from the actual life in which it had been embedded.

By the 1940s and 50s the education of children became inextricably linked to an external goal—the celebration of bar (and later bat) mitzvah.[2] Once bar/bat mitzvah was established as the raison d'être of Jewish schooling, it was only a short step to the conclusion that there was no reason to stay in Hebrew school after the age of thirteen. Attempts to prolong children's enrollment in religious school were also linked to external goals; by introducing the ritual of confirmation, congregations were able to keep some adolescents in the system for several additional years. But, by consensus, after confirmation one was certainly finished with one's Jewish studies.

It should come as no surprise that formal Jewish education, as found in supplementary schools, was rarely effective. Taken out of the context of enculturation, instruction is like a plant without roots. Imagine what it would be like to learn how to read in a society in which few people actually read, or to learn math in a culture that has no use for numbers. Living in an environment that does not particularly value what is taught in Jewish schools and provides few opportunities for this knowledge to be utilized, how could people retain what they have learned from year to year, not to mention over a lifetime?

Why Is Jewish Learning Important?

Today, learning is a still a central activity for Jews who consider themselves bound by *halakhah*. For example, many Orthodox Jews study a page of Talmud each day. They do not need to ask themselves why they are studying; that study is a mitzvah (a commandment) is reason enough. But what of those Jews who do not feel commanded by God, and who do not observe all of the mitzvot? Is learning an intrinsic Jewish value for them as well?

I would argue that learning is even more important for these Jews who value their autonomy, yet want to retain their connection to Jewish tradition. Jews who do not feel commanded by God, but who identify with the Jewish people and want to participate in Jewish life, need a foundation for understanding their Judaism and for enabling them to decide what traditions to follow. The Reform principle of *informed choice* speaks to this point: If one is going to be selective about one's Jewish practice, one had better be fully informed. While informed choice may not be a central principle for other movements in Jewish life, becoming fully informed is every bit as important for *anyone* who wants to live as a Jew. Full participation in Jewish life requires not only *keva* (regularity) , but also *kavanah* (intentionality). Jewish practice requires more than behavior; it requires thought and feeling. The more one knows about the significance of Jewish rituals and ceremonies, the more *kavanah* one is likely to invest in one's practice.

Today Jewish learning is more essential than ever. Americans, including Jews, have discovered that excessive personal autonomy results in isolation, and excessive skepticism leads to anomie. They have begun to search for community, for tradition, and for spirituality. Some have found these in Eastern religions and in a variety of cults; many more have found it in small groups that meet regularly for support or self-help. According to sociologist Robert Wuthnow, forty percent of Americans belong to a group of ten to twenty people that meets for an hour or two on a regular basis in a home, community center, or at a church or synagogue. Interestingly, nearly half of these groups include Bible study in their meetings.[3]

All Jewish learning, whether it is devoted to a study of sacred texts, Jewish thought, or Jewish history, enables learners to connect their personal struggles to larger social and ethical ideals. When a group of learners engages in this type of discussion over an extended period of time, the bonds that form among the participants are strong and durable. Though the participants' original purpose in joining the group may have been intellectual stimulation, the solace they find in the text and the emotional and social connections they form with fellow learners are what keep them coming back.

Learning creates a larger sense of community as well, a community that links Jews through time and space. When one reads *parashat hashavuah* (the Torah portion of the week) one can imagine Jews all over the world puzzling over the same verses; the commentaries to these verses connect us to the rabbis of third-century Palestine and eleventh-century France, and to the generations of Jews who studied these same verses with the same commentaries.

Overcoming Resistance to Jewish Learning

Given an opportunity to reflect on eternally compelling questions, to become part of something larger, and to gain psychological support, many congregants might, like Lisa Engel and Susan Wolfe, find that learning adds a new dimension to their lives. But while synagogues offer a variety of adult-education programs and classes, the people who need these programs the most are those who are least likely to participate because they are too busy, too intimidated, or too ambivalent about Judaism.

Judaism is not easily accessible to the uninitiated. Despite the fact that the vast majority of synagogue members are college educated, and that many have accumulated advanced degrees and impressive professional credentials, they are, for the most part, Jewishly illiterate. They have had limited exposure to Jewish texts, the Hebrew language, or Jewish thought, and assume that Jewish learning is accessible to only select groups of rabbis and scholars.

Psychologist Diane Schuster studied a small group of adults who participated in change efforts at several congregations. Despite their accomplishments in the secular world, and despite the contributions they had already made to their congregations, many believed themselves to be inadequate and even inauthentic Jews. As part of their participation in the process, they studied Jewish texts. For many it was their first exposure to text study, and they approached it with hesitancy and insecurity.[4] In the words of a thirty-eight-year-old psychologist:

> I felt inadequate and kind of inept, kind of not knowing what to do with it. It felt out of context to me. So I struggled with the first time that we did it, and I had that déjà vu experience of "Uh oh. This is gonna be an alienating thing in which I feel like I don't know, I don't have enough history."

A businesswoman who had long served on the board of her synagogue, chairing numerous committees, remembered:

Oh: I felt total fear. This is uncharted territory. . . . I felt like I was in school again, like a little kid. You know? You don't want to look stupid. And you look around and you can see who's confident and who's maybe as ill-equipped as you are.

A third interviewee described fears of having her ignorance exposed:

People are embarrassed by what they don't know and afraid they might be confronted by that lack of education. They're embarrassed by their lack of background.

Another person felt uneasy and self-conscious about how his lack of knowledge would be perceived by his rabbi:

I really wanted to participate at a level where I wouldn't be intimidated in front of the rabbi and feel like a third-grade student with a teacher who knows a lot more than I do.

Once past their initial feelings of discomfort, however, these novice learners reacted with pleasure and excitement. The following quotations reflect the enthusiasm of the respondents:

I think of text study as a deepening process. . . . It provides a context with which you look outward, and then you bring it inward and find the meaning, and then come out with it again. I don't know what it leads to—what the continuation of that is. But it's real exciting because I think that religion is about personal meaning and so to be able to look at something and then be able to filter through your own values, etcetera, and then come out with your own sense of where you want to go is pretty valuable experience.

I love to find the meaning, it makes me so much closer to it. It's like—there's some pride in where you've come from. In that freedom of discovering yourself. I love that.

The combination of a safe and comfortable context and compelling and meaningful content enabled the learners to get past the barriers, to become fully engaged in learning.

The Benefits of Learning in a Congregation

For learners who are eager to engage in study and who have overcome their initial hesitancy, opportunities for learning abound. Every year more Jewish books are published and more college courses in Jewish studies are offered. Jewish Internet sites continue to sprout. Study programs for adults, including weekly classes, day-long marathons, week-long retreats, and even year-long intensives, have proliferated. So *why,* one might ask, is it important for a synagogue to become a center for learning?

While Jewish learning has been rewarding, and even transformative, for individuals, its impact on their families and communities has been more limited. Because the most attractive and sophisticated learning opportunities exist apart from ongoing communal life, the opportunity to share one's learning with family and friends has been lost, and its impact on the local community has been diffused. In fact, it is not uncommon for powerful learning experiences to leave individuals feeling isolated from, rather than connected to, their families and communities. Hence the need for learning in a congregational setting. While community can be created temporarily at a retreat center, or even on the Internet, a congregation can be the center of an ongoing communal life that is rooted in families and in neighborhoods. In a synagogue setting, discussions and debates that begin in class can reverberate for weeks. Issues can be decided based on values that have been discussed; rituals can be expanded or revised in accordance with principles that have been studied. Synagogue life provides multiple opportunities to link what is studied to what is practiced—to translate abstract ideas into concrete actions, to weave pieces of information into a tapestry of meaning and symbols.

The learning that transformed the lives of Lisa Engel and Susan Wolfe, enabling them to go from onlookers to participants, has the potential to transform the lives of thousands of Jews in hundreds of congregations. These Jews are likely to have joined a synagogue without thinking much about what they wanted for *themselves.* They may have felt that their young children needed a religious "anchor," or that their school-aged children should become bar/bat mitzvah. They may have joined as a gesture of solidarity with other Jews, or been pressured into joining by their families or friends. They probably attend services on the High Holidays, send their children to religious school, and have been drawn into other synagogue activities, such as Mitzvah Day, the Hanukah bazaar, and an occasional prayer service. They may even have served on a committee or two. But, like Lisa Engel, they are likely to have felt that they were still very much outsiders, observers of a pageant in which they were unable to participate fully.

To reach their "marginally affiliated" members (who comprise the majority of the congregation) synagogues need to rethink the way they approach learning. They need to go beyond offering classes to incorporate learning that is active, participatory, and enjoyable into all of their activities. This learning could happen anywhere and everywhere—in the hallways and on the front lawn, at worship services and committee meetings, in people's homes and in their places of work. But creating these learning opportunities requires a different mindset—a fundamental rethinking of the role of learning in the congregation. It requires that a synagogue envision itself as a *congregation of learners.*

What Is a Congregation of Learners?

A congregation of learners is a center for authentic Jewish learning—learning that is viewed as a lifelong endeavor, that grows out of the life of the community, and which, in turn, strengthens the community. The congregation of learners is both a means to an end and an end in itself; it is an instrument for enculturating individual members into active participation in Jewish life, but it is also a model for Jewish community.

What does a congregation of learners look like? If one visited such a congregation, what would one see? First of all, one would see many people learning in many different ways. There would be formal classes, of course, but also informal discussion groups, arts workshops, and story-telling, as well as lots of one-on-one tutoring. Ideally, everyone in the congregation would be engaged in learning on a continuous basis. More realistically, learning would be seen as the norm, rather than as the exception. New members would be brought in with the expectation that they, and not just their children, would be engaged in learning in some form. It would be understood by all that Jewish learning extends throughout one's life, far beyond bar/bat mitzvah, and far beyond confirmation.

To accommodate its diverse membership, a congregation of learners would have to think in unconventional and creative ways about Jewish teaching. It is unlikely that funds could be found to provide truly professional teachers for everyone. Instead, teaching would be seen as a communal obligation, with the mitzvah of "teaching them [words of Torah] diligently to your children" expanded to include the entire community. In a congregation of learners, *everyone* would be a potential teacher, from the history buff teaching a course on the Golden Age of Spain to the teenager tutoring youngsters in Hebrew, and the amateur singers who lead song sessions. Everyone would be encouraged to assist someone else in learning, whether that involved becoming someone's study partner, leading an activity, collecting educational materials, reading aloud to preschoolers, or teaching a formal class.

A congregation of learners would be a congregation that acknowledges that there are many possible learning styles—that some people learn best through the arts, others through discussion, and still others through reading, listening to tapes, or surfing the Internet. Such a congregation would be committed to offering a variety of teaching modalities to its broad array of learners. Its goal would be to make learning both serious and enjoyable, accessible to everyone, but also challenging. Its educational programming would be conducted as a grand experiment, continually being evaluated and adapted.

Beyond the proliferation of learners, teachers, and teaching techniques, the hallmark of a congregation of learners would be what educators call a *culture of learning.* Learning would permeate every aspect of the congregation. To take just a few examples: Torah study would be incorporated into Shabbat services; the social action committee's work in a homeless shelter would be preceded by a study of texts related to *tsedakah* (which means both charity and justice); board members would study together, not simply as a perfunctory opening for a meeting, but as a way of grounding their decisions in traditional sources. Every activity and every space, from the bake sale and the Purim carnival to the hallways and offices, would be viewed as opportunities for learning. For example, items at the bake sale might come with tags that list the appropriate *brakha;* booths at the Purim carnival might actually teach something about the Purim story; bulletin boards in the hallway could contain famous quotations, challenging questions, or the Hebrew phrase of the week. Tidbits of learning, whether in the form of a skit, a song, or displays on the wall, would become regularities, and would be seen as part of "the way we do things around here."

Moreover, these instances of learning would not be isolated fragments. Congregational leaders would see to it that discrete activities were set in an overall context. There might be a theme for the year or a more elaborate multiyear plan. Either way, a group of people, such as a learning task force or council, would be responsible for promoting learning and for creating a synergy between the various programs.

And what of the subject matter? *What* would members of this congregation be learning? This is a question every congregation would have to answer for itself. Four thousand years of Jewish history have yielded a vast body of culture and lore, more than anyone, even the most learned scholar, can master. Part of the task of creating a congregation of learners is the process of deciding what a curriculum of lifelong learning might look like. Some congregations might decide to coordinate their offerings, so that everyone would have a common core of knowledge. Others might prefer a cafeteria approach, encouraging personal exploration and a wide diversity of topics. Some might encourage the development of skills, such as leading prayers and reading Torah; others might prefer to focus on modern history and contemporary sociology. What would distinguish the congregation of learners is its commitment to open, informed discussion of the various possibilities, and to the tracking and feedback necessary to see that the programs chosen are succeeding.

It would be my hope that in every congregation, one type of learning would receive a special emphasis, and that is the study of Torah. Not only in the narrow sense, meaning the Five Books of Moses, but also in the broader sense of the canon of texts that have been essential to the Jewish people—including the remaining thirty-one books of the Bible, the many volumes of biblical commentary, the Talmud and other legal texts, and possibly even great works of Jewish philosophy and literature. While every congregation would have to decide for itself how much emphasis to put on text study, and while more general subject matters, such as Jewish history and Jewish art are also important, I would argue that text study—the most traditional form of Jewish learning—ought to be a central part of Jewish learning because it allows the learner to get inside the tradition while maintaining a critical stance. When conducted in pairs or in small groups, and with proper facilitation, text study creates community and promotes informed choice. I will have a good deal more to say about the whys and hows of text study, as well as what counts as a Jewish text in chapter 9. For now, I will simply note that the *brakha* over Torah study states that Jews are commanded "to engage in words of Torah," not simply "to study," and not even "to be Jewishly literate." In other words, the primary goal of learning is not the *acquisition* of *knowledge*, but rather the *process* of engaging continuously with texts.

Where Does the Religious School Fit In?

One possible component of the congregation of learners that does not receive much attention in this book is the congregational school. Does a school for children belong in a congregation of learners? If it does, what would it look like? In the chapters that follow, few references will be made to the education of children, apart from the overall context of congregation-wide learning, for two reasons. First, a good deal has already been written about the congregational school, including ethnographies, curriculum guides, handbooks for teachers and administrators, and a compendium of "best practices."[5] Second, to imagine the ideal religious school in a congregation of learners is, in my opinion, to put the cart before the horse. First and foremost, children should be seen as an integral part of the community; initiatives to improve children's learning are neither more important nor more urgent than initiatives for adults. In fact, one might argue that because the influence of parents (with whom children spend many more hours than they spend in religious school) so far outweighs the influence of the school, adults are more important. But I don't need to go that far to establish the point that parental attitudes make a critical difference. Parents who value Jewish learning and who enact that value by participating in learning themselves are sending a strong message to their children, who are likely to internalize that value themselves. Conversely, parents who drop their children off but rarely enter the synagogue also send a strong message to their children—that attending religious school is a necessary nuisance, the price one has to pay for a bar or bat mitzvah.

Once a congregation has evolved a culture of learning, and once learning among adults has become the norm, the number of options for successful learning among children will multiply. Some congregations may decide to eliminate the school altogether, incorporating children into the ongoing learning activities (both formal and informal) that are available to everyone. Others may decide to retain formal instruction for children as part of an overall program of enculturation. Still others may incorporate parents and other adults into the structure of the school in any number of interesting ways. Set in the context of a deepening appreciation for learning, and the realization that learning is the responsibility of the entire community and not just the teachers, these changes will not seem so drastic; in fact, experience has shown that when a core of adults is clear about the place of learning in Jewish life, and they themselves are committed to learning, creative and meaningful learning opportunities for children arise in a natural and organic way.

Two More Tales

This chapter began with the stories of two novice learners for whom learning was the path to a more meaningful and active Jewish life. It ends with the stories of two learners who, having completed the cycle, returned to the community a portion of what they received. Lee Hendler, author of *The Year Mom Got Religion: One Woman's Midlife Journey into Judaism,* began her studies six years ago. No longer a novice, she now serves as the President of Chizuk Amuno Congregation, a 128-year-old Conservative congregation in Baltimore in which over 2,400 adults participated in some form of learning last year. Here she describes an experience in which she took her learning to the next level—teaching.

When I began six years ago, I thought that being a learner in a learning community was mostly about the learning. The receiving of it. The intoxication of it. The euphoria of it. The satiating of a newfound appetite for brain and soul food. Wasn't coming to the table enough? Wasn't being there enough? For a long time—nearly too long a time—I was almost overwhelmed by that appetite. Fortunately, time, teachers, and a wonderful congregation intervened. Together they offered the mediating influence I needed but could not summon alone. Now, nearly six years later, I look back with fondness, awe, and some amusement at that period of awakening. And I realize that the chief reason I can look back with such equanimity is that I had the tremendous good fortune to have undertaken this journey in the midst of a congregation so deeply committed to its adult learners and animated by the vision of what it means to be a learning community.

Earlier this year, Rabbi Seltzer, principal of our religious school, asked me if I would teach a favorite passage from *Pirke Avot* (Sayings of the Fathers) to a seventh-grade class at our day school. I was flattered by the request but immediately countered with a volley of concerns. I didn't have enough time to prepare. I needed to know more about the kids. How open-ended could the class be? How long? What would be the context for the lesson? Rabbi Seltzer simply smiled and said, "So you'll do it, then!" When I asked him later how *he* knew I would agree, even before *I* did, he responded, "You answered like a teacher."

I selected a teaching from Rabbi Rami Shapiro's *Wisdom of the Jewish Sages: A Modern Reading of* Pirke Avot. Rabbi Shapiro's translation expanded Ben Hei Hei's classic "in accord with the effort is its reward" to the lyrical "We are here to do and through doing to learn; and through learning to know; and through knowing to experience wonder; and through wonder to attain wisdom; and through wisdom to find simplicity; and through simplicity to give attention; and through attention to see what needs to be done. . . ." I had planned to explore this on its own as a statement about the responsibility of being a Jew or to contrast it with Judah Ben Temah's teaching about the various ages at which certain studies and experiences are appropriate. I saw in the cyclical nature of each statement a potential connection that middle-schoolers might find "cool"—that is, worth considering.

After the prerequisite five minutes of middle school settling-in time, Rabbi Seltzer gave me a gracious introduction, citing my roles as author, speaker, and president of the congregation. This was greeted with the predictable polite disinterest that one would expect of a normal group of well-behaved seventh graders. So I took the next few minutes to establish my *real* credentials. I was a mother of four, the youngest of whom was their age. I had also, incidentally, once been their age myself. I confided that I actually liked thirteen-year-olds. In fact, I had sat next to a number of them on the *bimah* (pulpit) during the past year as they celebrated becoming bar or bat mitzvah. But none of that explained why I was really standing there. Why did *they* think I was there? "Because Rabbi Seltzer asked you to." "Because you're thinking about being a teacher and wanted to try it out." "Because you're trying to set a good example for us." All true. And then a shy, soft voice expressed the insight born of gentle disbelief. "Because you *want* to be here?"

We talked of cycles. Of how one thing leads to another. I challenged them to relate Jewish values (for example, *betselem elohim*, being made in the image of God; *hakhnasat orchim*, hospitality to strangers; *kavanah*, intentionality) to each phrase Rabbi Shapiro had so carefully constructed. We spoke of experiences in their own lives that highlighted the truth of this teaching. We wondered how doing could lead to learning or whether it ought to be the other way around. It took immense concentration on my part to keep the discussion focused, to choose which comments to pursue and which simply to acknowledge. It took effort to appear effortless and completely at ease with my material. As I listened to what they were saying (instead of planning what I wanted to say next) and felt more than thought my way into my role as their guide, I suddenly realized with delight—the way a young child will, when days of effort are finally rewarded with a successful bike ride—that I was teaching . . . actually teaching! Not with the mastery I would like, not with the art I would aspire to, but with an energy that is contagious and a passion that is essential.

The class ended. The kids seemed cheerful and stimulated. We had all concluded that my wanting to be there was an expression of what it means to be a member of the community we call Chizuk Amuno. We agreed that if I could not demonstrate to them what mattered to me, then I couldn't possibly expect that they should connect their lives to mine or attempt to find shared meaning in our lives together as members of the same community. I did not have to *tell* them that I used my learning as a way of attending to what I see that needs doing. They *saw* it in my comfort with text, the multiple source connections I readily made and the enthusiasm for learning I eagerly shared with them. And they saw it by my being there. Suddenly the *being there* I had judged sufficient six years ago had taken on another meaning altogether. Being there for myself was no longer enough. Not if I wanted to claim membership in this community I had come to love so deeply.

I understood then that the teaching I had just engaged in was the natural outcome of the learning I had experienced. I could call upon a foundation of knowledge that was authentic—earned by dint of my own hard work at the communal table of learning set so grandly before me for the past six years—because I had seen how skillfully my teachers wove their own knowledge into our learning. I even moved in the space the way I had seen my teachers move, using the environments they had taught in— exuding the casual confidence that inspires students to take risks yet feel safe at the same time. I do not fool myself that it was a great lesson. But it was a good one, and I saw in it the shimmering outlines of a future for myself that fulfills some of the promise that my learning holds.

The Hebrew word for tradition, *masoret,* is from the root that means *to transmit,* not to receive. Communities depend on the reliable transfer of tradition for their viability. When our children see adults whom they admire learning and teaching, they receive a clear message: We, the adult members of your community, consider Jewish learning essential; without it our lives are incomplete. When our study leads our children to study, then we adult learners become transmitters of our wonderful Jewish tradition, assuring that it will continue to inspire and instruct for generations to come.

Finally, here is the story of Perry Oretsky, a longtime member of Temple Emanuel of Beverly Hills and a seasoned adult learner. For several years Perry has served as a mentor to students studying for their bar or bat mitzvah.

Growing up in an Orthodox congregation, I learned a great deal by rote, but had much less opportunity to see the Torah as a living document that related to my life.

As I approached midlife, I found myself searching for deeper meaning, and was drawn more deeply back to Judaism. As I studied with different teachers, I began to appreciate how dynamic Torah study might be. I found that I could directly link concepts in the weekly Torah portions to my life. For example, in reading the Genesis story, I was struck by the choices made by the principal characters and the impact these choices made on their lives. I could see how choices I had made had similar longtime effects.

I attended a seminar on spiritual eldering, and began to entertain the idea of teaching Torah to others. Could I pass on to others what had been missing in my own religious education?

An opportunity arose when my congregation, Temple Emanuel of Beverly Hills, decided to offer a mentor for every candidate for bar/bat mitzvah. The mentor would meet with the student once a month over a period of six months. They would study the content of the student's Torah portion, and work together on the student's *d'var torah* (Torah teaching). In the course of these meetings, it was hoped that the student would establish an important relationship with an adult outside of his or her own family who could serve as a Jewish role model. I became the first lay mentor.

Since that time, I have mentored ten students over four years. I begin by getting to know the student, his or her family, hobbies, and interests. Then we look together for a window into the *parashah* (Torah portion), something that intrigues the student. While every *parashah* contains important insights that go beyond the student, I find that beginning with the student's interests provides the best route to these larger issues. I try to instill in the student both a sense of moral values that can be found in his or her particular *parashah* and I also try to show that Torah is timeless, and has lasting value in his or her current and future life.

For example, a recent student and I studied *Bereshit* (Genesis). He was fascinated with the story of Cain and Abel, and decided to focus on the issue of choice. We looked at choice from the standpoint of all the choices that were made in the story: God chose to create the world; Adam and Eve chose to eat from the fruit of the Tree of Knowledge; Adam chose to hide what he had done from God; Abel chose to give the best of his firstlings; Cain chose to give the poorest of his crop and ultimately chose to kill Abel. Ultimately, God chose to be merciful.

This student was able to see through the words and stories the nature of choice and its impact on the future of his life. As he discussed in his speech, he had to think about the impact his decisions would have on his future. What this boy learned was how to approach a Torah text and to find the connection between the text and his life.

As for me, each time I mentor a student, I find new insights into the Torah, and how it affects my life.

From the Ideal to the Real

For some readers, the above descriptions of a congregation of learners may sound utopian and abstract. These readers might wish a more concrete and realistic picture of a congregation that embodies the principles outlined above. To the best of my knowledge, no congregation exists—yet—that does so fully. However, a growing number of synagogues have set for themselves the goal of creating a congregation of learners, and many of them have undertaken important initiatives in this direction. The next chapter contains vignettes suggesting the variety of ingenious ways that congregations have approached this goal.

3

Images of
Congregational Learning

Throughout North America, dozens
of synagogues have set out to become congregations of learners. Over
the past decade, these congregations have created many new learning
opportunities for their members and generated a palpable sense of excitement in the process. Though none would claim to have fully reached their
goal, all can point with pride to congregants whose Jewish lives have been
enriched, programs that have flourished, new traditions and expectations
that have been established, and, perhaps most importantly, enthusiasm
for learning that continues to grow. If this book had a companion video
or CD-ROM, readers could see for themselves what congregational learning might become. Failing that, the next best thing was to assemble a com-
posite picture of some possibilities for a congregation of learning, a collage
of images drawn from congregations throughout the United States.
Included in this chapter are eleven vignettes from nine synagogues and
two congregational consortia that were chosen to highlight different facets
of congregational learning.

By necessity, this is an incomplete collection. The vignettes included
in this chapter represent only a fraction of the learning opportunities

available at these congregations. And the congregations themselves represent only a sample of those that are experimenting with new modes of learning.[1]

There is no right way to learn. The statement that begins "The best way to teach X . . ." is bound to be proven false. Some people are most comfortable in formal classes, complete with lectures and reading assignments; others, who feel constrained in a formal class, might find themselves most engaged in informal, experiential settings, such as retreats or arts workshops. Some people learn best individually, while others enjoy learning with a partner, or even in a small group. A congregation of learners is one that has a wide enough range of formats and environments to accommodate many different types of learners. The examples in this chapter were selected to represent this range of options. Taken together, they suggest the variety of learning experiences a synagogue might offer: individual and group; formal and informal; intellectual and spiritual; one-shot and long-term, and varying lengths in between.

In selecting these particular accounts, my purpose is to give the reader a sense of the range of exciting learning opportunities that can be created in a congregational setting, and *not* to suggest that these learning opportunities should be found in every congregation. Theoretically, a congregation with infinite resources might offer programs in every permutation and combination of these variables. In reality, however, congregations need to make choices about where to invest their time and energy and financial resources. Every synagogue is different—each is located in a different milieu, adheres to a different ideology, and has a different membership with a different set of expectations. The type of learning that fits perfectly into one setting may not be appropriate in another. As I will argue in great detail in the next chapter, synagogue revitalization involves much more than replicating programs. The remainder of this book describes a process through which a congregation might make choices that fit its own special set of circumstances.

A most natural response to any of the vignettes in this chapter would be: *Wow, this is so terrific! We should do this at our congregation!* But I would ask you, the reader, to resist this urge and think instead about how these outstanding programs came to be: What enabled these congregations to create such innovative learning experiences, and to attract large numbers of their congregants to participate? In every one of the cases described here, the learning experience is but one example of a program that grew out of a larger vision, an attempt to become a congregation of learners. The creators of these programs did not think about congregational learning as an accumulation of programs, but as a process of discovery—with the staff discovering the needs and interests of the congregants, and the congregants discovering the excitement and satisfactions of Jewish learning.

The vignettes in this chapter fall into three categories: intergenerational learning, adult learning, and learning that is woven into the fabric of congregational life.

Intergenerational Learning

As the inherent limitations of the afternoon and weekend religious school have been felt more acutely, congregational educators have increasingly turned to family education. They have found that teaching prayers and rituals in a family setting increases the chance that the rituals will be practiced at home, and that the entire family will attend prayer services together. Other elements of the religious school curriculum, including Bible stories, rabbinic legends, ethical precepts, and Hebrew phrases, have a much better chance of being retained when they can be discussed and reinforced at home. When the entire family becomes involved in Jewish learning, a clear message is sent to the children that what they are doing is important.

Family Education

The following vignette tells of a small congregation's experiments in family education. The Shorashim (Roots) program integrated family education into the structure of the religious school in a variety of ways over a three-year period. It is written by Dr. Simone Schweber, the congregation's former educator:

> Etz Chayim is a young congregation; at the time of this writing, only five years old. Its Hebrew school, called Shorashim (Roots), is only three years old. And though Etz Chayim's membership is rapidly growing, fewer than 200 families are currently affiliated, many of them having never been affiliated with a congregation before. In some ways, precisely because of these congregational factors—its youth, size, and newness—Etz Chayim's educational programs have had tremendous freedom to experiment, if limited resources. (For lack of a better metaphor, it's easier to change the course of a small sailboat than that of a luxury liner.) As a result, the family education component of the Shorashim curriculum has taken radically different forms over the last three years.
>
> At the beginning of its first year, Shorashim's student body numbered only twelve, and the parents of those students were highly involved in shaping the formal curriculum, monitoring the administration of the school, and helping with classroom supervision. The program followed a one-room schoolhouse model where, for four hours each week, a single teacher (me) taught Hebrew, Bible, and prayer to all the students who ranged in grade from fourth through seventh. Though there were only a few formal family education events in the course of the year—that is, times when all the parents and children studied Torah together—many parents learned along with their kids when it was their turn to help out in the classroom. The family education component was thus mostly informal that year, but it was embraced with a rare enthusiasm; the few families who had taken the risk of enrolling their children in Shorashim shared a sense of excitement at being involved in something so new. I think that almost regardless of what I had planned, the parents' enthusiasm and excitement would have helped the family education component succeed in its goals of cultivating a strong sense of community, increasing knowledge of Torah, and cementing a dedication to Jewish learning among the families involved.

The next year, the Shorashim student body swelled to forty-four, and the education committee members and I became more ambitious about the family education component of the curriculum. In addition to our previous goals, we hoped to incorporate families with children in Jewish day schools into the family education program, which meant that the curriculum of the program would need to be distinct from Shorashim's and from the local day school's. We chose to study *klal yisrael* (the interdependence of all Jews) through the concept of Jewish denominations in American history, a timely topic for the congregation as it was to consider affiliation with a movement the next year.

The program met once a month for ten sessions and each session included joint and parallel learning times. Divided into three large groups, families spent the first hour of each session investigating the history or practices of a movement through a programmed activity. Then, after a bagel break, the parents met to discuss assigned readings based on the topic, and the kids met in age-graded classes (from first through eighth grades) to pursue a thematically linked activity. A quick example from the first session on Reform Judaism: During the first hour, families read aloud a brief one-page reading on some of the issues that sparked the creation of Reform Judaism in Germany. Then, the kids and parents were separated into two groups and assigned to debate the issues (whether parts of the worship service should be conducted in the vernacular, whether an organ should be introduced, etc.). In the second hour, the parents discussed an article on the history of the Reform movement (in the same three groups) while the kids designed synagogue spaces to correspond to the Reform movement's innovations.

Overall, this program, which we called B'Yachad (together), succeeded beyond our wildest hopes in some areas and failed dismally in others. The parents loved the parents-only times; they raved about the lay-led discussions and enjoyed, for the most part, reading the articles—many parents found the information itself new and fascinating. The joint learning times, on the other hand, worked well only for those families without kids below fourth grade. The sometimes subtle ideological distinctions between denominations were hard for younger children to grasp, if, indeed, they could sit still through the reading selections at all. We were most disappointed, though, to realize that holding sessions once a month was too infrequent to facilitate the integration of day school and Shorashim students. Finally, while many parents reported feeling a strong sense of community in the school as a whole, some were frustrated not to have an opportunity to meet in groups by class. These problems prompted us to redesign the family education strand again.

In the third year, the student body almost doubled but we were unable to rent more space to accommodate larger-sized family sessions. As a result, we gave up on the idea of integrating day school families, and we chose not to include younger siblings in the family education program. While this did compromise our desire to educate (whole) families, we had few alternatives given our budgetary constraints. Instead, we divided up the family education component according to the Shorashim curriculum. So, for example, the families of bar/bat mitzvah students had their own family education strand linked to the students' studies of *trope* (cantillations), *TaNaKh* (Bible), and mitzvot. Likewise, the third graders had their own family education strand that focused on the *siddur* (prayer book), and the fourth, fifth, and sixth graders, who were studying Jewish history that year in mixed-grade groups, had their own family education strand.

This model worked exceedingly well conceptually. For the students, the family sessions reinforced the Shorashim curriculum. For the parents, the tightly intertwined curricula allowed the students to serve sometimes as their teachers. (At one session of the Jewish history track, for example, the Shorashim students ran a series of stations teaching their parents about the Inquisition.) The family strands also allowed the parents of each graded group to get to know each other well. Because we had such limited rental space, however, only two of the three family education strands could meet simultaneously on a Sunday morning, which meant that only the bar/bat mitzvah group had more than four formal family education sessions, a definite drawback for our hopes of cultivating a strong sense of community and for strengthening Judaic knowledge among parents. Also, in part because there were so few meetings, the lay-led adult discussions didn't develop into cohesive groups. If all the family education strands could have met for one formal education session and one social activity each month, I think the program would have accomplished all of its goals with ease.

What did we learn from our experiments in Jewish family education? For starters, think big. It was worth having great ambitions for the programs despite our limited resources and physical constraints. Second, don't be afraid to make enormous and fundamental changes. (As is written in Joshua 1:9, "Be strong and of good courage; be not frightened, neither be dismayed.") Our family education program changed shape entirely from one year to the next in pursuing our definitions of success. And while we worried that this would compromise people's sense of security or consistency, instead it helped foster a continued sense of excitement among participants (even when they were dissatisfied). Third, be candid about your experimentation, explaining your reasons for structuring experiences as you do, requesting and taking seriously feedback from all your participants (kids and adults). Finally, always serve bagels and cream cheese at family education events. (It's good to have at least one nonexperimental aspect to a program.) Next year, Congregation Etz Chayim's experiments in Jewish family education will continue, hopefully with great success, but most likely with bumps along the way.

From Family Education to Congregational Education

While family education is a growing trend and is now offered by the majority of congregational schools, only some congregations have used it as a basis for congregation-wide learning. Indeed, in larger congregations it typically consists of a small number of family programs, organized by grade level, so that each set of parents participates with one of their children no more than three or four times a year. In an effort to expand the benefits of these programs, some synagogues are extending family education in two directions. First, they offer the existing programs to the entire congregation, and not just to families with children in the religious school. In this way, family education becomes congregational education, involving single people without children, parents who are empty nesters, and grandparents whose children live far away. Second, synagogues create new programs for a group of congregants that commits to attend weekly, usually on Shabbat. Thus the programming can go far beyond that of an isolated experience. Over time, knowledge and skills accumulate, and a community of learners coalesces.

Rabbi Richard Jacobs of Westchester Reform Temple, in Scarsdale, New York, describes an intergenerational program of this second type, called Sharing Shabbat:

> A chilling winter wind was blowing as the families arrived for Sharing Shabbat. Cars pulled up to unload children and parents, who huddled together while making their way down the stone path to Westchester Reform Temple's Center for Jewish Life.
>
> As the families arrived, the Schwartz family was busy setting up the kiddush they brought in honor of Max's birthday. Just a little after 9:00 A.M., most of the folks had found their usual seats and Cantor Angela Warnick Buchdahl began the service, leading everyone in a lively version of *modeh ani.* The service flowed freely with some reading, but mostly singing as people turned the pages of the specially prepared loose-leaf notebook *siddur.* After the *Shma,* almost all of the kids came forward to lead the opening phrases of *v'ahavta* through hand movements.
>
> During the *Amidah,* before the *modim* prayer, people had the opportunity to share with the congregation things for which they are grateful. One family said how lucky they feel to be sitting together in our warm sanctuary, looking through the large windows at the snow blowing through the trees.
>
> When the *Amidah* finished, the cantor called up the Chernick family to lead the Torah service. As a family they took the scroll from the ark and proceeded to carry it through the congregation. The kids helped undress the scroll before it was put down on the reader's table.
>
> Bob Chernick introduced the Torah portion, *Vayak'hel,* by saying that he hadn't really spoken publicly about a Torah portion since his bar mitzvah. As he read over this one he was struck by the manner in which the ancient Israelites came together to create their desert praying place. The

Torah says that every person whose heart was so moved brought forth offerings for the building of the tabernacle. The idea that the ancient Israelites freely participated in this sacred building project seemed quite foreign, because ever since his childhood, nothing having to do with Judaism was voluntary—he was forced into every single Jewish act.

At first the idea that he had to accompany his family each week to Sharing Shabbat felt like yet another coercive Jewish act, except that now on most Saturday mornings he was a *nediv lebo*—a person whose heart moved him—to come be a part of this praying and learning community called Sharing Shabbat.

Bob and Ellen chanted the *brakha* before the reading of the Torah and then Ellen chanted the opening lines of the *parashah,* letting out an enormous sigh with the last word. Next, ten-year-old Emily read the translation of the portion in heartfelt but barely audible English.

After the Torah service, Cantor Buchdahl told the story of how King Solomon found the right place to construct the Temple. This well known *agadah* (legend) describes two brothers who seem at first to be stealing grain from each other, but, when confronted by King Solomon, it is revealed that each one is actually showing kindness and sensitivity to the other. That is when Solomon is convinced that the field of such caring brothers would be the perfect site for God's Temple. The story made everyone think about what values should be the foundation of all Temples, including our own Sharing Shabbat.

Before the kaddish several people stood up to share remembrances of members of their family. One woman stood and spoke of her mother who had died suddenly the week before without any warning. Throughout her life, her mother had been her source of bedrock support and strength. She described feeling emotionally paralyzed by her loss. She closed by thanking the Sharing Shabbat community for enveloping her with kindness and casseroles during *shiva* (the seven-day morning period)—she couldn't have imagined getting through those excruciating days without this community's love.

The Schwartz family came forward to lead the *kiddush* (blessing over the wine) and *hamotzi* (blessing over the bread), prefacing the blessings with a word about this season of the year when their family observes a wedding anniversary and Max's birthday. Following the *brakhot,* folks descended upon the refreshments in the center hall. Serious shmoozing and not an insignificant amount of eating filled the next fifteen minutes. Finally, Cantor Buchdahl yelled out that adult Torah study was about to start in the sanctuary, and that the kids should all find their way to their classes.

Over fifty adults gathered in a circle with UAHC Torah Commentaries on their laps for the Torah study. In her introduction, Cantor Buchdahl described the description in the *parashah* of the building of the ancient tabernacle. She spent a few moments talking about the name of the *parashah, Vayak'hel.* "It means to form together as a religious community, a *kehilah,*" she explained. "What was it about the act of building a praying place that made our ancestors into a *kehilah*—a holy community?" Ed remembered reading descriptions of Amish barn raisings—how, after a fire, neighbors came together and spent a day building a new barn. The work itself bound them together—they felt a sense of community as they worked together for a common purpose. Similarly, Ed suggested, the Israelites truly became a community when they worked together for the common purpose of building their sacred worship space.

Meanwhile, the children gathered together in their groups, sorting through the Torah portion. The kindergarten and first graders had a very hard time working cooperatively to build a miniature Temple out of Legos. Their teacher had given them a simple drawing of a Temple and then asked them to work together in building the model Temple. Needless to say, it was not all smooth sailing as the students built their "mini-*mishkan.*"

The fourth and fifth graders compared last week's Torah portion about the building of the Golden Calf to this week's description of the building of the tabernacle. They debated why the Israelites were forbidden to build a calf made of gold while they were commanded to build golden objects for the tabernacle. One boy said God acted sort of like his mom and dad— the way they tell him certain things to do and not do, and when he questions them they answer: "Because I said so." "God's just pulling that parent thing, by telling the Israelites only to build what they are told to build."

The teacher concluded by asking the students what they would choose to do with their talents and time—would they work for the good of the community or just do things for their own benefit—"Isn't that the same choice the Israelites had to make?"

At 1:15 kids and parents made their way to the atrium for the final blessing. As the students were excitedly telling their parents what they did with the *parashah,* Cantor Buchdahl asked families to join her in singing a blessing for one another. "We'll see everyone next Shabbat!" As people bundled up in their down jackets and wool caps, the atrium echoed with the sound of "Shabbat Shalom!"

Intergenerational Learning Through the Arts

Not all intergenerational learning in congregations takes place on Shabbat, and not all of it takes the form of formal classes. The arts are a promising venue for bringing generations together, as the following vignette by Stacia Kopeikin, a member of Temple Emanuel in Beverly Hills, demonstrates:

For the past three years, our synagogue, Temple Emanuel of Beverly Hills, has presented an annual intergenerational production. It is a unique program that showcases temple members, ages eight to eighty-eight, celebrating Judaism and tradition through drama and music.

My introduction to these intergenerational plays came two years ago when my nine-year-old son, Max, asked if he could participate. I said yes, not really understanding what it all meant. After the first meeting, he came home and said that the other kids' parents and grandparents were taking part. He asked if I would join in. I had never been interested in acting, nor had I ever performed on stage, so I kindly declined, and encouraged him to approach my talented mother, Esther (his Bubbie). She, of course, could not refuse his request. For the next four months they attended many rehearsals, culminating in a fabulous four-performance run. They both gained so much from the experience that I was jealous and decided then to explore the next year's show for myself.

The 1998–99 production was announced and this time my eight-year-old daughter Hannah wanted to perform, *with Mommy.* (My son decided to sit this year out.) I, in turn, asked both my mother and father to participate, and they agreed. My father (from whom I got my terrible voice) worked mostly behind the scenes, building sets and gathering props. My mother, daughter, and I happily attended countless and seemingly endless rehearsals, run by our multitalented, energetic director, Nili Kosmol. Our show, *Generation to Generation,* was a wonderful musical that tells the story of one woman's life in flashbacks. The scenes deal with many of the passages of Jewish life—birth, bat mitzvah, marriage, and death, as well as factual historical events (the Russian pogroms, the Holocaust, and the Israeli wars). It was an emotional play to perform and we became a close-knit group.

Being in this play was a multifaceted learning experience. Each of us learned about Jewish history and tradition, to be sure. We sang and danced about Judaism's triumphs and tragedies. But, just as important, we learned to work together as a temple family, young and old. We learned to appreciate each other's different perspectives on life. My daughter Hannah met elderly women from the sisterhood whom she now regularly visits with at Friday night services and holidays.

I continue to feel extremely connected to my temple family because of this merging with my immediate family. The intergenerational component of these productions is a unique, unparalleled educational experience.

Adult Learning

A key to developing a congregation of learners is engaging adult congregants in study, a goal that has often been elusive. Most congregations offer adult classes, including "Introduction to Judaism," beginning Hebrew, and some form of Torah study. Typically, however, no more than ten percent of the membership enrolls in these classes, perhaps because the range of options is so limited, perhaps because of the required semester-long commitment, or perhaps because the programs don't seem particularly exciting.

Rabbi Harold Schulweis attributed adults' disinterest in adult study to their miseducation as children, whose—

> questions were either given short shrift, answered with dogmatic curtness, or put off to an unspecified future time: "When you're older you'll understand." The religious questions were displaced by Hebrew reading exercises, a few ritual skills, some Bible stories, and preparations for the bar/bat mitzvah public performance. The unanswered questions dried up, and in their place a theological black hole formed. This vacuum was in turn filled with superstition, myths, literalist translations of profound religious insight, images of street theology that as adults we cannot accept.[2]

The result, according to Schulweis, is a profound boredom.

In his own congregation, Valley Beth Shalom in Encino, California, Rabbi Schulweis set out to combat this boredom three decades ago by subdividing his large congregation into *havurot*, small subcommunities that celebrate and study together. In the intervening years, numerous congregations have created *havurot* of their own, but few have managed to institutionalize learning beyond the occasional guest lecture. Today congregations are trying a variety of new ways to promote adult learning. The next four vignettes show the possibility of utilizing different formats, such as an intensive workshop, a Shabbat retreat, or preparation for an upcoming holiday. In contrast to the prevailing assumption that adult learners will only come for one-shot sessions in which they are passive listeners, these vignettes demonstrate that adults can commit themselves to ongoing learning and challenging assignments when their minds, hearts, and imaginations are actively engaged.

A Spiritual Seminar

Rabbi Neil Kurshan of the Huntington Jewish Center in New York has found that one way to hook his congregants into Jewish learning is by inviting them to explore spirituality, in both their own lives, and in Jewish texts. He offers workshops on the writing of spiritual autobiographies, which allow participants to reflect on moments of holiness in their lives.

When we are young we look ahead to life. As we grow older we look back at life. While there is some truth to these statements, life is never quite this sharply bifurcated. At every stage of our lives we look back and attempt to make sense and meaning of our lives, and that very process integrates our experience and allows us to see where we are heading in the future.

Three years ago I began leading workshops to help individuals write spiritual autobiographies. A spiritual autobiography is a narration describing moments of holiness in life and describing the themes that have linked these moments of holiness together.

I first became aware of the possibility of such moments of holiness when I was a graduate student living in Cambridge, Massachusetts. It was a cloudy, dreary day under a monotonous gray sky, typical of early spring in Boston. I did not have class until the afternoon and was spending a languid morning in my apartment. I remember pausing by the window and gazing out. The view was the same as it had always been—a short, stubby tree immediately in front of the window—its trunk darkened and dampened by drizzle earlier in the morning. Behind the tree a six-story apartment house next door blocked the view from my window of anything more distant. I felt the stillness of midmorning since most of the residents of the neighborhood had long ago left for work or class. Suddenly a deep inner peace enveloped me. For a moment time stopped and I felt at harmony and at home in the world. A sense of fullness welled up from deep within me, although at the same time I experienced this feeling as a reality external to me. The view out the window was sharpened—I saw grace and fluidity in a gnarled tree and order and symmetry in an apartment building. The feeling lasted only a moment but my awareness of the holy dimension of existence that previously had only been an intellectual abstraction was now a personal reality. Eternity had breathed a moment into my life, and I knew that the remaining days of my life would have to be lived in response to that moment.

For most of us these moments of holiness are rare, occurring only once or twice in our lives and perhaps more frequently on a less intense basis. Sometimes they change the course of our lives; sometimes they may simply reaffirm a direction; sometimes nothing in our lives changes, but we see the world, others, and ourselves with a greater sharpness and beauty.

In my workshops I ask people to write about these moments of holiness. I ask them to describe when they happened. What provoked them? Where did they occur? What did they feel like? How long did they last? How did they change life or perception of the world? Sometimes people describe an experience similar to my own that had no apparent provocation. More often they describe moments in a place of great natural beauty; moments during a life passage such as a birth, bar/bat mitzvah, wedding or death; or moments of deep encounter with another person in a friendship or marriage.

Evoking these moments allows participants to pause from the busy pace of life and to recall the times they have touched a deep reality. Reflecting upon what has led up to these moments and what has followed them allows participants to extract the themes that have shaped their lives from the bewildering accumulation of detail and life experiences. As a result of these workshops, participants are better able to integrate their past lives into some patterns of meaning and to emerge from the workshop with a clearer sense of where they can go in the years ahead.

The workshops attract a variety of individuals. A somewhat greater number of women than men have pursued this work with me. Most of the participants are in the early years of midlife or older. Sometimes they are drawn to the course because they feel mired in their situation in life and unable to move ahead. Others join the course because they have gone through an experience of great sadness or joy that has left them profoundly changed and with a need to find new moorings. Others join simply because they want to pause to reflect upon their lives or to look at them through a different lens.

The series of eight workshops is divided into three components. The first four sessions consist of exercises to elicit the thoughts and memories necessary to write the spiritual autobiography. A pause of a few weeks allows participants to compose their autobiography. The workshop concludes with participants reading the autobiographies aloud to the group. The ideal size for the workshop is eight to twelve individuals. Groups smaller than eight diminish the diversity of experiences shared in the course, and groups larger than twelve make it more difficult to create a sense of intimacy and to allow the time for everyone to share their experience with the group.

In the opening sessions some of the exercises require that people recall significant moments in their lives directly, exercises through which individuals draw the present and then describe their picture to the other participants; recall a room in a childhood home that had pleasant associations and sketch the floor plan; describe a mentor who was a significant influence during adolescence or young adulthood; describe a place that is a sanctuary in adulthood—a place of safety and deep at homeness.

Other exercises elicit remembrance of the past through Jewish texts. Biblical texts, for example, are used to elicit the significant turning points in individuals' lives. Thus the stories of Jacob in the book of Genesis are used to highlight and recall life-changing experiences such as a moment of holiness (Jacob's vision of the ladder reaching to heaven); a life cycle event (Jacob's marriage to Leah and love for Rachel); a betrayal of trust (Lavan's deception); a significant disappointment (Rachel's childlessness); entrance into spiritual maturity (Jacob's wrestling with the angel); healing and *tshuvah* (Jacob's reunion with his brother); and homecoming (Jacob's return to Israel). Each of these stages of Jacob's life has the potential to recall life-changing moments in the lives of workshop participants.

The use of Jewish texts in the workshops is important. They help participants locate the experiences that are important in writing a Jewish spiritual autobiography. While a first dance, receiving one's driver's license, or admission to college may be significant moments in life, they are not necessarily central to a spiritual autobiography. In a spiritual autobiography we are seeking those experiences that have a connection to the realm of the holy. The use of Jewish texts legitimizes and identifies the realm of religious experience. Thus Psalm 30, which describes the ascent of the psalmist from despair to joyful closeness to God, is used in the course to sensitize participants to the moments of intimacy and distance from God in their own lives.

The reading of the spiritual autobiographies within the group in the final sessions concludes the course. Participants are asked to simply listen to the reader and to ask only questions that help the individual to clarify what he or she has written. All judgment, criticism, and even well-intentioned advice are avoided. Reading the autobiographies aloud within the context of an accepting group confers legitimacy upon the experience. Participants often comment upon the richness and complexity reflected in the unique story of each individual while at the same time noticing common themes repeated in each of the stories. The sharing of these autobiographies reminds participants both of the distinctiveness of each story as well as of the common humanity shared by each person in the group.

In writing their autobiographies some individuals focus only on one piece of their lives; others write an overview of their entire lives. One woman focused on the death of her father who, during her high school years, had not always been able to be a parent for her and her siblings because of working long hours at two jobs. The time they spent together before his death allowed them to heal the strains in their relationship. Though she has never again felt the spiritual intensity that she experienced when her father was dying, the time she shared with her father has allowed her to more fully recognize and appreciate the spiritual dimension of her life.

Many workshop participants do not single out one experience in their lives but rather define some of the themes that have shaped wide swaths of their experience. One young man described a creative tension that pervaded his life and was represented by the conflicting values of the two sides of his family, one more traditional and the other more Americanized.

> "So my mother's side was the traditional one—the big, warm, loving family, filled with people who would pinch your cheeks and proclaim something in Yiddish that, though it could never be understood, was enough to send any child blushing behind his mother's legs. My mother insisted that when we moved

to the suburbs, we join the synagogue so my older brother could go to Hebrew school. My mother's mother would come out for the holidays, and would tell me strange and wonderful stories about Irsava when I climbed into bed—about her house and her father, and my grandfather, and her store, and the mischief my mother got into when she was little.

"My father's side was nominally German Reform and, more accurately, philosophically opposed to religion. My father used to sit in the car at family weddings reading the newspaper rather than set foot inside the sanctuary of a synagogue. My father's mother in particular was horrified at my thickly accented maternal grandmother, who represented all that was backward and uncivilized about religion and Jews. What I could never quite understand was how my father went from rejecting Judaism to actively identifying with it; from being unwilling to open a book to ultimately being a (Jewish) teacher. I know the details—he took an adult education course, which inspired him, and he sought more and more information until his interest in observance surpassed my mother's."

The writer went on to describe his oscillation during his student days between his own secular and Jewish sides. As he became a young adult he felt the tug of his Jewish ancestry during a visit to Europe and Russia. In his conclusion he jumped ahead to the recent death of his father and writes:

"I have become more accepting of this tension in my life and family, and have been trying to resolve it, especially since my father's death, by coming to services, praying, reflecting on my own sense of connectedness to Jews and to God. I have not yet done so. I look to the example my father set: At some point he must have come to some realization about his own mind, his own understanding, that changed him from rejecting to relishing his Judaism. I wish I had asked him how he did this."

The autobiographies of the participants in these workshops span many emotions. They write of moments of intense joy and excruciating pain. They write of being embraced by God and of being abandoned. They write of moments of healing and of moments of regret for what will never be retrieved. As I have listened to participants describe their lives, I have often felt God peeking through the details. I have been impressed by the resiliency with which people have been able to face moments of despair and the gratitude they have taken away from the moments of joy and blessing. As I have listened to my students share their spiritual autobiographies, I have felt that I was listening to the reading of a sacred text. Each of these spiritual autobiographies has a human author, but is guided by a divine hand.

Retreats

Not all congregants are able to fit ongoing classes into their tight schedules, and some synagogues have found day-long or weekend retreats to be a popular alternative. In the next vignette Sidney Schwarz, founding rabbi of Adat Shalom Reconstructionist Congregation of Bethesda, Maryland, describes annual retreats, which served as occasions for study, the deepening of personal religious commitment, and the building of community:[3]

> Adat Shalom Reconstructionist Congregation of Bethesda, Maryland, was a community that I founded along with several friends in 1988. Its core organizing principles were the empowerment of the members, the strength of communal and interpersonal bonds, and a commitment to maximalist and serious progressive Judaism. The most unique part of Adat Shalom's educational program was the creation of a member-drafted communal Statement of Principles. It forced both the leadership and the membership of the community to struggle with what it meant to be a religious/spiritual community. It was drafted by a committee of members and then was presented to the community as a whole for feedback, discussion, and eventual ratification. Both the first statement, drafted in the first few months of the congregation's existence, and a more ambitious rewrite that took place five years into the congregation's history, became a vehicle that shaped the communal culture. Programs were evaluated based on their consistency with the Statement of Principles and my oral and written messages to the community were intentionally framed in the language of the communally sanctioned statement.
>
> An expansion of the Statement of Principles process took place in the

context of a program of retreats that we held every spring. We put the same energy into promoting the retreats that we did into launching our Shabbat morning services. It was a "happening" and you had to be there. In the early years attendance ranged from seventy to eighty percent of the community. As the congregation grew in size it dropped to closer to fifty percent of the community, yet there are few members who have not been to at least one retreat and virtually all would talk about it as a transformative experience.

In choosing the theme for the retreat, I looked for some aspect of Jewish life that had a direct bearing on our personal and communal practice of Judaism. I would then begin to assemble a sourcebook with biblical, rabbinic, and contemporary views on the topic. On occasion, when the material was voluminous, we would start the study of the material in adult-education sessions prior to the retreat.

At the retreat, three sessions were devoted to the topic. I would lead the sessions through an examination of traditional sources and then facilitate discussions on the extent to which the traditional *halakhic* standards had relevance to our own lives. By the Sunday session of the retreat, participants would work on personal and communal contracts in which they would try to articulate what of the traditional norm they would seek to integrate into their personal life and what standard they would like to see for the Adat Shalom community.

The theme of the first year was Shabbat (how we would observe, celebrate, and make that day special). In subsequent years we tackled other key issues that affected Jewish communal life: *tsedakah* (how we would use and/or share our wealth); *gmilut chasidim* (ways to extend acts of loving kindness to other members of our community); *tikun olam* (how we might address the injustices of our society and our world); *avodah* (how we engage in service to the community); Israel and the Jewish People (what our relationship is and how we express it); and eco-*kashrut* (what might guide our consumption patterns in an ecologically threatened world).

The theme never ended with the conclusion of the retreat. We would collect everyone's ideas for communal standards and then I would recruit several volunteers to take responsibility for putting the ideas into language with the express intention of creating guidelines for the entire community. At the High Holidays that followed the spring retreat I would devote a sermon to summarizing what we had studied and learned at the retreat and then announce that a committee was currently working on drafting guidelines that would be published by the congregation after proper review and ratification by the membership. This would always elicit several new volunteers and the committee commenced its work. Similar to the process of passing the congregational Statement of Principles, each set of guidelines was eventually ratified by the entire congregation. The guidelines are on display at our services and some of the language from each has found its way into revised versions of our Statement of Principles. They serve as educational tools for the congregation and are a source of great pride to the membership.

The process of creating each set of guidelines not only raised the knowledge of Judaism and of its texts among our members; it also raised consciousness about the way we might live our lives more in keeping with the spirit of the Jewish tradition. And many people became more observant as a result. Having been brought into the process of shaping the standards that might guide Jewish life, members became far more invested in how their personal or family practice might be a part of that vision of Jewish life.

Following the Calendar

Yet another vehicle for adult learning is to relate study to an upcoming holiday. Even Jews who don't live their lives according to the Jewish calendar find their thoughts turning to Jewish concerns around the time of major holidays. A consortium of four synagogues in Westchester, New York, capitalized on people's heightened awareness of their Jewishness around the time of the High Holidays, and joined together to create a series of communal study sessions to prepare their congregants for Rosh Hashanah and Yom Kippur. A special feature of the program is that the congregations were drawn from the four denominations—Orthodox, Conservative,

Reform, and Reconstructionist—and that the study sessions offered their congregants a rare opportunity to engage in serious discussion and dialogue with one another. Rabbi Gordon Tucker of the Conservative Temple Israel Center in White Plains, New York, was one of the rabbis who organized this program.

Shortly after I came to White Plains, New York, in 1994, a Reform colleague proposed that we form a *hevrutah* (study fellowship) of the various rabbis in the community and study together regularly. I readily agreed. We immediately got in touch with our Reconstructionist colleague, and we were quickly a threesome. Because the rabbi of the Orthodox synagogue in town was retiring that year, and a search was already underway for a successor, we decided to begin with the three of us and then invite the new Orthodox rabbi to the *hevrutah* when he arrived the next fall. Regularly study began on Wednesday mornings, and when the fall of 1995 came around, it was our delight to receive an enthusiastic positive response to our invitation from our new Orthodox colleague. Thus was born the White Plains Rabbinic Hevrutah, a fellowship of rabbis (and some educational directors) from four different synagogues of four different movements that studies Talmud every week.

The existence of such a transdenominational fellowship and friendship in a decade otherwise marked by great friction among Judaism's movements was not exactly unique, but it was highly unusual. But more important, the uncommon colleagueship that developed around common inquiry had some important results that stretched far beyond the contained world of the rabbis themselves. When tragedy struck with the assassination of Yitzhak Rabin, just two months after our "foursome" had been created, we were already close enough to be able to create a joint memorial service on which we could all agree, and to organize it in less than twenty-four hours. We also began to think jointly about the ways in which our teenage populations needed wider Jewish horizons, more exciting learning, and an opportunity to meet more Jews their age. Improbably enough, joint educational programs among our four high schools began to take shape, and slowly became a fixture of our schools. Word, of course,

got around that there was something special about the rabbinic community in White Plains that was a welcome model of dialogue, pluralism,
and mutual respect. But it wasn't until the fall of 1997 that what we had
done for ourselves in our small group really began to touch a chord in the
community at large.

In the spring of that year, I casually described to my colleagues the program I had run for several years in the fall before the Days of Awe: several
study sessions for the adults in my congregation that focused on the
liturgy, the theology, the history, and the music of the upcoming holidays.
Forty to fifty people had come each year, and they got a great deal out
of it in terms of preparing their minds and their souls for Rosh Hashanah
and Yom Kippur. The *hevrutah* immediately had the idea of expanding
this to the entire community, under our joint auspices. And so we got
started planning. With rabbis, cantors, and educational directors from the
four synagogues, it was a simple matter to put together a program that
would offer nine or ten multievening mini-courses on topics ranging from
an understanding of the Binding of Isaac, the history, laws, and theology of the shofar (ram's horn), and the Book of Jonah, to an analysis of
the concepts of sin and forgiveness in Judaism. Wouldn't it be wonderful
if forty to fifty people were to show up not just from Temple Israel, but
from each of the four synagogues? We would meet four times, once in
each congregation. People would get to know the physical layout of their
neighbor's house of worship. They would be encouraged not to study
with their own rabbi and cantor, but rather to see how Torah was understood and transmitted in counterpart synagogues. With hopes for an
attendance of about 150, we sent out invitations to the community and
waited expectantly on the evening of 2 Elul 5757 at Reconstructionist congregation Bet Am Shalom.

By the time the three-hundredth person entered the building, we knew
we had tapped into something quite important and attractive to the community. In all, 400 men and women came not just that night, but on each
of the other three nights, all eager to study, share insights into this highly
charged season of the Jewish year, and understand better how their Jewish
neighbors study and worship. The classes had an electricity about them,

as each of us who were teaching had the pleasure of guiding people only partially familiar to us through a study of texts that we all share, but that we interpret and apply very differently. It was in many ways what learning is supposed to be—not simply a reconfirmation of what we already believe, in a style with which we are all too comfortable, but rather a challenge, and a confrontation with ideas that we do not encounter every day. What a blessing to have lay people anxious to engage in such an enterprise! On one of the four nights, we planned for a community *bet midrash* (house of study). As people entered, we gave them texts relating to *Unetaneh Tokef,* a central prayer of the season, and matched them with four or five other people who were from the spectrum of the sponsoring synagogues. For an hour, the participants (again, 400 strong) studied together, debated among themselves, derived insights from their colleagues' interpretations and experiences, and left wanting more. The Elul program had been a smashing success, and it was, quite simply, the draw of Torah, the draw of encountering Torah with other Jews, and the desire to create peace and a greater whole in at least one Jewish community.

The last of the Elul programs that year was on the night of 23 Elul. Rosh Hashanah was a week away. No one wanted to end the experience, but there was no more time. And yet, people have a way, even if spontaneously, of making certain things that ought to happen actually happen. On the first day of Rosh Hashanah, in the late afternoon, my usual group of about 100–125 congregants walked over to a nearby creek (there is not much water in White Plains) for *Tashlich,* a ceremony in which we cast bread crumbs into the water, symbolic of our transgressions. As we gathered, along came similar numbers from the other synagogues. Four hundred people came to observe the Rosh Hashanah ritual together at the same place and time, because they did not want to let go of the important experience of learning together now that the holiday for which we had prepared together was really here. It was a moment not to be forgotten.

The Elul program has continued. It is a fixture in the community that the community itself will ensure happens each year. In 2000, a spring learning series among the four synagogues will be started as well. And in the meantime, the rabbis have finished their own study of tractate *Hagigah* and are about a third of the way through tractate *Gittin*. We've taken on another colleague from a neighboring town, and the chance to study together is one of the most precious things in our weeks. Our congregants have come to know, respect, and covet what we have. In a time when the commitment of Jews to traditional study can easily be doubted, and in a time when Jews of different movements too often make headlines by delegitimizing one another, a bit of a positive counterculture has been created.

It's been quipped, sardonically, that talmudic humor is epitomized in the phrase "Disciples of the wise increase peace in the world." Sometimes, however, when the conditions are favorable, and the Torah is just right, disciples of the wise can actually do it.

Linking Congregations to One Another

Finally, learning can be used as a powerful tool to connect members of far-flung congregations. Dr. Jeffrey Schein, director of education for the Fellowship of Reconstructionist Congregations and Havurot, describes a project in which groups of adult learners in different synagogues were paired to study the Book of Ruth in preparation for the holiday of Shavuot, in a program entitled Aytz Hayim We.

Aytz Hayim We began as one of literally hundreds of ideas emerging from a "future conference" for leaders of the Reconstructionist movement in June of 1997. The initial spark for this idea was a strong desire to provide materials that would focus the strong Reconstructionist commitment to adult Jewish learning (sociologically speaking, perhaps the defining feature of the movement from the 1950s through the mid-1990s) on Jewish texts. Jewish texts were part of every curriculum we had produced, but we had not until that point created a curriculum whose primary purpose was to increase literacy with classical Jewish texts. As we peered ahead to the twenty-first century, the small group of rabbis, educators, and congregants discussing a project that later would be titled Aytz Hayim We wanted to "privilege" the learning of

Jewish text amidst a whole range of other possible foci for meaningful Jewish learning.

Many other ideas generated at the futures conferences remained *bashamayim* (in the heavens) but this one became *ayn zo agadah,* no mere educational fantasy. Aytz Hayim We is a year old as an official project of the Jewish Reconstructionist Federation (JRF). The broadest conceptualization of the program includes these goals:

1. To provide an expanded opportunity for text-based adult Jewish learning.

2. To develop interpretive skills based on classical and contemporary forms of *midrash* that enrich the student's ability to glean the full range of Jewish and human meanings residing in the dialogue between the text and the reader.

3. To expand the Jewish knowledge base of the learner, thus helping him or her to move closer to the goal of being a "literate Jew."

4. To provide a common textual focus for Reconstructionists for a set period of the year.

5. To strengthen links between Reconstructionist congregations and *havurot.*

6. To lay the foundations for a more ambitious Reconstructionist Torah commentary, in which the community, as well as scholars, generate the commentary.

We knew that this kind of educational ambition had to be tempered by the rabbinic wisdom of *tafasta merubah, lo tafasta* (if you reach for everything, you often get nothing). Our initial letter to our JRF affiliates did not invite them to take on the world but rather to focus on the study of the Five *Megilot* (scrolls). We hoped in a three-year period to guide a group of our adult learners through all five of these rich groves of Jewish/human meaning. We intend to award a certificate for distinguished adult learning to congregations and individuals who complete the process.

But all great things have small beginnings. The initial commitment to Aytz Hayim We was only to find a *minyan* of learners that would meet five times between Pesach and Shavuot in the spring of 1999 to study the

Book of Ruth. JRF provided a study packet and a "sister/brother" congregation with whom participants could exchange insights about the book.

We were delighted that thirty-three congregations or *havurot* (from a JRF institutional membership of ninety-seven) responded to our invitation to participate in Aytz Hayim We. The project was designed to allow for "rolling admissions," and we anticipated that at least another dozen congregations would join the project in the fall of 1999, when we continued with the second of the Five *Megilot, Kohelet* (Ecclesiastes).

The thirty-three congregations joining Aytz Hayim We represented the spectrum of adult Jewish learning in Reconstructionist congregations across North America. Several of these congregations included Aytz Hayim We as one offering among dozens of others in a sophisticated repertoire of adult learning classes. For other congregations and *havurot,* Aytz Hayim We facilitated their first attempt at ongoing adult study. In between these two extremes was our initial intended audience, congregations and *havurot* that had done adult learning around many themes and topics, but had never focused their adult learning endeavors on Jewish texts.

The Five *Megilot* are accessible beginning points for Jewish study. But while these books are simple in comparison to some other texts, they are neither simplistic nor simpleminded. They are each rich in interpretive possibilities. Our hope is to build the interpretive capacities of individuals, congregations, and the movement over time in order to take on the more challenging Jewish texts.

The demography, size, and philosophy of the Reconstructionist movement all point toward designing materials that can be led by either rabbinic or lay leadership. In a number of instances, the study of the Book of Ruth was facilitated by both a rabbi and a lay member of the study group. In her evaluation of the curricular materials provided by Aytz Hayim We, one of our participating rabbis wrote:

"We held our first class session last week. The response of students was enthusiastic, to say the least. I believe the opportunity to take part in a national study program enhances the students' motivation. All the students were excited about the opportunity to connect with another congregation and to share insights across the miles. One congregant is especially pleased that her mother, who belongs to a Reconstructionist congregation in another state, is studying the same material at the same time that she is. I believe that this approach has the potential to strengthen our movement and our ties with one another."

As they begin their study of *Kohelet* in the fall of 1999, many of our Aytz Hayim We study groups have doubled in size. One participant in the electronic list serve for the project posted the following comment:

"Kohelet is the ultimate monotheist. He doesn't flinch from critiquing even his own skepticism. He knows that even his own dark questioning will pass on to a lighter, brighter perception of reality. This demoting of our strong ultimate judgment into penultimate opinions is exactly the humility needed for any authentic monotheism."

Ken yirbu . . . may Aytz Hayim We generate many other such insights.

When Learning Becomes Part of "The Way We Do Things around Here"

Thus far, the vignettes demonstrate the variety and range of programs that can be offered with the goal of creating a congregation of learners. But to fully embody this vision, a congregation needs to go beyond simply offering programs and classes; it must incorporate learning into *all* of its activities, including worship, social justice, community-building, and decision-making.

Learning as Prayer

Rabbi Harold Schulweis pioneered this form of congregational learning two decades ago by instituting interactive study sessions in place of sermons. "I, the rabbi, become the *meturgeman* (the translator). In between the *aliyot* (when people are called to say the blessing over the Torah), I raise questions, asking: Why is this important? Do you really believe this happened? People come up with remarkable insights, and they come prepared with their own questions. Then I will quote some answers: What did the tradition say about this? This goes back and forth, and takes an hour. The importance is to frame a question that really means something to people."[4]

Increasingly, other congregations have begun to follow Rabbi Schulweis' example, replacing the sermon with interactive text study. At the New Emanuel Minyan at Temple Emanuel of Beverly Hills, Torah study is done in small groups, as explained by Rabbi Laura Geller.

The morning service includes a prayer for our bodies, for our minds, and for our souls. This suggests that for prayer to be meaningful it needs to incorporate the physical, spiritual, and intellectual. I learned this as a young rabbinical student when I was part of the Westwood Free Minyan. We moved our bodies when we prayed; we sang the liturgy in Hebrew or in English, and we wrestled with Torah through wonderful Torah study. Because I was a novice at praying, the place in the service that was most comfortable and exhilarating for me was Torah study. That experience taught me that Torah study was its own kind of prayer, and that lesson has carried over into the services that I now lead as rabbi of my own congregation.

In a typical service, the rabbi gives a sermon. As powerful as a sermon might be, it does not offer the congregation an opportunity to respond. The rabbi preaches or teaches; the congregation listens. Torah study, on the other hand, can be both engaging and interactive.

At the New Emanuel Minyan, Torah study has become a central part of the worship experience. Each week, the prayer leader (usually, but not always, one of the rabbis) prepares a teaching on the Torah portion. The leader sets the context for the study with reference to a personal or communal experience or anecdote, and then hands out a study guide with a central text from the portion, a few commentaries, and some guided questions. The goal of the questions is to lead the congregants through a process that begins with comprehension and moves into deeper levels of analysis, synthesis, and evaluation. Congregants turn their chairs into groups of three or four, and in these study partnerships wrestle with the text and each other.

For many congregants, Torah study in the *minyan* is the only Jewish learning in which they regularly participate. Ideally, then, learning at the *minyan* ought to introduce congregants to the many different ways Jews study Torah. The prayer leaders meet monthly to reflect on upcoming *parshiot* (portions), with attention given to presenting Torah through different interpretive lenses. Sometimes the study focuses on literary motifs, other times on the different sources reflected in the *parashah,* and still other times on a *midrashic* or a feminist approach to the text. Torah study in the *minyan* context has two ultimate goals: first, to give worshippers the skills they need to study Torah, and second, to help individuals engage with the text on a personal level.

With astonishing regularity, the Torah portion just happens to raise an issue completely relevant to the issues of the moment. Let me give just one example. In the summer of 1999, a racist gunman burst into the Jewish Community Center not too far from our synagogue and let loose an avalanche of bullets on children and staff of the JCC. It was a horrible moment for everyone. People came to the *minyan* the following Shabbat hoping for consolation and comfort and looking for guidance as to how to respond.

The Torah portion that week was *Shoftim,* which contains a long list of laws, including one that seems, at first, confusing: If a murder has been committed and no one knows who did it, the elders of the town are to break the neck of a cow in a ritual sacrifice, wash their hands, and then say: "Our hands did not shed this blood nor did our eyes see it." The study sheet for that Shabbat began with the verses as they appear in Deuteronomy 21:1–9. The first question helped clarify what was actually going on in the text: What is the reason the Torah requires the elders to make this declaration? The next text, from the *Mishnah* (Sotah 46b), argued that the intent of the declaration is neither transparent nor simple, but shows that the community's leaders might, in fact, be culpable through negligence. Three additional texts from three additional sources, the Talmud and medieval and Hasidic commentaries, helped focus the conversation on whether individual members of a community share the blame for allowing a climate of violence to develop. The final question asked directly: How ought we to respond to the shootings at the JCC and to the proliferation of gun violence?

The study that morning was intense and heated, as the worshipers sharpened their own ideas through discussions with their partners. By the end of the allotted half-hour, people wanted to continue their conversations into kiddush and lunch. Many felt that Torah was speaking directly to them and to their concerns. They were clearly challenged by their experience of reflecting on such an important event through the lens of Torah study.

As we chanted *Alenu,* the prayer that asks us to imagine a world where God really is the power that unites the entire world, it seemed that our wrestling with Torah had given us the strength to become partners with God in repairing the broken world. Torah study like this is indeed its own kind of prayer.

Owning Our Own Texts

Not only the Torah, but also the *siddur* (prayer book) merits close study. It has been likened to a "textbook of ideas, beliefs and values,"[5] yet few Jews who come to a service take time to study this textbook. Rabbi Sidney Schwarz tells an unusual story about Congregation Beth El of Sudbury, Massachusetts, whose rabbi, Lawrence Kushner, encouraged congregants to compile their own prayer book.

A course that Larry Kushner was teaching on liturgy over the course of several years highlighted the gap between the standard Reform prayer book and the kind of prayer experience that was taking place under Kushner's leadership. Several members of the class decided that they would write their own prayer book.

Some thirty members of Beth El began to work on a new congregational *siddur* that eventually was published in 1975 under the title *Vetaher Libenu* (Purify Our Hearts), edited by Nancy and Peter Gossels. Five years later, *Vetaher Libenu II* was issued. Edited by Nancy Gossels and Joan Kaye, it was more notable than its predecessor in one significant way. The editorial committee had decided that the exclusively male imagery used to describe God in the traditional liturgy was unacceptable. It led, in their view, to a form of idolatry.

The solution offered by the editors was to retain the Hebrew language [while alternating] "He" with "She" for God [in the English]. . . . The standard translation of the blessing formula was changed from "Blessed art Thou, Lord our God, King of the Universe" to "Holy One of Blessing, Your Presence fills Creation."

The most remarkable part of the creation of the prayer book was the fact that the rabbi was not part of the committee that created it. Though Lawrence Kushner, to this day, thinks that the Beth El prayer book projects would have been better off if they had been preceded with an extended exposure to a more traditional prayer book, he is unquestionably proud of what his members created. He deliberately kept his relationship with the respective efforts at a defined distance. When presented with drafts of sections that included questions about taking one direction or the other, he would offer his opinion and then say, "Whatever you do will be fine."

Nurturing the Teachers, As Well As the Students

A congregation of learners requires a special cadre of teachers who, aside from having the requisite knowledge and skills, are integrated into the fabric of the community. Given the severe shortage of teachers in congregational schools, many congregations find that they have to compromise and hire teachers who, for a variety of reasons, do not fit in well with the community. It takes special effort to nurture a cadre of teachers that shares the vision of the congregation and feels a stake in promoting that vision. The following vignette, written by researcher Dr. Lisa Malik, describes the ways in which Congregation Beth Am Israel in Philadelphia works with its teachers to make sure that they are an integral part of the learning community.

Beth Am Israel is a small Conservative synagogue in the western suburbs of Philadelphia, with a membership of 330 families. The synagogue has more than doubled its membership in the past decade, resulting in some "growing pains," as it evolved from a *havurah* to a small, burgeoning synagogue. As a consequence, its professional and lay leaders engaged in a process of reflection, which resulted in Beth

Am defining itself as a "community of engagement." Studying Torah, the "tree of life," and living by its precepts were embraced as key components of the congregation's identity. According to Rabbi Marc Margolius:

> Torah study is a conversation, but that doesn't mean that it's just a few Jews sitting around talking about anything. Torah is not "whatever I say it is." Torah is an intergenerational conversation that involves listening to the text as well as to each other's voices. Torah study also involves listening to what people said before you—such as Rashi and other commentators.

After interviewing several staff and lay people at Beth Am Israel, I began to take note of the recurrence of the phrase "Torah is a conversation." This phrase is part of what Education Director Cyd Weissman refers to as "Beth Amese," the shared vocabulary of the Beth Am community.

The common language employed by the various people whom I encountered at Beth Am Israel highlighted a defining characteristic of the congregation: consistency. It was truly remarkable to hear the same phrases being used repeatedly, and to note the similarity in educational philosophy among the teachers, rabbi, education director, and education committee chairperson. The consistency of values and educational approach reminded me of the philosophy of the Accelerated Schools Program, a holistic educational reform program in public schools that is targeted to at-risk students. The Accelerated Schools Program's three basic tenets are: 1) unity of purpose, 2) empowerment, and 3) building on strengths. Beth Am Israel's approach to Jewish education seems to embody all of these tenets. Most notably, Beth Am's shared language (Beth Amese) is a quintessential illustration of "unity of purpose." While the Accelerated Schools Program targets students who are "at risk" from a socio-economic standpoint, Beth Am Israel's educational initiatives seem to target families who are "at risk" from a Jewish identity standpoint, through either assimilation or alienation. Beth Am Israel's leadership aims to reduce these risks by creating a community of shared value and practice. Beth Amese, the shared language of the congregation, creates and reflects the community's shared value system.

Beth Am Israel's unity of purpose is also evident in its approach to change. A metaphor that Cyd Weissman uses to describe Beth Am's holistic approach to educational change is that of *tikun* (repair). According to Cyd, most synagogue supplementary schools do not work because they consist of "fragmented, broken pieces."

> We used to think of the supplementary school in fragments, with lots of separate components. For example, the curriculum was often publisher-driven and not driven by the needs of the individual synagogue. Teachers, curriculum, and teacher training were all viewed as separate entities. Our goal at Beth Am is to make everything connected. We want to repair the broken pieces. . . . Only when all parts of the synagogue work hand in hand with one another can the institution change in ways that can truly impact congregants in a meaningful way.

In an effort to educate its congregants holistically, Beth Am Israel created Beit Midrash, an alternative to Beth Am's Sunday–Thursday religious school program. Beit Midrash "is designed to bring children and adults into the rhythm of Jewish life." In addition to Hebrew studies for students in grades 3–6 on Thursday afternoons, students in grades K–6 who participate in Beit Midrash attend services and study sessions on Shabbat mornings. Torah study and family participation are key components of Beit Midrash, with parents attending Shabbat services and study sessions along with their children.

Beth Am's holistic view of learning was in evidence one Shabbat morning as I observed a staff learning session facilitated by Cyd Weissman. Cyd firmly believes that Jewish education can only be successful if it is embedded in a community of shared values and practices; thus, it is important to bring the teachers into the Beth Am Israel community to learn Beth-Amese. For Beth Am Israel to truly be a community, the teachers, rabbi, education director, and lay leaders all need to have a shared language.

For example, because Rabbi Margolius' pedagogical approach is rooted in the idea that "Torah is a conversation," the teachers' pedagogical approaches should also be rooted in such a philosophy. The consistency in pedagogical approaches between the rabbi, the education director, and the teachers should reflect a shared value system and a systemic approach to educational change in the synagogue.

In order to make sure that the teachers communicate the shared values of the Beth Am Israel community, Cyd Weissman and Alan Caro (a researcher and project director for Beth Am's new educational initiatives) have been teaching and modeling a certain type of educational approach to the teaching of Torah. During the staff learning session that I observed, Cyd reiterated the objectives of Beth Am Israel's educational program. According to Cyd, the "end goal" is to develop a meaningful Jewish identity:

> We need to be identity-builders. For example, our goal is not just to teach kids to recite the *Shma*. Our goal is to have our students learn the *Shma* in order to be able to go out into the world and live *Shma*. This would mean that students—children and adults—would strive for ways to make God's name one at school or at the office. . . . The goal of Torah study is not to become scholars but to encourage kids to engage in the Torah text and to feel that what is learned is relevant. We want the students to make meaningful connections between Torah and their personal experiences.

Cyd reiterated four steps that help build identity. She noted that a student is more likely to be engaged in Torah study when what is learned is:

1. part of his or her personal story;
2. distinct from other stories;
3. applicable to daily living (i.e. students view the world with a "Jewish lens");
4. shared and valued by the community.

At the staff learning session, Cyd stressed the importance of keeping Beth Am Israel's educational "end goals" in mind when planning lessons. After going over the end goals and the four steps that build identity, she posed the following questions to the teachers: How have you successfully used this formula with the teaching of Torah? How can we successfully transfer this formula to other subjects? The discussion that ensued was lively. One could feel the excitement in the air as the teachers enthusiastically shared their stories of how they help to build Jewish identity in their classrooms. One teacher described a lesson in which he read a story about *tikun olam* to his first-grade students and then asked them to answer the question, How can you bring *tikun olam* to the world? Another teacher beamed as he recounted an incident of a student who discussed the issue of *lashon harah* (literally, evil language) around the dinner table with his parents after having learned about *koach halashon* (the power of speech) at Beit Midrash.

As the teachers spoke about lesson plans that enabled students to make connections between the Torah and their daily lives, one could hear the chanting of *Etz Hayim Hi* ("It is a tree of life to them that hold fast to it") through the walls. Torah as a "tree of life" is an idea that literally and figuratively permeates the walls of the synagogue and its educational programs.

Study That Informs Congregational Decision-Making

The ultimate hallmark of a congregation of learners is decision-making that is informed by study. Rabbi Gordon Tucker of the Conservative Temple Israel Center in White Plains, New York, describes one such experience:

The synagogue had not that many years before adopted an egalitarian stance in its ritual practice, following a difficult period of discussion and debate. But the equality of men and women had become, in fairly short order, a matter of pride for the congregation—part of its very identity. No distinctions whatsoever were made between men and women of any age in synagogue services. Indeed, the synagogue would, just a year or two later, engage a woman to be its assistant rabbi.

But the congregation's Ritual Committee now had before it the following question: Should the congregation's practice of always reserving the first and second *aliyot* at each Torah reading for a *kohen* (priest) or *levi* (levite), respectively, be continued? Or should we make all congregants eligible for all *aliyot,* so that a *yisrael* could get the first *aliyah* and a *kohen* could get the sixth *aliyah*? Since the congregation had become egalitarian with respect to sex, for which distinctions were rather more prominent in the tradition, should it also become egalitarian with respect to "priestly status"?

The Ritual Committee is charged, by the synagogue's by-laws, with considering and recommending to the Board of Trustees changes in the synagogue's liturgical practice. The rabbi of the congregation is to be the Ritual Committee's advisor on Jewish law, and the committee and the Board of Trustees are forbidden by the by-laws to institute any practice that the rabbi believes to be a violation of Jewish law. Vetoes of that nature are, of course, hardly desirable. Much more constructive is a process in which those involved in the decision-making can educate themselves and understand the matters of law and policy that are impinged upon, and come to a meeting of the minds, perhaps entailing compromise, that approximates consensus and is also true to the principles of Jewish law.

On the question of how those of priestly or levitical descent should be treated with respect to *aliyot* to the Torah, there were on the committee divergent points of view. Some saw a tight connection to the gender egalitarianism that we had recently adopted and felt that distinctions between a *kohen,* a *levi,* and a *yisrael* based solely on family lineage were obsolete and undemocratic. Others, however, thought that there was something very deeply rooted about these distinctions, and that in any event, they helped bolster a sense of Jewish identity and connection to the past among those who were *kohanim* and *leviyim.* It was clear to me, however, that the issue should not be decided on the basis of impressionistic views such as these, and that, in any event, one of the "perks" of being on the Ritual Committee ought to be an opportunity to engage in some meaningful study.

Thus, the committee (about twelve members) undertook to study the history and legal aspects of the matter at hand and, only then, try to come to some overall decision. I prepared materials that included some of the early rabbinic texts on the subject (from the beginning of the era in which the Torah was read regularly in the synagogue at all), representative selections from the medieval codes that reflected differences of opinion in the Middle Ages, and recent writings from the Conservative Movement's Law Committee (the opinions of which guide, but, in general, do not bind individual rabbis and congregations).

The study that we engaged in for two meetings of the committee did indeed turn out to be a perk. Ritual Committee members who had an experiential but not a book knowledge of synagogue practice found themselves reading and evaluating talmudic texts for the first time. Everyone learned about the dates, locations, and cultural settings of such medieval authorities as Rashi, Maimonides, and Joseph Caro. Differences of interpretation from the classical period inspired members to venture their own interpretations of texts and to disagree collegially with one another. Members also learned that the oldest reason given for the priority given to *kohanim* and *leviyim* is that doing so would promote community peace by preventing large-scale bickering over who would get the first *aliyah* when the Torah is read. This then challenged our modern decision-makers to determine what the contemporary equivalent of community peace would be, and what direction that might point us in. At this point, it was widely recognized that we had a somewhat different problem to deal with. Today, we do not face bickering over the first *aliyah,* but rather the problem of how to accommodate with Torah honors bar or bat mitzvah families with multiple *kohanim,* and conversely, how to avoid having one or two *kohanim* and *leviyim* control twenty-eight percent of the *aliyot* each Shabbat when many other congregants, including those celebrating important religious milestones, feel they are entitled to be called for an honor.

The discussions were lively, sensitive, and respecting of the underlying texts and precedents, though not enslaved to them. In the end, the Ritual Committee had to devise a strategy that would meet the actual needs of the congregation in allocating *aliyot* to the Torah, and at the same time not ignore a long-standing tradition of priestly status that means a great deal to those who have been raised to take pride in it.

A lawyer (himself a *levi*) on the Ritual Committee proposed the approach that carried the day. The needs of "community peace," he said, today require that we open all *aliyot* to all Jews. It is also true, he argued, that based on our study, we should feel that there is more than sufficient warrant in the Jewish legal tradition for such a position. But there should always be a reminder, a liturgical footnote, if you will, that this practice is preempting an entitlement that the *kohanim* and *leviyim* historically have had. How to construct this reminder? Let us stipulate, he proposed, that the Ritual Committee is empowered by the congregation to speak on behalf of its members on liturgical matters. And let us stipulate that since our study of the sources has convinced us that the *kohanim* and *leviyim* of the community ought to waive their historical entitlement in the interest of the community, that this entitlement has in fact been waived. And then let us, each time we call a *yisrael* for the first or second *aliyah,* call that person up "by virtue of the priests' (or levites') waiver." A bit of a more cumbersome way to call people for *aliyot,* but an elegant solution nevertheless: true to the sources, consistent with synagogue needs, and respecting of those who take pride in their heritage.

The suggestion was adopted unanimously, and just about everyone was happy. The committee was delighted with its experience of working the issue through in an authentic way, and with the feeling that it could really justify its decision before anyone, no matter how learned. The reasoning was written up in digest form in the synagogue bulletin, and today, some years later, it is standard practice in the congregation. And even those who may still have reservations can tell anyone inquiring why it is that this synagogue does what it does, and how it is continuous with the tradition. This was surely a triumph of learning together, and it illustrated in a concrete way the power that the study of Torah in a historical mode can have to bind a community together and create constructive compromise.

Creating a congregation of learners is a never-ending journey; like any journey, it has its peaks and troughs, moments in which one proceeds full steam ahead, and moments in which one is mired in mud. Alongside the wonderful learning opportunities depicted in this chapter, there exist, in each of the synagogues mentioned, a set of opportunities that were missed, programs whose bugs have yet to be worked out, and problems that seem, for the moment, intractable. As proud as these congregations are of their accomplishments, they are also painfully aware of the work that remains. There are always more people to be reached, programs to be improved, higher standards to be set.

The remainder of this book charts the course of a journey that any congregation might take to fulfill its vision.

4

Becoming a
Congregation of Learners:
An Overview of the Process

Taken together, the images presented
in chapter 3 offer a new perspective on congregational education. A synagogue that offered its members a range of learning opportunities similar
to those described in chapter 3 would convey two important messages:
Learning is an essential part of Jewish living, and learning together is key
to building and perpetuating community.

How have some synagogues been able to move learning from a peripheral activity that is largely for children to one that is central? How have
they persuaded ordinary American Jews, who were raised with the notion
that Jewish education ended after bar or bat mitzvah and who lead extraor-
dinarily busy lives, to become engaged in learning?

Some of these congregations were founded on the principle of active
lifelong learning. Others were inspired by charismatic new leaders who succeeded, by dint of personality and persistence, to engage congregants in
learning. But for many synagogues the ideal of becoming a congregation
of learners was neither established at the outset nor the brainchild of a per-
suasive individual. Rather, it evolved over a period of years, as lay and pro-

fessional leaders worked together to create a community of meaning.

In some congregations this evolution was serendipitous and unplanned, the confluence of the right people being in the right place at the right time with the necessary resources. For others, the changes were deliberate, the result of conscious reflection and years of planning. The earliest congregations to undertake planned change had to navigate on their own, drawing on the expertise of consultants in unrelated fields. Over time, as change projects at the local and national level sprang up, synagogues were able to adopt and adapt each other's methods.

The remainder of this book focuses on planned change; it describes one particular approach to planning, an approach that has been successful in over twenty congregations over the past decade. It was first developed by the Experiment in Congregational Education, and consists of five overlapping phases: readiness, visioning, experimentation, outreach, and exploration, each of which will be described more fully in subsequent chapters. In this chapter I offer a brief description of each phase and discuss four assumptions that undergird this approach.

My confidence in this model of change has been bolstered not only by its success but also by the literature on organizational change, which dwells repeatedly on the following four principles:

1. Change Involves More than Good Programming

Visitors to congregations renowned for their learning are often impressed by the profusion of programs and activities. As a result, they focus on the number of participants, how the staff is recruited, and how funds for these initiatives were raised. Rarely, however, do they ask the more important questions: What motivates members to participate? How did these learning activities come to be seen as defining features of the congregation? Concentrating on the programs themselves, rather than on how they originated, evolved, and became established, has led many to the erroneous conclusion that synagogues can be changed by the replication of success-ful programs. It is true that creative and effective learning opportunities are necessary, but they are hardly sufficient. As I argued in chapter 2, a con-gregation of learners is pervaded by an ethos of learning, an expectation that learning is a central communal function. The content or format of the congregation's offerings are less important than the context in which they are set, and the way in which they are perceived by members. As any backyard gardener knows, selecting and sowing the seeds is only a small part of growing a garden. The ground must first be prepared, and painstak-ing maintenance must be done afterwards. Just as gardening consists of much more than planting, creating a congregation of learners goes far beyond programming. More important than the theme of a program or its innovative teaching methods is that members buy into the assumption that to belong to their congregation means to engage in a variety of learn-ing experiences.

A program that succeeds in one congregation may fail in another, depending upon the needs of congregants, the interests and abilities of the staff, the synagogue's history, and the type of learning available at nearby institutions, among many other factors. Synagogue archives are filled with flyers and memos promoting inventive programs that failed to attract an audience, or were popular for a year or two but then lost ground. However exciting the concept, and however talented the teachers, congregants were not sufficiently invested in the programs' success. This leads directly to the next assumption.

2. The Recipients of a Change Must Be Actively Involved in Making It Happen

The fact that synagogues are voluntary membership organizations has pro-found implications for how a synagogue operates. Leaders of a congrega-tion can't just create a new learning initiative and simply require everyone to participate; many members would either ignore the requirement or leave the congregation.[1] For change to succeed, members must be actively involved in its planning and implementation. This point is best articulated by Peter Senge, who writes that the active involvement of participants in an organization is critical to that organization's ability to fulfill its mission in a changing, and often competitive, environment:

- Organizations are products of the ways that people themselves think and interact.

- To change organizations for the better, you must give people the opportunity to change the ways in which they think and interact.

- This cannot be done through increased training, or through command-and-control management approaches. No one person, including a highly charismatic teacher or CEO, can train or command other people to alter their attitudes, beliefs, skills, capabilities, perceptions, or level of comfort.

- Instead, the practice of organizational learning involves developing tangible activities . . . for changing the way people conduct their work. Given the opportunity to take part in these new activities, people will develop an enduring capacity for change.[2]

Though Senge is writing about corporations, this argument applies even more pointedly to synagogues whose membership is voluntary.

In the change process outlined below, the proposed activities for both congregants and staff include reflecting on current realities and problems, envisioning a different kind of future, and considering the ways in which the gap between the ideal and the real might be bridged. In my experience, after a year or more of discussions of this sort, a group of congregants becomes so heavily invested in the future they have imagined that they voluntarily take on the role of change agents—serving as vocal advocates for increased learning, organizing new programs, recruiting their friends to participate, and raising the necessary funds. Because these congregants have created their own vision, rather than having one that is handed down to them, their level of commitment is much stronger.

How many congregants need to be involved in the process? And how actively do they need to be involved? There is no single answer that will work for every congregation. Obviously, the more people who participate, the higher the level of investment and the greater the likelihood that the initiative will succeed. But it would be impossible, not to mention unwieldy, to involve everyone. The more people present in a room, the less opportunity for individual participants to become engaged. The way out of this conundrum is to remember that not everyone needs to be involved at the same time or at the same level. A core group, representative of the congregation at large, must be integrally involved on a continuous basis. Others can be brought on board in connection with specific tasks. Still others (such as those on the board of directors or key committees) need to be informed on a continuous basis, but need not be actively engaged. For the majority of congregants, participation can consist of attending a single parlor meeting where their voices can be heard and taken into account.

In the planning model I will discuss, two groups serve as the incubators for change. The first is a task force, the core group whose composition may range from twenty to fifty members. This group meets every four to six weeks over a period of two to three years. The composition of the group will be discussed in chapter 6, and the activities in which it engages in chapters 7–11. At this point, I simply want to stress that the task force must reflect the congregation in its diversity. At the outset, those congregants who are avid learners will serve as the standard bearers and role models. But to include only those who are already engaged in learning would be preaching to the converted. Also represented should be those who have little experience with Jewish learning, and those who have not, for a variety of reasons, chosen to make it a priority. Only a diverse group will be able to arrive at a vision that has broad appeal; and only a diverse group will be able to inject a sense of reality into the dreams of the visionaries and ideologues.

Directing the task force is a second, much smaller group, which I have termed a leadership team.[3] It usually begins with four members and expands, over time, to include as many as ten. In chapter 5 I will have a great deal to say about the roles played by the members of this leadership team, and the characteristics and skills they should possess.

3. Participants in the Process Should Experience a Taste of the Final Product

Firsthand experiences of the changes that are under consideration will enable members of the task force to understand these changes more concretely and to become strong advocates for change. Applying this principle to the process of becoming a congregation of learners means that Jewish learning should be an integral part of the change process itself.

It is difficult for those who haven't had powerful Jewish learning experiences to become believers in and advocates for the value of Jewish learning. This is the challenge facing many members of the task force, whose formal Jewish education probably did not extend past their adolescence, and who may not have had informal learning experiences as adults. The first step toward developing a new mindset is to make learning an integral part of the change process. Task force meetings must include learning experiences that are rich and varied, so the members will themselves become "hooked" on learning. When it is time to reach out to the congregation, a taste of the kind of learning the task force hopes to promote should be offered at every opportunity.

· Making learning a part of the "business" of synagogue life may take some getting used to. Committee meetings in the workplace or in civic organizations don't usually include learning. People come to meetings ready to "work," and may be disconcerted when asked to read a text or discuss a topic that seems unrelated to the work at hand. My experience, however, is that when the atmosphere is welcoming and the study interactive and engaging, people's initial resistance gives way to enjoyment and to a desire for further study. I believe strongly that text study in particular should be part of all congregational meetings. In chapter 8 I will explain why and discuss some of the teaching methods I have found to be particularly effective.

4. Change Takes a Long Time

The kind of profound change required to become a congregation of learners takes a long-term commitment. It is usually two or three years before a synagogue experiences significant change, and even these are only preludes to the deeper changes that come after five or six years. While this may astonish those who think of change in terms of implementing new programs, it will not surprise those knowledgeable about the culture of organizations. Organizational culture is a term that refers to the sum total of customs, attitudes, and beliefs held by an organization's members. Some of these beliefs and behaviors are so pervasive that they constitute a kind of unwritten code of conduct. The most tenacious are often unacknowledged, and may even be unconscious, which makes them most difficult to challenge and modify.

For example, many congregants arrive at services or other synagogue events with the expectation that they can sit back and be inspired by a teacher, cantor, or rabbi. They hold that leader responsible, whatever the outcome. While there might be much talk about increased participation, the actions of both leaders and congregants may belie this professed goal, such as when the majority of the liturgical music that is chosen does not allow for participation, when teachers lecture without providing time for discussion, and when congregants choose to sit in the back of the room. Both the rhetoric of participation and the nonparticipatory behaviors are part of the congregation's culture, as are the cantor's, teachers', and congregants' underlying reasons for behaving as they do.

A new culture can't be created by simply introducing a few new customs. In fact, as Edgar Schein points out, a culture can't be *created* at all:

You cannot create a new culture. You can immerse yourself in studying a culture (your own or someone else's) until you understand it. Then you can propose new values, introduce new ways of doing things, and articulate new governing ideas. Over time, these actions will set the stage for new behavior. If people who adopt that new behavior feel that it helps them to do better, they may try it again, and after many trials, taking as long as five or ten years, the organizational culture may embody a different set of assumptions and a different way of looking at things, than it did before. Even then, you haven't changed the culture; you've set the stage for the culture to evolve[4]. . . . If all this seems complicated and time consuming, you are perceiving it correctly.[5]

One of the tragedies of American life is the shortsightedness and impatience of the American people. We think only of the end product and we expect to see it produced quickly. When our goals are difficult to define, and when they defy simple quantification, we become uneasy and doubly impatient. American Jews, unfortunately, are no exception, which is why we tend to equate success in a synagogue with numbers of members and attendees. We become so fixated on the bottom line that we forget to think about the quality of the synagogue experience, and we don't distinguish between the active and inactive member, between the number of programs and the value of those that can really transform people's lives.

If we want to truly revitalize our synagogues we will need to think about more complicated outcomes over much longer terms. We will need to help congregants evolve from consumers to cocreators. It will take time for people's prior ambivalences to surface and be overcome. It will take even longer for the cumulative effect of exposure to new learning experiences to sink in, and for people to embrace Jewish learning wholeheartedly. The result may not be an immediate increase in membership—in fact, it may be a drop in membership, as those who wish to remain consumers turn elsewhere. Eventually, the congregation will be filled with people whose commitments are deep and abiding. But all of this will take time.

An Outline of the Change Process

The five-phase process outlined below responds to all of these challenges: to actively involve a core group of congregants in a meaningful discussion of Jewish learning, and its role in Jewish life; along the way, to give them a variety of stimulating learning experiences; to engage them long enough so that they will develop a deep commitment to learning; and to accomplish all of this in an institution whose resources are limited, and which is sustained by volunteers.

It bears some resemblance to strategic planning, but differs from it in several respects. Like strategic planning, this model includes visioning and focus groups. Unlike strategic planning, however, it does not assume that the goals are tacitly known, and simply await articulation. To the contrary, it presumes that few participants have had extensive experience with Jewish learning, or have thought deeply about synagogue life, and that few, therefore, will be able to articulate their goals at the outset. Because of this, text study is built into every meeting, and the process of visioning extends over a long period of time.

Whereas strategic planners use focus groups because they are an efficient way to collect data, this model sees focus groups (which are renamed "community conversations") as serving an important function beyond that: investing congregants in the process. Therefore, even when the answers people give become repetitious, the congregation may want to continue running these groups because they can reach people in a way that bulletin articles and sermons often don't. Whereas strategic planners typically hire paid researchers to facilitate focus groups, this process relies on volunteer facilitators, knowing that few synagogues can afford to hire paid consultants, and that having congregant-facilitators sends a powerful message of congregant investment. Whereas strategic planning usually specifies target dates for specific results, this process is more open-ended, because we see the process as having inherent value.

Hopefully, engaging in this process will be so rewarding that it will inspire people to continue their deliberations indefinitely, setting goals that become more and more ambitious. The result will be not only a congregation of learners but also a learning congregation, a concept that is discussed in depth in the final chapter.

In this model, change takes place through five stages:

The *readiness* phase consists of a preliminary set of sessions in which a group of congregants learns about the congregation's history and begins to articulate and interpret its culture. The exercises in this phase enable participants to learn about one another, about the congregation, and about the type of learning that is currently available. Most importantly, these exercises, and their text study components, give participants a concrete sense of what they could expect if they were to enter the next phase. Upon completion of the readiness phase, some participants may decide that this process is not for them; in fact, the entire group may decide that the process is not appropriate for their congregation for any number of reasons. If they do decide to proceed, the readiness phase will have helped them identify some promising members of the leadership team, and think about the additional congregants needed in order to round out their task force.

In *visioning,* the task force engages in a variety of exercises to articulate their vision of a congregation of learners. Text study continues, which helps focus the vision further. This phase does not necessarily culminate in a vision statement; even when a preliminary statement is drafted, the assumption is that it will continue to undergo revisions.

Experimentation may begin even before visioning is completed. This is the point at which the task force creates a small number of innovative programs that have been suggested in the course of visioning, and that are relatively easy to implement. These programs give congregants a taste of a different kind of learning, and a concrete sense of what it might mean to become a congregation of learners. Borrowing a term from the literature on organizational change, these programs could be called "low hanging fruit," because they are the fruits that are easiest to pick. Over the years, the garnering of fruits should continue, with people's reach getting higher and more ambitious.

Outreach is the phase in which the task force conducts a series of "community conversations" to promote the idea of a congregation of learners, to brainstorm ideas for innovative learning and, if a preliminary vision statement has been produced, to get some feedback on that statement. Though these community conversations require a great deal of person-power, this phase is typically very energizing because congregants respond so enthusiastically. Following the community conversations, the task force reviews the responses of participants and the ideas that were offered, and narrows its focus to a small number of themes (such as adult learning, Hebrew, or Shabbat) for further exploration.

Exploration is the phase in which committees form to investigate each of the themes. For example, if the theme is learning for adolescents, the committee might do some of the following things: survey or interview adolescents and their parents to determine their interests and needs; become informed about some issues in adolescent psychology by reading selected articles or inviting people with expertise in this area to speak; gather information about notable programs for adolescents at other religious institutions; experiment with a number of programs and innovations and monitor these changes carefully; devise a long-range plan for improving adolescent education; and discuss staffing and fund-raising possibilities. For other themes the content would, of course, vary, but the steps would be comparable.

These five stages, though sequential, overlap. Experimentation, for example, might begin before visioning ends, and should continue throughout the phase of exploration. After outreach, the task force might decide to go back to visioning for a period of time. The timetable for the phase of exploration may be different for different areas of interest.

As has already been mentioned, text study and reflection should be built into all of these phases. Wherever possible, congregations should stay in touch with others that have gone through a similar process. These congregations can provide invaluable information in a number of areas: from exercises that worked well for their task force to strategies for conducting community conversations. Congregations that have been doing this work for several years may have developed some new programs that can serve as inspiration for those who need to see concrete reflections of their ideas. It would be important, however, to impress on people that another congregation's programs might or might not be appropriate for their own congregation, depending upon the results of the outreach and exploration phases.

As noted above, the timetable for each of these phases can vary. One congregation completed all five phases in a year and a half, but most take considerably longer. The pace appropriate to a congregation will depend on the other projects in which it is involved (Is there a capital campaign underway? Are there plans to build a new facility?), on the availability of staff and lay leaders, and on the availability and patience of members of the task force.

What happens after exploration? This too varies from congregation to congregation. Some congregations have created a long-range plan that was submitted to the synagogue's board of directors and then used to solicit the necessary funds. Other congregations phased in the innovations that were suggested as resources (which include volunteer time, staff time, and money) became available. Some congregations have declared an official end to the process, while others continue to find new areas of exploration for the task force. Several congregations have created second-, and even third-generation task forces. All these possibilities will be discussed in the final chapters.

5

The Readiness Phase

Imagine that several leaders at your congregation, both lay and professional, have read the first part of this book. They are inspired by the vision of becoming a congregation of learners, and intrigued by the vignettes presented in chapter 3. Still, they have many questions: Will this ideal appeal to others? Will its appeal be strong enough to galvanize people into action? Does their synagogue have what it takes to embark on this journey? What *does* it take? Is the timing right? In short: Is this congregation ready to engage in a change process with the goal of becoming a congregation of learners?

In this chapter I will deal with the issue of readiness from three different perspectives: First, I will discuss some of the a priori conditions that enable a congregation to succeed at change. Second, I will describe the composition of the "readiness team," the group that should be convened to decide if the congregation is ready. Third, I will offer suggestions for the kinds of exercises such a group should engage in, which will enable them to determine, over a number of months, whether the process outlined in this book is appropriate for this particular synagogue at this particular time.

What Not to Worry About

Before listing what I perceive to be the factors necessary for readiness, let me begin with a brief discussion of the variables that are irrelevant, such as size, location, and wealth. The model of change described in this book has been successful with a congregation of 250 member-units, a congregation of 3,000 member-units, and everything in between. Every size has its advantages and disadvantages. Large congregations have larger professional staffs, enabling one or two staff members to participate more actively in the work of the task force. However, they are also likely to have a larger percentage of peripheral members who attend infrequently, and this presents a special challenge. In a large congregation it is easy for members to go unnoticed; congregants whose talents might be of use in this change effort may not be known to the leadership. Smaller congregations tend to have fewer professionals and a smaller support staff, but they often have a stronger tradition of volunteerism. Members of small congregations are less likely to disappear into the woodwork; they know they are needed, and are willing to help out.

Similarly, every location has both benefits and liabilities. A synagogue located in a metropolitan area with a large Jewish population has an abundance of resources for learning available close by, such as Judaic studies professors, Jewish libraries and museums, and adult learning opportunities at the Federation, the JCCs, and the community at large. On the other hand, these other opportunities may draw the most committed learners away from the congregation. A synagogue that is more isolated may have fewer resources to draw on, but may have an easier time building a community of learners. The challenge of having to "grow one's own" talent can also be a big motivator.

My father used to say, "rich or poor, it's good to have money." This truism certainly holds in the case of synagogue change. But it is important to point out that engaging in the change process does not require a great deal of money (the budget for such a process is discussed in chapter 6). Developing the ideas, investigating and documenting the need, and generating enthusiasm can all be done inexpensively. Eventually, the long-range plans that are developed may indeed require additional staff, and even an expanded facility, but there will be ample time to investigate potential sources of funding. A growing number of donors and foundations are funding a variety of projects related to Jewish education. It has been our experience, thus far, that good ideas filling a demonstrable need, with an enthusiastic clientele, end up finding the support they need.

What Makes a Congregation Ready?

If size, location, and wealth don't matter, what does? The following factors have proven to be important:

1. A core group with an interest in learning

A good place to start is with a core group of adult members that is interested in Jewish learning as a lifelong endeavor. This core might include any of the following: participants in the synagogue's existing adult-education programs; people who have participated in regional and national programs, such as the Wexner Heritage Program, the Melton Adult Mini-School, and study retreats sponsored by denominational groups; people who are voracious readers; people who use the Internet to study Talmud or *parashat hashavuah,* the weekly Torah portion; parents of school-aged children who would like to be able to answer their children's questions; Jews-by-choice who participated enthusiastically in an Introduction to Judaism class; and those who have had an adult bar or bat mitzvah. The broader the range of experiences, the better. This core group need not be very large, but it must contain at least a few people with the potential to be both leaders and cheerleaders (more on this below). A rabbi or educator who wishes to create a congregation of learners but cannot identify a core group of learners will have to spend some time recruiting, teaching, and mentoring potential leaders. As mentioned in the previous chapter, some rabbis and educators, by dint of their charisma, have managed to galvanize congregants and reinvigorate the congregation single-handedly, though we have no way of knowing how many failed in similar attempts.[1] In any case, the process described in this book requires group leadership, rather than that of a single person.

2. A critical mass of reflective leaders

Prior learning experiences are a necessary precondition, but they are not sufficient. Those involved in the process must also be able to think critically about the place that Jewish learning might play in their lives and in the life of the congregation. They must inquire about the needs and interests of a wide spectrum of members, and weigh the pros and cons of a range of possible innovations. This kind of sophisticated planning can only be done by people who are thoughtful, self-reflective, and open to new ideas.

3. A cadre of capable and competent workers

No synagogue project can succeed without a core of committed and able volunteers. A project that seeks to involve so many congregants in decision-making is especially labor intensive. There are phone calls to be made, minutes to be taken, materials to be gathered, and so on. Even when a synagogue has sufficient funds to assign the typing to a secretary and the arrangements to a paid coordinator, a good deal of work must be done by members of the leadership team; no outside person can be hired to do their thinking and planning for them.

One of the readiness exercises described below, an inventory of the congregation's current learning activities, is designed to test the ability of both the lay and professional leadership to gather and analyze information. It serves as a good test of people's ability to break a project down into component parts that are assigned out, to have the assignments completed in a timely fashion, and to synthesize the results. If the readiness group seems incapable of completing the work, they will need to expand their group to include members with the necessary skills and commitment; alternately, they may conclude that they are not ready to embark on the next phases of the process, which involve more work and more coordination.

4. A willingness to share leadership

Taken together, the first three attributes may seem daunting. Where on earth can one find reflective leaders who have a demonstrated commitment to

Jewish learning and who have the time and energy to devote to a variety of demanding tasks? It is unlikely that one could find many who qualified on all three counts. But if, instead, we look for people who have two of the three necessary qualifications (for example, workers who are reflective, or learners who are able to devote time to volunteer work), the universe of possibilities expands. Of course, this solution depends upon the ability of the core group of leaders to function as a team. In fact, the entire process is dependent upon teamwork and on the sharing of leadership.

Everyone holds a piece of the puzzle, and all of the pieces are needed in order to complete the picture. The rabbi and educator, for example, probably have a well-articulated vision of Jewish learning. But they can't, on their own, transmit it to the entire congregation. They need a group of committed learners who can function as both role models and advocates. But for these congregants to have ownership of the vision, they must participate in its articulation. Thus, the rabbi and educator need to be able to share their leadership, to give the others time to formulate their own ideals. Similarly, the leaders of the task force cannot, on their own, reach the entire congregation. They must involve others, who, as the price of involvement, will bring in their own ideas both about the vision and about the project's organization. And so on.

Shared leadership is both an ideological commitment and a learned skill. It would be too much to expect participants to have mastered this skill; but the ideological commitment and some indication that potential leaders have the rudimentary skills for working as a team should be there at the outset.

5. A congregation with both a modicum of stability and an openness to change

The first four prerequisites for readiness focus on characteristics of the individuals who will form the leadership team and task force. In contrast, the fifth and last prerequisite concerns the synagogue as a whole and the degree to which it is both stable and open to change. A synagogue that is in crisis is not in a good position to engage in a long-term change process. Financial problems, personnel conflicts, or issues that are deeply divisive demand so much energy and attention that the leadership may have difficulty focusing on goals that are less immediate and much less concrete. A beleaguered staff person may have difficulty acknowledging the flaws in the current system; in a politically charged atmosphere, even thoughtful and justified critiques become weapons. On the other hand, a synagogue that is very stable and unused to change may have difficulty mustering the energy that it takes to rethink and reconfigure programs that have been operating, seemingly successfully, for a long time. Why invest energy in fixing something if it doesn't seem to be broken?

Several congregations have undertaken change initiatives when either the rabbi or the educator (and sometimes both) had been on board for only one or two years. Yet these congregations had a good deal of stability in their lay leadership. A number of congregations have engaged in a change process at the same time that they were constructing a new building or facing a budget deficit; these certainly slowed the process down, but did not derail it entirely. In the absence of more research on congregations going through the process of change, it is impossible to determine the appropriate degree of stability, on the one hand, and openness to change, on the other. The best one can say is that a balance between the two must be struck.

The Readiness Group

The readiness process is the first of three occasions where a diverse group of congregants and staff, many of whom may not know one another, will be brought together to think about Jewish learning. Who should be involved in this preliminary process? The question of inclusion will recur at every juncture in the change effort. Finding the appropriate mixture of insiders, whose talents are known, and outsiders, whose potential is untested, is a perennial challenge. Among congregants, prospective invitees fall into one of three categories:

1. Active members who have taken various leadership positions in the past;

2. People who have been less active, but performed well when given certain responsibilities;

3. Members who are known to have certain talents or abilities, but who haven't volunteered in the congregation.

Unfortunately, it is impossible to gauge accurately whether those who are untested will fulfill their potential. Yet it would be a big mistake to include only the current synagogue leadership because part of the goal is to continually reach out to a new pool of potential leaders; hence the dilemma.

The process works best when there is an equal representation from each of these categories, so that there is a good mix of insiders, outsiders, and those in between. Aside from their proven abilities, those in highly visible leadership positions (such as a past president or a current member of the board) lend credibility to the effort. But because these members are likely to be both overburdened and invested in the status quo, it is important to bring in new leaders who have original ideas and the time and energy to give to the initiative. Additionally, this sends a signal that this effort represents a departure from "business as usual," and that new ideas and new perspectives are being sought.

The readiness phase is an especially good opportunity to bring in fresh faces because it is limited in scope. From the perspective of the invitee, a commitment to attend four to six meetings over a few months is much less onerous than a commitment to meet regularly for a period of two years or more. From the perspective of the congregation, a short-term commitment is a good way to "audition" potential new leaders. At the end of the readiness phase, those who don't work out (for example, those who are unable to attend with regularity, or who tend to dominate the discussion) can be thanked for their time and not invited to participate in the next phase.

Ideally the readiness group will form the kernel of the task force, so it should consist of potential task force members. In thinking about whom to invite, three factors should be considered: the roles people play in the synagogue, their character and personality traits, and their areas of expertise. The following is a list of characteristics to consider in each of these categories.

1. Synagogue roles

Taken together, the members of the readiness team (and, later, of the task force) should be representative of the synagogue as a whole. Included should be:

- A few key staff people, including the rabbi, the educator, and at least one teacher
- A few members of the board of directors
- Chairs of key committees, such as the religious school committee and the adult-education committee
- People who participate actively in adult learning in the congregation
- People who have volunteered regularly for events like the Purim carnival and various fund-raisers
- People who come infrequently
- People who are involved in Jewish learning outside of the congregation
- People not currently involved in learning, but who have given some indication that they would like to become more involved
- Some veteran members, including at least one past president
- Some members who have joined only recently
- Young adults
- Parents in the various schools
- Empty nesters and senior citizens

- A teenager in the confirmation program and/or youth group
- At least one Jew by choice and, perhaps, the non-Jewish spouse of a member

Of course, any individual member is likely to fill several of these positions. For example, s/he may be a long-time member who is an empty nester and has been a past president; a Jew-by-choice who is a new member and has children in the preschool; or a young adult who is involved with adult education and volunteers in social action projects.

2. Character and personality traits

In addition to their roles as representatives of various constituencies, the members of the readiness team must demonstrate certain key characteristics. Though no one person can have all these, the group, as a whole, should include:

- People who can serve as cheerleaders for the project, who are good at promoting an idea enthusiastically
- People who are very organized and can think systematically about a series of interconnected tasks
- People who know "how to get things done"
- People who are thoughtful and reflective, and who enjoy discussing issues
- People who are doers, who enjoy making phone calls and arrangements
- People who enjoy creative brainstorming
- People who are enthusiastic about learning
- People who ask challenging questions
- People whose ideas don't get in the way of their ability to listen
- People who are able to create harmony when disagreements arise

Ideally, these traits should be in abundance among the group as a whole.

3. Specific skills

In the group there should be at least one person (and preferably two or three) with each of the following skills:

- Facilitating and leading discussions
- Taking good minutes
- Writing reports and grant proposals

In addition, people with the following kinds of skills, if they can be found, will be helpful later on in the process:

- Experience conducting focus groups
- Experience with social science research, such as conducting a survey or doing interviews
- Experience with fund-raising

Inability to locate people with the latter set of skills should not, however, cause undue concern. Over time, appropriate congregants may emerge; if not, outside consultants with this expertise can be hired.

While all these attributes and skills are important, the most important factor is the ability to work together as part of a team. The chemistry among the members is as important as their individual talents. Of course, this can't be known in advance, which is what makes the readiness phase so useful. After four to six readiness sessions it should become clear who works well with whom, and which individuals don't fit in, for whatever reason.

Goals of the Readiness Process

The overall goal of the readiness process is to give the key players a sense of what it would be like for the congregation to engage in a long-term exploration of Jewish learning. Those who enjoy the exercises, text study, inquiry, and introspection are likely to become strong advocates for this effort; those who do not are afforded an opportunity to voice their objections before a decision is made. In some cases the opposition may be so strong that a congregation will decide not to proceed further. If a strong majority reacts positively, the congregation may proceed to the official "launch" with confidence.

A second goal is to determine whether the focus on learning is appropriate, the work involved manageable, and the timing right. If there is insufficient interest in learning, or if the level of learning is already fairly high, worship or social justice might be better areas to focus on. Alternately, despite having identified both an interest in and a need for learning, the group might decide that the congregation doesn't have the person-power to support an intensive effort at this point in time. All of these concerns are best aired before a decision is made to proceed.

A third goal is to "audition" potential members of the leadership team and task force. Responsibility for facilitating exercises and text study sessions, and for organizing the inventory of learning opportunities, should be given to various members of the readiness group; this will provide a built-in opportunity to assess people's skills and get a sense of their ability to work together as a team. If, after these four to six sessions, the congregation decides to embark on the next phase, a number of individuals should be invited to form the leadership team. The roles and desired characteristics of leadership team members will be discussed in the next chapter; it is best to resist the temptation to appoint these people before the conclusion of the readiness phase.

A fourth aim is to raise the task force's consciousness about the importance of Jewish learning, and to expose participants to text study in small groups. Though the entire task force process will be devoted to the topic of learning, it is helpful to have as many members of the task force as possible begin with a heightened awareness, having had some new and engaging learning experiences.

Similarly, the readiness sessions should prepare future members of the task force to embrace change, rather than to be anxious about it. Change is often upsetting. At the very least, it requires everyone to make adjustments; at its most extreme, it can lead to major disruptions in an organization. Though it will be at least two years before the synagogue makes any substantive changes in programming, staffing, and volunteer responsibilities, some people may take that time, or longer, to adjust. It is, therefore, important to create an appreciation for thoughtful, planned change.

A sixth goal is to inform future members of the task force about the history of the congregation and the range of learning activities currently available. When we refer to the synagogue's "membership" in the singular, we tend to lose sight of the fact that congregants and staff members joined the congregation at different points in time, and that those who joined more recently may not know a great deal about the congregation's past. Before discussing the future of the congregation, it is essential that people have a sense of the bigger and more complete picture. Everyone should have an understanding of how and why certain traditions evolved and decisions made. People should have an opportunity to share their own perceptions of the culture of the congregation, and to hear the perceptions of others. And everyone should be informed of the full range of programming that relates to learning. In my experience, few people are aware of all the congregational activities that relate to learning. For example, empty nesters may be unaware that the religious school now includes family education; men may be unaware of the women's *rosh chodesh* (celebration of the new moon) group; and so on. Even if going through the readiness exercises leads a synagogue to conclude that it does not want to enter the full planning process, sharing this type of information is inherently worthwhile.

The last goal is to get participants to be more reflective about synagogue life. Staff members who are overworked and lay leaders whose lives are already full apart from their responsibilities for the synagogue rarely have time to reflect on the current reality, or to envision an alternate one. But introspection and imagination are critical for thoughtful planning and are built into the entire process described in the book. Their inclusion in the readiness phase signals that the discussions of the task force will be thoughtful and deliberate.

Exercises for the Readiness Team

There is no "right" way to prepare a congregation to undertake a major change. With the above seven goals in mind, one might design an infinite number of exercises and activities for the readiness group. What follows is a selection of the activities created by the ECE staff for this purpose. Before using any of these, the following questions should be asked:

- Is this activity appropriate for our congregation?
- What might make this exercise more effective?
- How long will it take? Have we allotted sufficient time?
- What other activities can be done at the same session?
- What kind of introduction will begin the entire meeting? How will the meeting be brought to a close?
- What skills are required to lead this exercise? Who has these skills?
- What kind of advance preparation is necessary?
- What kind of support does the facilitator need?

Text study sessions appropriate for the readiness phase are included in chapter 9.

Reviewing the Congregation's History

This exercise is designed with two goals in mind:

1. To give participants some essential information about the history of the congregation. Since the readiness group is, by design, diverse, its members will have joined the synagogue at different points in time. Everyone will be acquainted with different aspects of the congregation's history, but few will have a broad perspective. The more informed group members are about the congregation's past, the better able they will be to deliberate about its future.

2. To inform (or remind) members of the group about deliberate changes that were instituted in the past, and to have them reflect on the impact of these changes.

Preparation:

Before this session two members of the team are assigned to research the synagogue's history and make two presentations to the entire group.

The first presentation recounts the major historical events; it can be organized around the following questions:

- When was the congregation founded?
- How many members were there when the congregation began?
- Who were the founders of the congregation?
- Why did the founders believe there was a need for this congregation?

- Where was the congregation's first building?

- Has the congregation moved since its founding? If so, where and when?

- How and when has the membership grown and shrunk, and why?

- Which changes in building/location and membership were planned and which were a result of circumstances?

The second presentation focuses on change. Some guiding questions for this part would be:

- What changes have occurred in the congregation? Which were planned changes and which were a result of circumstances? Why did they happen?

- What issues and/or conflicts has the congregation grappled with over the years?

- Which issues or conflicts were a result of circumstances and which were introduced deliberately?

- What changes, if any, resulted from grappling with these issues or conflicts?

- What are some of the innovations spearheaded by the professional staff?

- What are some of the significant innovations spearheaded by lay leaders? Who were the innovators?

Though the presenters will undoubtedly collect a great deal of fascinating information, it is important that their presentations be short and concise—no more than ten minutes each.

The facilitator prepares in advance a long timeline on which significant events can be noted in writing large enough for everyone to see.

Grouping of Participants:

The presentations are made before the entire group; for the follow-up discussion, divide participants in groups of three.

Time Required:

Approximately one hour: 20 minutes for the presentations; 10 minutes for questions and comments; 15 minutes for the small groups; and 15 minutes for the groups to report back.

Facilitation:

During the presentations the facilitator records major events on the timeline. After the presentations, small groups of three are formed and given the following instructions:

- Pick one change or innovation from the time line.
- Imagine what forces, events, and/or factors inspired the change or innovation.
- Describe and/or imagine the reception (and resistance) to the innovation: What was the impact of this change or innovation on the congregation?
- Prepare a 2-minute report of your discussion and choose a spokesperson.
- Think now about some aspects/characteristics of the congregation that are precious and enduring and have not changed. List a few to share with the group when you reconvene together.

When the group reconvenes, have each group of three share its report and the characteristics of the congregation that have endured.

Record Keeping:

A summary of the congregation's history should be compiled and saved, along with the timeline. It will be useful in the orientation of new leaders, both lay and professional, both during the learning initiatives and in the future.

Exploring the Congregation's Culture

As explained in the previous chapter, the less reflective the members of an organization, the more resistant they are to change. Conversely, the more aware people are of the norms, values, and assumptions that govern their behavior, the easier it is to change the institutional culture. This exercise provides an opportunity for the readiness group to reflect together on the culture of the congregation.

Preparation:

Before this session, participants should be asked to present to the group an artifact or tradition that teaches something about the congregation's culture. Artifacts might include a copy of the synagogue's bulletin, budget, or membership form; a tradition could be the yearly break fast after Yom Kippur services or an annual fund-raising project. After explaining the artifact or tradition, participants should be prepared to explain what it can teach us about the congregation's norms, values, or assumptions. Participants may find the following definitions useful:

Norms are rules that tell people how to behave. They are the "ropes" you must know in order to "fit in" with an institution.

Values reflect the institution's philosophy and mission, its goals, ideals, and standards.

Assumptions are beliefs that members hold:

- About themselves and other people and their relationship to others, and

- About the nature of the institution and their relationship to it.

Assumptions are rarely articulated, questioned, or even recognized; therefore they are taken-for-granted beliefs and are very difficult to change.

Grouping of Participants:

Part 1 is best done in a group of 10–15. If more than 20 are present, the group should be divided in half. Part 2 is done in small groups of 3–4.

Time Required:

Part 1: 3 minutes per person, plus an additional 30 minutes for general discussion (this could include reports, if the group has been divided in half). Part 2: 15–20 minutes in small groups and 15–20 minutes for sharing.

Facilitation:

PART 1:

Each participant tells:

- What artifact or tradition s/he brought,

- Why s/he chose this artifact or tradition,

- The norms, values, or assumptions s/he thinks it reflects

The facilitator lists both the artifact and the assumption on a flip chart and asks, "Does anyone have a different interpretation of what norm, value, or assumption this artifact represents?" None of the answers should be challenged at this point; all should be listed.

When all the artifacts/traditions have been presented, the facilitator asks, "Did anyone find an artifact particularly interesting or surprising?

"Can you think of any additional artifacts or traditions that reveal something important about the culture of our congregation?"

PART 2:

Divide participants in groups of three or four to work on the following quotations and their accompanying questions. Debrief the answers to both questions.

> Culture is neither legislated nor designed; it emerges. That is, group members—not necessarily leaders—establish norms, accept values, and learn assumptions by sharing an organization's history. . . . At critical points in its history the organization's members confront [certain] problems, arriving at solutions that become accepted through active agreement or silent acquiescence. If these solutions remain stable (i.e., they continue to be accepted as solutions in future confrontations of the same problems), they become part of the culture. [pp. 225–226]

- **Thinking back on our discussion of defining moments in this congregation's history (in the previous exercise), can you think of a period of time in which a new norm, value, or assumption became assimilated as part of this congregation's culture?**

> Organizational members' assumptions about themselves and other people, their relationships to other people and to the organization, and the nature of the organization and its relationships to the outside world form the core of organizational culture. These beliefs and assumptions accumulate subconsciously, go unrecognized and unarticulated, and become taken for granted. . . . [Thus] they are very hard to change. If they change at all, they do so slowly, and only under certain conditions. . . . To make cultural change succeed, managers must provide leadership in creating a new system for making sense (answering basic questions) out of a changing world. This involves leadership, but it also requires understanding of the process of cultural formation. One does not deliver a new culture, pristine and complete, to the waiting masses for their approval. Rather, the members of an organization generate its culture. Changing that culture is a process of influence. At best,

managers can hope to take to take the lead in that process. [pp. 226–227]

- **The ultimate goal of this change effort is to have more congregants engaged in more Jewish learning. If this goal is to be achieved, what norms, values, and assumptions of this congregation might have to change? What can we do to take the lead in changing these norms, values, and assumptions?**

Record Keeping:

A record of the artifacts, and of the norms, values and assumptions should be kept. It would be interesting to repeat this exercise a year or two later and compare the lists.

From "Corporate Culture" by Robert M. Weinberg[2]

Surveying the Learning Opportunities That Are Currently Available

The purpose of this exercise is for the members of the readiness team to be familiar with the full range of existing programs and classes. What is being offered? Who is doing the teaching or facilitating? Who is participating? What groups are underrepresented among the learners?

Preparation:

Rarely are all learning opportunities that a congregation provides (both formal and informal) widely known; in fact, quite often only one or two people have the full picture. A few members of the readiness team should be designated to compile a list of learning opportunities and to prepare posters that display the relevant data: the types of programs offered; the number and age of the participants in each; the teachers; the time frame; the subject matter; how information about the program is disseminated; and anything else that people might be curious about, in relation to learning.

Facilitation:

This exercise has two parts: First, participants circulate around the room, gleaning as much as they can from the posters about the current state of learning in the congregation. Then, the entire group debriefs together, with the following questions asked: What generalizations can we make about the state of learning in our synagogue? Who are the learners? Who *isn't* learning, and why? The facilitator should be careful to steer people away from either evaluating the learning or suggesting concrete solutions. This is not an appropriate point to critique either the classes or the teachers; nor is it the time to decide on new programs. Instead, the purpose of the discussion is to understand the current situation as fully as possible. What are the special characteristics of each program? Who is the target audience, and is that audience being reached? What factors might deter participation? Is the time convenient? Is the setting conducive to learning? What is being done to promote the program?

Time Required:

Approximately a half-hour for looking and 30–45 minutes for discussion.

Record Keeping:

Both the data and its interpretation are critical for the work of the task force, assuming the readiness team decides to continue the process. A detailed but easy-to-read summary of both the data and people's interpretations should be produced.

Evaluation of the Readiness Experience

Evaluation is an important component of any planning process. Aside from allowing the facilitators to assess the effectiveness of their sessions, the evaluation models the introspection and shared interpretation that are so critical for successful change. The following form might be distributed toward the end of the last readiness session, with time built into the meeting so participants can fill it out on the spot. Following this, participants should have an opportunity to share some of their reactions with one another. Completed forms should be read by future members of the leadership team, and anyone who is interested.

Making a Decision

At the end of the readiness phase, a decision must be made about whether or not to proceed further. There are at least four separate steps involved in making this decision. Since synagogues differ in their governance structures, the importance of each step and the way it is carried out will vary from congregation to congregation.

Step 1: The readiness group should discuss the feasibility of continuing; this can flow quite naturally from the kind of evaluation discussion suggested above.

Step 2: The staff and key lay leaders who initiated the process should read the evaluation forms and meet to make a tentative recommendation.

Step 3: If the decision is made to continue to the next phase, there should be a discussion about whom to invite to the leadership team, and about the level of funding that will be required. The roles and characteristics of members of the leadership team, as well as the cost of the planning process, will be discussed in chapter 6.

Step 4: A formal proposal should be submitted to the board of directors for their approval.

Readiness Evaluation Form

Please check each readiness session you attended (fill in with number of sessions and dates).

I enjoyed participating in the "readiness" experience . . . *(check one)*

☐ not at all   ☐ somewhat   ☐ a great deal

The part I enjoyed the most was . . .

The part I enjoyed the least was . . .

I enjoyed the text study components . . . (Please explain.)

☐ not at all   ☐ somewhat   ☐ a great deal

One thing I learned in the text study sessions was . . .

One thing I learned about my congregation was . . .

One of my congregation's strengths is . . .

One of the congregation's weaknesses is . . .

I think that my congregation is . . .

☐ not at all   ☐ somewhat   ☐ very much

ready to participate in a long-term planning process because . . .

One of my concerns about embarking on a change process is . . .

Is there any additional feedback you would like to give at this time?

6

Leading the Initiative: The Task Force and the Leadership Team

All living systems start small. Each of us once began as an embryo, smaller than a fingernail. The mighty sequoia tree begins in the humblest seed. It is no different in growing a new organizational culture. Once we surrender the myth that a "heroic CEO creates change," we understand that all great things have small beginnings—and we begin thinking naturally of "pilot groups." Unless some kind of pilot group can coalesce, new ideas in an organization have no incubator, no place where concept can become capability, where theory can meet practice.[1]

In this planning process, two pilot groups serve as incubators for the change—a task force of twenty to fifty people, and a leadership team of four to ten, which functions as the executive committee of the task force. This chapter deals with the membership of these two groups and with some of the steps that might be taken to help them operate most effectively.

The Task Force

If the readiness phase has been successfully completed and a decision has been made to proceed, a significant percentage of the readiness group should be eager to join the task force. (If this does not happen, the congregation should think again about whether it is really ready.) The next step should be an assessment of this group, bearing in mind the list of roles, characteristics, and skills delineated in the previous chapter. The following questions should be asked: Was a balance struck between doers and thinkers, between those who enjoy process and those who like to see results? Were facilitation or organization skills in short supply? The watchwords here, as with the readiness group, are diversity and complementarity. This is the perfect time to make sure that the task force represents the diversity of the congregation. It is likely that several constituencies were not sufficiently represented in the readiness phase; perhaps they were overlooked, or perhaps it was difficult to persuade people from these groups to participate. Members of the readiness group can be asked to recommend people with the desired characteristics and skills to fill in the gaps.

Before too many newcomers are invited, it is important to consider the optimum size of the task force. This will vary from congregation to congregation. Some have done splendidly with a task force of twenty; others worked equally well with a group of fifty. Congregations with 1,000 member-units or more may require a larger task force to mirror the full diversity of the membership. The strength of the lay leadership and the percentage of congregants who are active volunteers should be taken into account as well; it might be better to have a smaller group of active and committed members than one that is large, but in which attendance is spotty. Bear in mind, as well, that the size of the task force will determine, to some extent, the nature of its meetings. An open-ended discussion with a group of fifty is difficult to negotiate; the larger the task force, the greater the requirement for small group discussions and skillfully facilitated exercises.

Invitations to join the task force should be carefully orchestrated.

Consider the following questions: Who should do the inviting? The congregation president? The educator? The rabbi? What kind of time commitment is required? It is likely that the task force will meet over a period of eighteen months or longer. Will meetings be held in the evenings? On Sundays? Over two-day retreats? Potential members should be given an estimate of the time parameters. Is it advisable to include people who may not be able to make such a serious commitment, in the hope that they will become more committed over time? Conversely, would it be better not to invite these people, whose erratic participation might undermine the morale of the group? The answer varies from place to place.

New members of the task force who did not participate in the readiness sessions will require some sort of orientation prior to the first meeting. This might include: a summary of the discussions relating to the congregation's history, culture, and learning opportunities; an exercise related to one of these topics; and, of course, text study.

Finally, it is important to keep in mind that volunteers require special nurturing. A letter may not be sufficient to remind people of a meeting, for example; phone calls or e-mail messages may be needed in addition. Participants who miss a meeting are more likely to remain involved if someone stays in contact with them, informing them about what they have missed. Just whose responsibility this is will be discussed in the next section.

The Leadership Team

An executive committee of sorts, the leadership team, should be given the responsibility of planning and facilitating the meetings of the task force and maintaining its esprit de corps. Some congregations have found the term *leadership team* to be too elitist, and preferred to use terms like *steering committee* or *core group*. Whatever it is called, this team should comprise at least four people—a chair, a coordinator, the educator, and the rabbi— whose roles are delineated below.

The Task Force Chair

The task force chair is the key lay leader identified with this effort. Ideally, this person is well-known and well-respected, with a proven track record. A past president or chair of a key committee who has also been an active learner would be the perfect candidate, because his or her stature will reflect on the task force. As the public face of the planning process, the chair may be called upon to give reports to the board or make presentations to potential donors. But even more important is his or her role as a behind-the-scenes cheerleader. The chair must become the primary champion of learning in the congregation; s/he should use every opportunity to promote learning and the work of the task force.

In the best of all worlds the chair would be both a visionary and a doer, able to inspire groups in public and nurture individuals behind the scenes; and in the ideal world s/he would have unlimited time to devote to this project. In the real world, however, a leadership team that, as a group, embodies these qualities, will do quite nicely. The more easily the team is able to share leadership and utilize the skills of its members, the more effective it will be. Thus it is critical that the chair understand his or her strengths and limitations, and learn to rely on his or her teammates when necessary. If the chair does not have group facilitation skills, for example, s/he may have others lead discussions and exercises. If s/he is more of an organizer than a visionary, it would be important to add at least one visionary to the team. Some congregations have preferred to appoint a pair of co-chairs.

The Coordinator

Throughout the process, communication is key: Notices must be sent to task force members, and minutes taken at meetings. Phone calls before and after the meeting should be made to help members feel connected. As the initiative gathers steam, the level of behind-the-scenes activity will increase: The experimentation phase will require program planning, coordination, and publicity. In the outreach phase, invitations to community conversations must be sent, and facilitators and researchers trained. After the community conversations, the data must be organized and summarized. In the exploration phase, coordination and communication are required between the various sub-groups. These tasks taken together easily require ten to fifteen hours a week. In most congregations, these tasks have been handled by a single person who serves as the glue that holds both the task force and the leadership team together.

The type of person chosen to serve in this position may vary from congregation to congregation. Some synagogues have been fortunate to have a volunteer come forward who is willing to put in the necessary time on a regular basis. These volunteers tend to be long-time members who have worked in a similar capacity at other organizations but, for a variety of reasons, no longer want or need a paying job. In other synagogues, a person with a similar abilities has been hired to work between ten and twenty hours a week (the actual number of hours depends on the size of the congregation, the pace at which the process proceeds, and the abilities of other leadership team members to take on various assignments). In a few congregations, the educator has assumed the role of coordinator, with an assistant hired to take over ten to twenty hours of his or her work.

The most important qualifications for the coordinator are organizational skills, the ability to get things done, a commitment to moving the process forward, and a congenial personality. Throughout the life of the initiative, dozens of volunteers will be asked to contribute their time and energy to this effort. The deployment of these volunteers must be handled with enthusiasm, efficiency, and grace. If the coordinator is also well connected in the congregation, a good facilitator, and a visionary, all the better; if not, lay leaders with these qualities can be brought in.

To state the obvious, the coordinator is *not* a secretary. In fact, s/he must be given secretarial help in order, for example, to send out various mailings. Unless s/he prefers to work at home, a desk, a telephone, a computer, and access to a fax machine are necessary to making the coordinator's work load manageable.

Other Lay Leaders

If possible, the leadership team should include one or two additional lay leaders who complement the task force chair in terms of the constituencies they represent and the skills they bring. Over time, even more lay leaders with very specific skills may be added. For example, in the outreach phase, a person with experience running focus groups could be an invaluable addition, as would a person with experience conducting or analyzing social science research. As experimentation gathers speed, one or two people with experience in arts education, informal education, or a related field, might be helpful.

Members of the leadership team should be asked to make a commitment of two to three years, depending, again, on how quickly or slowly the process proceeds. If the process is going well, replacing these leaders, should that become necessary, will not pose a major problem because potential candidates will have been identified at the task force level and through the community conversations.

The Role of the Professional Staff

Because this entire change process is predicated on the principle of shared leadership, it is critical that at least two members of the professional staff serve on the leadership team: the senior rabbi and the educator. Time permitting, other professionals, such as an assistant rabbi, the synagogue administrator, or the cantor, may wish to join the task force (though probably not the leadership team). These professionals may feel awkward at the outset and have some difficulty defining their roles. They are likely to have spent their entire careers developing a vision of congregational education and honing their expertise in one area or another. As members of the leadership team and the task force, they will find themselves engaged in discussions with congregants who may not have thought much about Jewish learning, who are, for the most part, far less knowledgeable, and who may be intimidated. In the words of one long-time member of a leadership team, "There was a sense from people: 'Who are we to do this? What do *we* know?' . . . The leadership team and the task force needed to learn how to gradually let go of their image of the rabbi in control."[2] The task force will be working toward a shared vision, which will evolve slowly as its members engage in study, discussion, and debate. The professionals will need to trust the process and not impose their own views.

Lay leaders have an understandable tendency to defer to professionals because of their learning, their title, and the role they have played at key life-cycle events. Moreover, it is often taken for granted that the vision of a congregation is synonymous with the vision of the rabbi. But if the rabbi and educator fully accept the need to evolve a shared vision, they will realize the value of exercising restraint, and ensure that their contributions do not overwhelm those of the other team members. Thus, professionals face the challenge of holding back their opinions while remaining fully engaged in the discussion, or else their restraint will be interpreted as indifference. Professionals who miss meetings regularly, or read their mail during the meetings they attend, are sending a message that the process is not important to them. An article by Eugene Borowitz on the need for professionals to practice *tsimtsum* (contraction, or forbearance) in their work with congregants has assumed the status of a classic.[3] Yet this kind of restraint is more easily preached than practiced.

For their part, the lay members of the leadership team will need to get past their awkwardness at having their rabbi as a teammate. This generally runs counter to learned behavior. Take the first leadership team meeting at one congregation. The coordinator placed packets with participants' names around the table; without thinking, she put the rabbi's packet at the head of the table. Both the task force chair (who expected to be at the head of the table) and another member of the team (who objected to having *anyone* at the head) complained about the seating arrangement, to which the coordinator replied, "But he *is* the rabbi."

Lay persons on ECE leadership teams have often found themselves challenging the rabbi for the first time in their lives. At another congregation, a heated debate broke out between the rabbi and a member of the team. Later in the day, this lay leader realized that she had never challenged any of her rabbis before. Though an experienced and highly regarded professional, in her capacity as a synagogue leader she had always instinctively deferred to the rabbi. The fact that she had stood her ground in this debate signaled an important change in their relationship.

If a team is aware of the tensions and prepared to discuss them openly, they will, over time, get past this awkwardness. Professionals will come to trust the judgment and commitment of the lay leaders; lay leaders will come to realize that they have a great deal to contribute. Once a mutually respectful relationship has developed, the members of the leadership team can decide together how the professionals' time, which is always in short supply, can best be used. At which meetings is their presence critical? From which meetings may they be excused? What roles can they play behind the scenes, rather than at meetings?

Becoming a Team

Each member of the leadership team will bring to the process his or her own values, beliefs, and working style. The readiness experience should have tested the chemistry between them and resulted in the creation of a team with the potential to work well together. But it will take time for these individuals to become a true team, a group "with complementary skills, who are committed to a common purpose and approach for which they hold themselves mutually accountable."[4] Organizational consultants Jon Katzenbach and Douglas K. Smith, who have conducted research on "high performing" teams in a variety of settings, suggest that newly formed teams spend a good deal of time together, especially at the outset. The most successful leadership teams meet weekly, for an hour and a half, or biweekly for a longer period of time. In addition to formal meeting times, team members interacted in a variety of ways, spending time one-on-one, on the phone, or communicating by e-mail.

One technique most teams find to be quite useful is that of responsibility charting. This technique has members of a team work together to list the tasks they will perform and decisions they will make, and review each task to determine who is responsible, who must approve, who must be consulted, and who must be informed. Since the tasks and responsibilities shift over time, these charts should be revised on a regular basis.[5]

But the most important predictor of a leadership team's success is the willingness and ability of its members to acknowledge and manage tensions. The enthusiasm that characterizes the early stages of the team's work together is tested when disagreements arise either over substantive issues or over personal and working styles. This is such a common occurrence in the life of groups that Tuckman and Jensen, in their research on the stages of development of working groups, characterize the second stage as "storming."[6] If tensions are allowed to simmer, the result can impede, or even destroy, the group. On the other hand, when potential conflicts are identified, articulated, and discussed openly, they can be managed, even if they are not entirely resolved. The diffusing of tensions is not so easily accomplished by those who are on the inside; at key junctures, it may be necessary to bring in an outside adviser to keep the process from bogging down or disintegrating.

The Role of the Adviser

Each ECE congregation was assigned an adviser, a paid consultant who spent an average of twenty days a year working with the congregation, over a period of three to five years.[7] Advisers who lived near the congregation were more likely to pop in and out for short meetings, while those who lived a considerable distance arranged to have a series of longer meetings that took place over the course of two or three days. In either case, the consensus of both the congregations and the project staff was that advisers added immeasurably to the congregation's ability to achieve its goals.

The majority of the adviser's work was done behind the scenes, meeting with the leadership team or working individually with some of its members. The adviser helped team members define their roles at the outset, and redefine them over time. S/he prodded the team to reflect on its strengths and weaknesses and expand the leadership pool when necessary. The adviser reviewed and critiqued plans for task force meetings, often suggesting suitable exercises and texts. S/he helped train the facilitators and notetakers for the community conversations. Early on in the process s/he helped prepare members of the task force to lead text study at meetings, and later helped the professional staff assume a similar role. It was the adviser's role to look down the road and identify potential problems, create mechanisms for preventing these problems, and help solve those that did arise. Ultimately, the adviser's goal was to equip and empower members of the leadership team to do this kind of problem solving on their own.

The adviser to one congregation recalls intervening at several key points in the process by: a) encouraging the original team to recruit additional lay leaders; b) assisting the staff in learning to accept and respond to critiques of existing programs; c) helping them understand that they were feeling "stuck" because they had not fully articulated their vision; and d) encouraging them to discuss their differences before the underlying tensions erupted, and to resolve these tensions amicably. Over time, this leadership team developed the ability to identify potential problems themselves, and to discuss them openly. They became advocates of "truth-telling," a phrase derived from Chris Argyris,[8] which is the belief that any and all opposing views should be stated openly, rather than behind closed doors or in the parking lot after the meeting.

Though not all synagogue change projects utilize advisers, a number of them do, so that there is now a cadre of educators, communal workers, and organizational consultants who have had experience working in this area. If a congregation can afford to hire an adviser, that money will be well spent, especially at the outset.

Support from Other Congregations

Between thirty and fifty synagogues have gone through an intensive change process related to learning, either on their own, through the ECE, or through other change projects. Another thirty or so congregations have been working in the areas of prayer and healing, under the auspices of Synagogue 2000. These congregations constitute another invaluable resource to a congregation that is just getting started. Members of the leadership teams and steering committees at some of these "veteran" synagogues have been quite generous with their time, spending hours on the phone offering advice, hosting and educating visitors, and even visiting other congregations to make presentations. The ECE maintains a roster of participating congregations, as do other change projects.

The Need for Continuous Communication

A final word of advice: As a disparate group of individuals coalesces into a well-oiled team, it develops a lingo of its own, as well as a set of common rituals. These help the group operate most efficiently and most effectively, but they become problematic when they serve to exclude others. As the authors of *The Dance of Change* explain:

> In many ways, zeal and isolation are the most insidious unintended consequences of profound change initiatives. The deeper and more effective the change that occurs in the pilot group, the more easily they can come into conflict with the larger organization. The more people do change, the more different they become, in their thinking and acting, from the mainstream culture. . . . Ironically, the more personal and business results they achieve the more arrogant and intolerant they can become.[9]

A member of one leadership team made a similar point:

> It is important not to assume that people in the larger group have the same understanding you do. There is always the risk

of the leadership team becoming isolated from the task force. This is an important thing to stay in touch with—there is the potential to get side-tracked in our own process and forget there is this other group out there.[10]

It is inevitable that some division will occur between the leadership team and the task force, on the one hand, and the task force and the congregation, on the other. This gap can be narrowed through continual communication. The leadership team must actively work at spreading its vision, especially to the board of directors and key committees. A team that has grown too insular may wonder why people don't understand what it is they are doing. "After all," they may say "Our task force has been announced from the *bimah* (pulpit) and explained in the bulletin dozens of times!" If leadership team members remember (or are reminded) how hard it was for them to envision a new kind of learning, they will be more tolerant of and generous with the "outsiders" who don't "get it," and better able to communicate with the entire congregation.

7

Evolving a Shared Vision

In Genesis 12:1 God summons Abram on a journey:

Go forth from your native land and from your father's house to the land that I will show you. I will make of you a great nation, And I will bless you; I will make your name great, And you shall be a blessing.

We can only marvel at God's ability to inspire and Abram's capacity to trust. God's call comes in verse 1, and by verse 4 Abram has already begun his journey, bringing along his wife, Sarai, his nephew Lot, his servants, and all their possessions.

Compare Abram's situation to that of the newly convened task force on congregational education. Abram received a direct command from God. Though he had probably never been to Canaan before, he could trust God to show him the way.

Task force members, in contrast, are not being asked to uproot themselves physically, and their journey, which is metaphoric, will only affect a part of their lives. However, having been summoned by human beings, rather than God, they will be much less certain about the destination, and will need to plot the journey on their own.

The task force will, therefore, need to begin by clarifying its ultimate goals. While an individual, or even a family, might enjoy taking a hike with no predetermined endpoint, institutions do not usually benefit from aimless wandering, which is usually accompanied by a squandering of resources, confusion, and, ultimately, conflict.

The task force's ability to envision its end-point will take time. It is, by design, a diverse group. It is unlikely that more than a few members have had experience setting the goals for any institution, much less a synagogue. The phrase "a congregation of learners" is only the sound-bite summary of a vision that requires further elaboration: Why is learning important? What kinds of learning does the congregation wish to promote? What results does it hope to achieve? Few members of the group will have had an opportunity to consider these questions, whose answers will lead to a collective vision of a congregation of learners.

This chapter outlines a process that a task force might use to do just that and to ensure that the vision is concrete enough to plan for the future, yet flexible enough to evolve over time. But before I describe the process, I need to explain in greater detail what an institutional vision is.

What Is a Vision and Where Does It Come from?

If you are a parent, you probably recall the vision you had for each of your children when s/he was born. You may have imagined that child as an excellent student, a great baseball player, a creative artist, a loyal friend. Undoubtedly, you fantasized about his or her future as a loving sibling and spouse, a compassionate and ethical citizen. Where did this vision come from? What served as your inspiration? Most likely, your vision was derived from three sources: your values, your experience, and your imagination. Our hopes that a child grow to be loving, loyal, ethical, and compassionate are a reflection of our values, the qualities we consider to be most important in a human being. But values are abstract, and somewhat vague; if your vision consisted only of values, it might sound like a batch of disembodied and disconnected ideas. Experience, the second source of one's vision, translates the abstract ideal into a more concrete, three-dimensional character. Your vision of your child as a talented musician or a brilliant mathematician probably came from personal or vicarious experiences that made music, math, or any other endeavor pleasurable and important. When you imagined your child as a loving parent, you were able to call forth memories of your own parents, perhaps when they took you on a special outing, or taught you to drive. A negative experience can be as powerful as a positive one—for example, if you once came close to drowning, you might be determined that your child should be a strong swimmer. But experience alone is still not enough. Some of our ideals for our children go far beyond what we can see or feel today; they come from our imagination. The Zionist pioneers envisioned their children as citizens of an independent Jewish state. Blacks involved in the civil rights movement in the 1950s envisioned their children as fully integrated into American society.

Over time, your vision of your child probably changed a great deal. For one thing, the child had another parent, whose vision may have differed, at least to some degree, from yours. Second, as the child grew, his or her own talents and inclinations were factored into the equation. A child who is tone deaf is not likely to become a great musician; on the other hand, he or she might exhibit unexpected talent as a gymnast. Finally, as society changed, your vision may have changed with it. For example, parents in the 1950s may not have envisioned their daughters as having high-powered careers; until the 1980s few parents envisioned their children as computer geniuses.

A vision enables a parent to see in a very small infant the full potential of a grown human being. It inspires one to make certain opportunities available. It serves as a touchstone when disciplinary action seems called for. It helps sustain one in moments of doubt, reassuring one that beyond the tantrums of the two year old and the sulking of the adolescent lies a person who could grow up to embody one's evolving ideal. Specific details change over time, but the fact that one *has* an ideal inspires one to be the best parent one can be. Ultimately, the *content* of the vision is less important than the *process of visioning.*

Institutional Vision

Parents don't always express in words their vision for their children; sometimes they are not even aware of the values, experiences, or aspirations that guide their actions. Articulating a vision may only become important when a conflict emerges, such as when two parents disagree, or when a child does something that seems inappropriate or wrong. On the other hand, an institution that does not have an explicit vision is headed for trouble, particularly if it is a synagogue with hundreds or thousands of members. If a synagogue's vision is not clear, it can easily find itself buffeted by opposing factions, unable to reach one destination before it is pushed to pursue the opposite course.

What is institutional vision? Drawing on the work of Burt Nanus,[1] organizational consultant Robert Weinberg defines it as "a compelling organizing image of a desired future of an organization." In contrast to an organization's *mission,* which summarizes what that institution *does,* a *vision* expresses what the organization could *become.* A synagogue's *mission* is to be a house of prayer, a house of meeting, and a house of learning; its *vision* sets forth the *kind* of prayer, meeting, and learning it would like to offer, how it hopes people will respond, and the kind of community it hopes to create. For example, the vision of Congregation B'nai Jeshurun is "to inspire and require." The vision of Temple Emanuel of Beverly Hills is "Passionate, Activist, Visionary, Artistic, Caring, Spiritual: We take our inspiration straight from Torah."

A vision of a congregation motivates and sustains its leaders, enabling them to make decisions and set priorities, mindful of why these priorities are appropriate. For example, every synagogue, consciously or not, makes decisions about the style of worship it offers; whether it will use only Hebrew, or a combination of Hebrew and English; whether the music will be traditional or contemporary; whether participation will be encouraged or discouraged; and so on. An institution's vision guides its deliberations, increasing the chances that the decisions will be thoughtful and consistent. It is always necessary to set priorities. No matter how well endowed, a congregation cannot afford to mount an endless number of learning opportunities. A vision supplies the rationale for choosing some options over others. Finally, a vision reminds both congregants and the staff why they are doing what they are doing, and what they aspire to become. It is easy to get caught up in the details of scheduling, planning, and fund-raising and forget the ultimate point of all this activity. Like the *mizrach* plaque that hangs on an eastern wall to remind us of the Temple in Jerusalem, a vision helps us remember what is really important.

Articulating an institutional vision poses a number of challenges. The vision must be broad enough to inspire the institution's diverse constituents, concrete enough to guide its decisions and priorities, and yet flexible enough to evolve over time.

The typical congregation operates under the tacit assumption that its vision should be set by its rabbi, in conjunction, perhaps, with a small core of lay leaders. There are two reasons to question the validity of this assumption and to include a much broader coalition of congregants (and staff) in articulating the vision. First, congregants may question whether they want to perpetuate this hierarchical model of leadership. If a synagogue belongs to the community, and not just the rabbi, as many members of the community as possible must have a stake in envisioning its future. In the past decade people who work in business, government, and education have increasingly been exposed to organizational theories that view leadership not as a quality that resides in an individual, but as an activity that can and should be shared by many. Anyone can be a leader, according to these theories, if s/he acts in the interest of the organization as a whole and inspires others to do the same. In an age of employee ownership of businesses and shared decision-making in public schools, religious leadership, too, will increasingly be seen as more of a joint responsibility.[2]

If the first reason is theoretical, the second reason for seeking broader participation is more practical: A charismatic leader can indeed motivate people to *begin* learning, but if the motivation is not internalized, it will be difficult to sustain this activity over time. The ultimate goal is for congregants to engage in learning on a continuous basis because they value learning, and because they experience it as enjoyable and rewarding. Why not harness the potential energy of ordinary members from the outset, involving them in articulating this vision? The activity of shaping a vision can invest congregants in learning to the point that they will not need charisma to motivate them.

Congregants who participate in a process of visioning will have an opportunity to: think about some important Jewish questions; explore their Jewish values; recall formative Jewish experiences, both positive and negative; share their ideas and experiences with others; and imagine what their ideal congregation might look like. This process of visioning may well be the first time these congregants have been challenged to consider these issues, and the first time they will have heard the voices of their fellow congregants. Their thoughts will evolve over time. Whereas their first thoughts might dwell on particularly negative experiences in Hebrew school, later they may remember more positive experiences they had as teens or adults. At first a formative public celebration might come to mind; later, experiences that were more private, but equally powerful, may surface. If the process of visioning is combined with the study of texts, these texts will challenge people further and deepen their appreciation of the tradition. Congregants will undoubtedly disagree with one another's values and conclusions, at least at the outset. But just as the vision of the parent develops and changes, so can the vision of the stakeholders in a congregation.

The Use (and Misuse) of a Vision Statement

A *vision statement* is a document that evolves from a series of conversations about vision, a written record of the group's consensus. Writing down the main ideas that have been discussed and shaping them into an inspiring paragraph or page accomplishes two purposes. First, it creates a record of the conversation, keeping the participants in the process of visioning "on the same page." Though they may disagree in their interpretations of the statement, they will have reached at least a modicum of agreement. Second, the statement enables those who engaged in the visioning process to communicate their conclusions to others in the congregation.

However, the vision statement itself is only a pale representation of the wealth of insight and experience that led to its creation. In the absence of the conversations that animated them, the words of the vision statement can ring hollow, sounding like motherhood and apple pie. This is why it would be inadvisable to simply adopt the vision statement of another congregation. To date, two or three dozen congregations have attempted to spell out what it would mean to them to become a congregation of learners; examples from three such congregations appear in this chapter to convey a sense of what the end product of a visioning process might look like. After going through the exercises outlined in this chapter, your congregation might arrive at a statement very similar to one of these. But, being the product of a series of conversations, your own version will have considerable resonance; reading it will remind you of the value statements, experiences, and imagination that were its building blocks.

For the same reason, it would be a mistake to simply publicize the vision statement your task force creates and leave it at that. In as many ways as possible, the vision statement should be used as a jumping off point for other members of the congregation to reflect on their own values and experiences, and to exercise their own imagination. Suggestions for doing this will appear on the following pages.

Five Steps to a Vision of a Congregation of Learners

The task force should devote at least four sessions (of two to three hours) to visioning exercises; many ECE congregations devoted considerably more time than this, and felt that this time spent up front, clarifying their goals, enabled them to operate more efficiently later on. The exercises included in this chapter fall into five categories: reflecting on experience; identifying and clarifying values; unleashing one's imagination; drafting a vision statement; and interpreting the vision statement. Since these exercises are cumulative, I suggest that records be kept and placed in a "vision folder." These contributions will serve as the raw material for the vision statement.

Reflecting on Experience

The easiest way to begin articulating a vision of learning is to recall those moments in which one learned something in a very powerful, engaging way. The moment could be as short as a half-hour, or as long as a summer or a semester. What was learned may have been information, but it could also have been an idea, a skill, or an attitude. Given a few minutes to reflect, nearly everyone can recall learning experiences that were deeply satisfying, perhaps because they were so enjoyable (like playing an instrument or reading a great novel), perhaps because they served as a stepping stone to a significant achievement (like driving a car or being able to communicate with strangers in a foreign language), perhaps, even, because they were transformative (leading to an important insight or inspiration). Beginning with positive experiences allows people to get past their bad memories of their own terrible fourth-grade Hebrew teachers, or their child's difficult time in religious school the previous year. These will undoubtedly come up in the course of discussion, and that will be fine; but it is important to keep task force meetings from becoming gripe sessions. Hearing one another's experiences gives participants a sense of the many different perspectives on learning represented in the room. Some experiences will be highly intellectual, others emotional; some will involve learning in a group, while others will be more private. In a subtle, nondidactic way, Exercise 1 and Exercise 2 deliver a message about the need for a variety of approaches to learning.

The learning experiences people reflect on need not be Jewish; in fact, congregations have had great success utilizing two different exercises, one that focuses on Jewish learning, the other on secular forms of learning.

Identifying and Clarifying Values

Having warmed up by sharing and analyzing their experiences, members of the task force are now ready to delve more deeply into the values that are associated with learning. Why is Jewish learning important? What values should guide our choice of what to teach and how to teach it? Answers to these questions could fill (and have) volumes of philosophical writing. The point of these sessions is not to arrive at definitive answers, but to expose participants to a range of views and to stimulate their own thinking. Two very different types of exercises help with this: Exercise 3 involves reading and analyzing short texts; Exercise 4 invites participants to think metaphorically.

Additional Activities That Might Be Used for an Exploration of Values

1. A discussion of a short article or selection from a book on synagogue life or Jewish learning.

2. Presentations from two or three individuals who have different visions of the ideal congregation.

3. An analysis of the vision statements of other congregations. Three such vision statements are included at the end of this chapter, along with some sample questions that might be used to guide discussion.

A Memorable
Jewish Learning Experience

This is a simple and relatively short exercise that many task forces have used in their orientation session. It asks everyone to describe in a minute or two a memorable Jewish learning experience. Experiences that are mentioned might include cooking with one's mother or grandmother, studying for an adult bar/bat mitzvah, reading a book, and attending a Passover seder. After everyone has spoken, people can be invited to reflect on what they have heard. They are likely to focus on the diversity in the room.

Preparation:
No preparation is required.

Grouping of Participants:
The ideal group for such an exercise is 10–15. A smaller group may not be sufficiently diverse, while the stories of a larger group could get repetitive and boring. This means that the task force will need to be divided in half, and possibly even in quarters. Time should be allotted at the end for someone from each group to report briefly on the similarities and differences they have heard.

Time Required:
Allow 2 minutes for each participant, 10 minutes for general comments.

Facilitation:

This exercise requires no special facilitation, just someone to ask the initial question, call on participants, and ask for reflections.

Record Keeping:

There is no need for the answers to be displayed. However, it might be worthwhile to place a list of the different activities that were mentioned in the vision folder for future reference.

Reflections on Our Own
Best Learning Experiences

This is a more complicated exercise whose purpose is for people to extrapolate from their non-Jewish learning experiences some general principles about what makes learning particularly powerful, enjoyable, and meaningful. Handout 1 (below) suggests one way in which this assignment might be framed.

Preparation:
An instruction sheet for participants will be required. See Handout 1 for a possible model.

Grouping of Participants:
Small groups with five participants each.

Time Required:
30–40 minutes for the small groups, and 1–2 minutes for each group to report back.

Facilitation:
Each group can work on its own, following the instruction sheet.

Record Keeping:
The "principles" should be placed in the vision folder.

Reflections on Our Own Best Learning Experiences

In Small Groups:

Think for a moment of a very positive learning experience you have had, either learning a skill or a new subject. For purposes of this exercise think of something you learned that was *not* particularly Jewish.

- **What factors or conditions made this a particularly positive experience for you?**

- Take turns sharing both the experience and the factors that made it so successful. As people talk, have someone list the factors or conditions. Notice how many of these are mentioned more than once.

- After everyone has had a turn, spend some time analyzing and prioritizing the list: Which items can be combined? Which seem to be most important?

- Pick your group's top five priorities.

- Turn each of these five into a sentence that explains what the factor is and why it is important. Write them on a flipchart or a large piece of butcher paper to be shared with the other groups; keep a copy to place in the vision folder.

Deriving Values from Texts

The Jewish tradition is full of texts extolling the virtues of learning, describing the qualities of the ideal teacher, and suggesting methods for teaching. The advice offered by one text may contradict that of another; likewise, the values implicit in one text may differ sharply from those embedded in another. While these texts teach us about the traditional place of learning, they also serve as a springboard for clarifying our own values.

Preparation:

- Select a small number of texts, perhaps only two or three. Handout #3 (below) contains a number of texts that have been used by ECE congregations, but part of the fun is finding texts of your own. Texts that at first seem puzzling or ambiguous, and therefore invite interpretation, work best as triggers for discussion. When two texts by noted authorities seem to contradict each other, that too engages the discussants. Select small, carefully edited excerpts so as not to overwhelm participants with long or complicated sentence structures or tangential issues. If your text contains a number of unfamiliar Hebrew terms, prepare an accompanying glossary.

- Select a facilitator for each small group. Give the facilitators an opportunity to review the texts prior to the session. Introduce the session by explaining that this exercise has two goals: 1) To identify the values that were traditionally most important in Jewish learning; 2) To explore the question of whether these values remain important today, or whether they need to be replaced by other values.

Grouping of Participants:

Small groups of 3–5.

Time Required:

Allow 15–20 minutes per text, and about 15–20 minutes to write the value statements.

Facilitation:

See Handout 2 for a suggested facilitator's guide. Rather than sharing the value statements out loud at the end (which would be difficult for listeners to grasp and impossible for them to think about seriously), these might be typed up and mailed to participants after the meeting.

Record Keeping:

The value statements should be collected in the visioning folder.

Facilitating Text Study
as Part of the Visioning Process

Working in small groups:

Read each of the selections assigned to your group. As you read, note what each text seems to imply about the value(s) we derive from Jewish learning.

After reading the texts:

- What does each of these texts tell us about the value(s) that Jewish learning can bring to our lives?

- In what ways are the values suggested by the texts different?

- Are these values relevant to us today? If not, how might they be restated to be more relevant?

- Can you think of any other values derived from Jewish learning that are not mentioned in these texts?

- Think of an experience you had learning something Jewish in which you felt that you had gotten one of these values. What conditions made this experience so valuable?

Based on the experiences of members of your group, write some statements about the value of Jewish learning and the conditions that help make this learning a valuable experience.

A Selection of Texts
to Be Used in the Visioning Process

Behold, a good doctrine has been given to you, My Torah; do not forsake it. It is a tree of life to those who hold it fast, and all who cling to it find happiness. Its ways are ways of pleasantness, and all its paths are peace.

Etz Chayim, prayer said upon returning the Torah to the Ark

This is what Rabbi Leib, son of Sarah, used to say about those rabbis who expounded Torah:

"What does it amount to—their expounding Torah! A person should see that all his actions are a Torah and that he himself becomes so entirely a Torah that one can learn from his habits and motions and his motionless clinging to God."

Martin Buber

Throughout the past this is what the Torah did for the Jew: It set up definite standards of behavior. Conformity with its tenets and practices made one a good Jew, and the reverence in which the Torah was held made one wish to earn that title. In the course of his Jewish studies, the Jew should nowadays be fully apprised of the causes which have rendered the Torah, in its traditional form, largely irrelevant to his needs. This knowledge would clear the ground for that process of reinterpretation which would make the Jewish tradition a means of stimulating our people to resume its quest for a good life. It should be the purpose of adult Jewish study to train the Jew in that process of reinterpretation, so that the tradition of his people, even if not infallible, might function as a potent influence in shaping the ethical and spiritual ideals which alone can render life worth living.

Mordecai Kaplan, *The Future of the American Jew,* p. 476

These are the things, the fruits of which a person enjoys in this world, while the stock remains for him in the world to come: honoring the father and mother, the practice of charity, timely attendance at the house of study morning and evening, hospitality to wayfarers, visiting the sick, dowering the bride, attending the dead to the grave, devotion in prayer, and making peace between man and his fellow; but the study of the Torah is equal to them all.

Mishna Peah 1:1

Judaism is a process of ongoing commentary. To be a Jew is to be a student. To be a self-affirming Jew is to love and study Torah. It is no small matter that the rabbis considered study equal in value to all the other mitzvot combined as one. We are a people devoted to a text. . . . We can affirm this fully without denying the human origins of the Torah. We can celebrate it along with recognizing the fallibility of the text, along with agonizing over its moral imperfections, its ancient, rather than modern, sensibilities. A fallible text is one all the more in need of commentary, our way of bringing our past into the present before we hand it on to those who will create the future. . . . As we struggle to add to tradition, to reshape it for each new generation, the text is also given a chance at reshaping us, at making a real demand on the way we think and live.

Arthur Green

The study of Torah was not restricted to any special group. It had to be open to all. Was not the Torah given by God in the free desert, in the open places, so that everyone feeling the desire for it might receive it? Even as the desert is open to all and is not privately possessed, so is the Torah accessible to all and the private property of none. When the School of Shamai ventured the opinion that only those should be taught "who are wise, modest, of good family, and wealthy," the School of Hillel objected, countering with the prevailing view to "teach everyone, for when there are sinners in Israel and they are brought to the study of the Torah, many righteous, pious and worthy Jews will come from them."

Israel Goldman, *Life-Long Learning Among Jews,* p. 50

Metaphors of a Congregation/ Congregational Learning

Exercise #3 approached the issues of values from an intellectual perspective. But values are not only formulated intellectually; often we discover them through our emotional response to certain situations. This exercise in metaphors, devised by Dr. Susan Shevitz, approaches the question of values in a more imaginative way that taps into one's emotions. Participants are asked to think of something (it could be animate or inanimate, large or small) to which their ideal congregation (or their ideal sense of congregational learning) might be compared, to draw that metaphor, and to interpret the metaphor for others. For example, one task force member compared the congregation to a garden that required tending to make it bloom. A second drew an image of a hospital in which patients interacted with the staff, but not with one another.

Preparation:

Large sheets of newsprint and markers, while not essential, might free the participants' imaginations. Otherwise, no preparation is necessary.

Grouping of Participants:

Participants may be offered the choice of working individually or in groups of two or three. Ideally, 8–10 drawings should be made and shared, so consider dividing the task force into a number of small groups.

Time Required:

20–25 minutes for the drawing and the analysis; two minutes for each explanation.

Facilitation:

The facilitator will need to give instructions, watch the time, and keep the presentations moving along. Some participants may be resistant to thinking metaphorically, or to producing a drawing. Employing humor, and without being defensive, the facilitator should encourage (but not force) people to participate. After people finish their drawings they should be asked to "unpack" them: What assumptions about synagogue life and/or Jewish learning are embedded in this metaphor? What values does this metaphor stress? What values does it downplay? For example, in the garden metaphor, what are the congregation's equivalents of sunshine and water? Who are the gardeners? Embedded in the hospital metaphor is an assumption that doctors, not other patients, are critical to restoring health; expertise is valued highly, but community is not.

Record Keeping:

Some congregations found that this exercise served as an important turning point, giving them great insight into the congregation and into one another. One congregation saved the drawings and repeated the exercise two or three years later; a juxtaposition of the two sets of metaphors enabled them to discuss how far they had come.

The Ideal Learning Community

Preparation:

Each participant is given 25 large Post-it notes (five each of five different colors) and a medium point felt-tip pen. Posted around the room are five pieces of butcher paper, each coded with one of the five colors of the Post-its, and given one of the following titles: WHO? WHAT? WHERE? WHEN? HOW?

Grouping of Participants:

Part 1 is done individually; for Part 2, divide the larger group into 5 sub-groups.

Time Required:

Part 1: 20–25 minutes; Part 2: 20–25 minutes

Facilitation:

PART 1:

Participants are asked to dream about the ideal learning community. The key words on the butcher paper (WHO? WHAT? WHERE? WHEN? HOW?) are intended to inspire people to dream as broadly as possible. Each dream should be written down (legibly, in rather large print) on the Post-it of the appropriate color. After 10 minutes, invite participants to post their notes on the corresponding sheets of butcher paper.

Participants then walk around the room to read the notes.

PART 2:

After dividing into five groups, each group is given one of the pieces of butcher paper. In this group, they will use a technique called "affinity grouping"—silently, they are to group together Post-its that have a common theme; if they don't agree with the grouping someone else has created, or want to add another Post-it, they should feel free to rearrange things. Doing this silently will prevent discussions of which notes belong together and why. The goal is to achieve consensus silently, having all the notes grouped to everyone's satisfaction.

After consensus is reached, the group gathers together to describe each of the categories of Post-its in a sentence. The sentences are written on the butcher paper, over the individual comments.

Then the butcher paper is posted again so that everyone may view the summary statements.

Record Keeping:

The statements are compiled, typed, distributed to participants at the next meeting, and placed in the vision folder.

The Synagogue Bulletin of the Future

The synagogue bulletin of the future is simply a device for people to imagine the kind of learning that might take place once the planning process is completed. This activity will work best if it is done toward the end of the visioning phase. No preparation is required.

Grouping of Participants:

Small groups of 3–4.

Time Required:

30 minutes

Facilitation:

This requires very little facilitation. Participants are asked to imagine what the synagogue's bulletin might look like in 7–10 years, after the synagogue has become a congregation of learners. One group might be assigned to write the calendar of events; a second, the lead article; the third, the rabbi's column; etc. Rather than being shared orally, these might be typed up and distributed along with the minutes of the task force meeting.

Record Keeping:

Of course, a copy of this fantasy bulletin should go into the vision folder.

Challenging Our "Limiting Assumptions"

Preparation:

No preparation is required.

Grouping of Participants:

The first part of this exercise can be done with the task force as a whole; the second should be done in small groups of 3–5.

Time Required:

45 minutes for the first part; 30 minutes for the second. You may decide to have some task force members continue working on Part 2 on their own or in small groups prior to the next task force meeting, at which they will have an opportunity to review the rewritten assumptions.

Facilitation:

PART 1:

Participants sit in a semi-circle (with two or three rows, if necessary); two flip charts are at the front of the room, with a recorder at each one. The facilitator asks people to brainstorm the assumptions they, or their fellow congregants, have about learning in the context of the congregation. Some of these statements may be true, and some false; these will be discussed in Part 2. Part 1 is a brainstorming exercise, so there are no wrong answers. The recorders take turns writing down people's statements. If participants get stuck, the facilitator can prompt them by asking some more specific questions, such as: "What assumptions do we have about students? Teachers? The subject matter? The parents? The goals of learning?" etc.

PART 2:

In groups of 3–4, participants make a note of the assumptions they believe to be true. Then they choose a small number they would like to challenge, and try to rewrite the statement so it becomes an assumption they can affirm. Their work can be posted on the wall.

Record Keeping:

The re-written statements (as well as the ones that are deemed to be true) should go into the vision folder.

Unleashing One's Imagination in the Visioning Process

The process of visioning is an opportunity to engage people's creativity and encourage them to imagine wonderful new possibilities, liberated, at least for a short while, from the constraints of budgeting, staffing, scheduling, and so on. In the end, of course, all sorts of realities will have to be factored in, but suspending them temporarily frees participants to dream. Exercises 5, 6, and 7 have been used to spur people's imaginations. Exercise 5 is a free-form dreaming exercise designed by ECE adviser Susan Huntting. Exercise 6, created by ECE consultant Robert Weinberg, asks participants to imagine their fantasy synagogue through the device of a synagogue bulletin of the future. Exercise 7, which has people articulate and challenge their "limiting assumptions," was contributed by organizational development consultant Edward Reynolds. If your group has the time to do all three exercises (over the course of two or three meetings), it would be advisable to do them in the order suggested here, warming people up by having them fantasize broadly, and then gradually narrowing their focus.

Drafting a Vision Statement

Even if the task force has done only one exercise from each of the first three categories, the vision folder should now be filled with interesting fragments, many of which will overlap. At some point, a small committee should gather to assemble these fragments into a first draft of the vision statement. It is likely that at least two meetings will be required for the first draft, which can then be sent to members of the task force for feedback (preferably in writing), and revised again (at least once). The task force as a whole should not engage in "word-smithing," which could become tedious and frustrating.

The committee should bear in mind that the purpose of the vision statement is both to inspire congregants to engage in learning and to create a set of guidelines for the kind of learning opportunities the congregation will offer. The statement needs to be connected to some overarching ideas, but written in language that is concrete enough for everyone to understand. It must be short enough so that people will read it, and long enough to be substantive. There is no one right way to write a vision statement. Members of the committee will feel less intimidated if they bear in mind that the statement will go through a number of revisions, so that they need not prepare a draft that is perfect.

Some of the ECE task forces found it useful to review and discuss vision statements created at other congregations, not in order to copy them, but to get a flavor of different possible formats. If brought in too early, vision statements from other congregations might, in fact, serve the purpose of cutting off discussion; their directness and simplicity might be intimidating. After the visioning exercises and prior to the actual drafting of the statement, however, analyzing and discussing these examples might get people past their "writer's block."

Sample Vision Statements

Following are three vision statements from three different congregations. The first, produced at Temple Shalom of Newton in Massachusetts, is introduced by a personal narrative from the congregational educator, Julie Vanek, describing the often laborious but ultimately energizing process the congregation went through. Those responsible for producing the first draft might want to read this narrative if they are feeling discouraged or overwhelmed. They will note that Temple Shalom put off writing its vision statement for quite some time, proceeding to the community conversations of the outreach phase, and returning to write the vision statement only after that phase had ended. This is a possible option for those congregations who find themselves totally stymied.

The second vision statement is from Congregation B'nai Jeshurun in New York City.

A third type of vision statement was produced by the ECE task force at Temple Emanu-El of Dallas. It was designed to resemble a traditional Jewish text, with the main text in the center, surrounded by commentaries. The document has two parts. In the first, a concise statement about the value of Jewish learning is surrounded by equally brief comments on values that are related to learning. In the second, citations from classic Jewish texts are woven together with quotes from congregants (recorded at the community conversations) and members of the task force, to produce a moving meditation on the importance of learning in the life of the congregation.

Following the three vision statements is a handout with a set of questions that might be used to analyze the vision statements in this chapter.

Interpreting the Vision Statement

The primary purpose of the vision statement is to engage congregants in discussions about Jewish learning in general, and about their potential as learners, in particular. One very successful exercise asks people to write a commentary on the statement.[4] An additional benefit of this exercise is that it teaches about the Jewish interpretive tradition and how the process of commentary continues to this day. The exercise is a good way to involve members of the board of directors and various committees, religious school teachers, parents, and even students.

Communicating the Vision

Vision statements are of limited use if they sit in a drawer, so once a "good enough" draft has been produced, it should be shared with the congregation in as many ways as possible. A primary vehicle for communicating the vision statement will be through the community conversations, which will be discussed in chapter 9. Other, simpler ways include reprinting the statement in the synagogue bulletin, posting it in several prominent places in the hallway, and featuring it on the congregation's web site. Bearing in mind that genuine communication is two-way, and that most people communicate most comfortably face to face, opportunities should be created to use this document as a springboard for discussion.

Creating a Vision of Learning
at Temple Shalom of Newton

We were almost two years into our process of re-visioning Jewish education at Temple Shalom before we finally began working seriously on creating a vision statement. Though we had made several earlier attempts at putting a vision down on paper, we always managed to push it to the back burner, claiming that "it was not the right time." At this point, however, it was time to clearly articulate our vision in order to be able to attract people and bring them into the process of re-visioning Jewish learning at Temple Shalom.

Our adviser helped us clarify some important issues before we began the work. We discussed why it had been difficult for us to get to work: a discomfort with lay people setting the vision in a system accustomed to looking to the rabbi as the authority, the need to let the vision evolve from our work, and the difficulty of focusing solely on Jewish learning. After these discussions our planning group (including four congregants, the educator, the senior rabbi, and our adviser) began to work, first individually, then in pairs, then bringing our contributions to the whole group. We began in January of 1997, and by mid-March we had a draft we felt good about. We knew, however, that it was important to create an opportunity for the members of the task force to really study the document. We designed an activity that divided our task force into small groups, based on their committee work. Each group was asked to find connections between the vision statement and its own projects (current or proposed). An important piece of feedback we got at this session was that our draft was too long. The planning group agreed to continue working, and to present another draft at the May 1st task force meeting. After several wonderful discussions and a few more revisions, we presented the penultimate draft to the full task force at the beginning of May. After a few changes, it went to the board for approval. Members of the task force who sit on the board read the statement out loud. When they were finished, the members of the board broke into applause!

We have tried to make our Vision of Learning visible to all members of the congregation. It was highlighted during High Holy Day services and in the temple bulletin, and appeared on the weekly Shabbat booklet distributed on Friday evening.

The ten goals articulated in the Vision of Learning provide us with standards to strive for and help us evaluate our accomplishments.

As the members of the Board of Trustees began to realize that the senior rabbi expected this to be a guiding principle for the future of the Temple, they expressed some discomfort that this was a vision of learning and not a vision of the congregation as a whole. It became clear that we needed to articulate a comparable vision for the entire congregation. The process we used to write the vision of learning was then replicated with members of the Board of Trustees. We began with a day-long retreat. Six months and many revisions later, the board approved a vision statement for Temple Shalom at its April meeting.

Our hope is that goal statements, comparable to those in the Vision of Learning, will be written for each of the additional five areas.

Vision of Learning at Temple Shalom of Newton

Temple Shalom aspires to be a congregation of lifelong learners, because we believe that Jewish learning has value for its own sake *(torah lishmah)* and that active participation in Jewish learning is a pathway to:

- Lifelong learning *(Torah Lishmah)*
- Enriching spirituality *(Kedushah)*
- Building community *(Kehillah)*
- Repairing the world *(Tikun Olam)*
- Sustaining Jewish continuity *(Brit Olam)*

Goals:

In order to build a Temple community that reflects and supports a commitment to lifelong learning, the membership, the lay leadership, the Board of Directors, and the professional staff of Temple Shalom will:

1. Develop opportunities for learning that are vibrant, stimulating and readily available to all members.

2. Assist individuals and families to design their own plans for learning.

3. Ensure that every event and gathering at Temple Shalom pro-

vides an opportunity for Jewish learning.

4. Build a religious school characterized by programs that assist students and families to embrace, understand, and experience their Judaism with commitment and love.

5. Provide learning opportunities that assist members of the congregation to increase their participation in rituals at home and in the synagogue.

6. Monitor and evaluate the effectiveness of learning strategies and programs.

7. Encourage members to see that learning and teaching are the province and responsibility of all.

8. Enhance the physical space to support the learning needs of the congregation.

9. Approve a budget that supports the learning needs of adults as well as children.

10. Promote an organizational and committee structure that reflects the central importance of Jewish learning to the life of the congregation.

Vision Statement of Temple Shalom

At Temple Shalom we aspire to be a congregation whose members find meaning and fulfillment in the practice of Reform Judaism. We believe that this meaning and fulfillment flow from personal engagement with the living tradition of Judaism. We invite our membership in all its diversity to participate in the religious, educational and communal life of our synagogue.

Together we are committed to the ongoing work of building a congregation whose everyday undertaking is shaped by the Jewish values of:

- Lifelong learning *(Torah Lishmah)*
- Enriching spirituality *(Kedushah)*
- Building community *(Kehillah)*
- Repairing the world *(Tikun Olam)*
- Sustaining Jewish continuity *(Brit Olam)*

Vision Statement of Congregation B'nai Jeshurun, New York, New York

[The following is the introduction to B'nai Jeshurun's vision statement, and the third section of the statement, which deals with learning.]

B'nai Jeshurun is a progressive, egalitarian, participatory congregation committed to synagogue transformation. While we are within the Conservative movement, we are committed to an expression of Judaism which is a bridge among all Jews without regard to denominational label. Our expression of Judaism is woven from the many strands that make up Jewish life.

We strive for a new model of synagogue membership in which each person takes responsibility for his or her own participation and spiritual growth while caring for each other. . . .

Study at B'nai Jeshurun should be a personal and spiritual engagement that connects the mind and the heart. It should move each of us to more fully encounter ourselves, each other, and God. Study should strengthen us as a community and inspire each of us individually and collectively to increase our level of observance and do our part to repair the world. Study also should reflect our commitment to Israel and Zionism.

Study and education at B'nai Jeshurun should be a program of continuous learning that encourages and enables members to commit to setting aside time regularly for Torah study. B'nai Jeshurun must make relevant and challenging formal and informal opportunities for study available to all members of the community from the youngest to the oldest, from the beginner to the most learned. Our program of study must be structured to allow students to progress to ever-increasing levels of learning.

Each member of B'nai Jeshurun should acquire at least a basic level of Jewish literacy. To fully participate in our services, that literacy should include basic prayer book Hebrew.

To achieve these goals, our current educational programming must be maintained and enhanced with effective and creative initiatives.

Vision Statement of Temple Emanu-El of Dallas[3]

God

Education is an opportunity for connection with God and the Jewish people that creates and nurtures spiritual experiences.

Diversity

Congregational education provides a variety of experiences and recognizes the needs of our diverse membership.

Community

Congregational education provides a warm and welcoming environment that enables the strengthening of family, friendships and community.

Identity

Learning enables us to develop confidence in our knowledge of Judaism, and offers ways in which to integrate Judaism into our lives.

Vision

Learning is an ongoing process through which congregants of all personal and educational backgrounds gain an enhanced knowledge of Judaism and its values and connections to God, Israel, and the Temple community, which provides comfort and an opportunity for transformation.

Values

Learning encourages us to incorporate into our hearts and our daily lives Jewish values from Torah and Reform Jewish tradition.

Torah

Learning provides us continuing opportunities to experience Torah, Talmud and Hebrew in the context of modern life

Transformation

Education continually challenges us to find a new understanding and awareness of what it means to be a Reform Jew.

Comfort

Learning provides us, irrespective of our backgrounds, a comfort zone in which to participate in a myriad of learning opportunities.

The educational life of our congregation bears intense and loving scrutiny. The journey for many of us began two years ago as we labored to learn how and why we as members of Emanu-El learned. Perhaps the words "learning" or "education" convey too narrow a picture, for, almost at once, it became apparent that our notions of formal education did not do justice to how we internalize "Jewish" knowledge as a congregation. The Proverbist writes: "If you will call for understanding, and lift up your head for wisdom; if you seek her as silver, and search for her as hidden treasure. . . . For wisdom shall enter into thy heart, and knowledge will be a pleasure to your soul." (Proverbs 2:3–10). This document, then, becomes our synthesis, and we hope a contemplation of the future of our journey as a learning congregation. Joining the voices of our group are those of our congregation, the scribes of our people, modern commentators, and interspersed throughout, the words of Torah and the prophets. We intend this to be a record that breathes—that is, to communicate both a strong sense of purpose and a dynamic sense of possibility, to invigorate us with resolve and to give us a center from which we can explore without and within.

At its core is the lifelong practice of learning. In the Sayings of the Fathers, Ben Zoma was attributed: "Who is wise? He who learns from all men. It is said: I have gained understanding from all my teachers" (*Pirke Avot* 4.1). We gain when we act to receive learning, whether in study, deeds or worship; whether through a formal or an informal process. And we mark our progress with one eye toward our long Jewish heritage and with the other eye toward our continuity, giving meaning to "You shall teach them diligently to your children and speak of them in your house and on your way, when you lie down and when you rise up" (*Devarim,* Deuteronomy 6:7). As one congregant reflects on her Jewish education: "My grandfather was a very learned and observant Jew. My mother performed all the rituals, but didn't fully understand why. As a child, I was raised in a Conservative synagogue. We observed the holidays, but little else. Since my 20s my interest in religion has increased each decade. My son had a bar mitzvah in 1995, and I had an adult bar mitzvah this past March. For me it is a meaningful step forward, but I still have much to learn." K.D. And so do we all.

Vision

Learning is an ongoing process through which congregants of all personal and educational backgrounds gain an enhanced knowledge of Judaism and its values and connections to God, Israel, and the Temple community, which provides comfort and an opportunity for transformation.

Questions to Guide Your Study of Another Congregation's Vision Statement

1. Does the statement define or explain Jewish learning? If so, do you agree with this definition? If not, can the congregation's definition be deduced from the statement? How important is it to define or explain learning?

2. Is it clear, from this statement, what the key values of the congregation are, in the area of learning? Which of these values seem particularly important to our congregation? What additional values, not mentioned in this statement, do we hold?

3. Do you find this vision statement inspiring? What "works" and what doesn't work for you?

Writing Commentaries on the Vision Statement

Preparation:

If the group has not studied commentaries before, this is a good opportunity to offer a short introductory lesson about the tradition of Jewish commentary. The facilitator can choose a short selection from the weekly Torah portion (or any other passage in the Torah), and select a few commentaries that raise questions about the text and offer a variety of answers. The vision statement might be placed in the center of a large sheet of paper, so that the commentaries can surround it, to mirror a traditional page of Bible or Talmud.

Grouping of Participants:

Small groups of 4–5.

Time Required:

30 minutes, plus the introduction.

Facilitation:

The introduction (with or without the text study suggested above) should explain how the writing of commentary is an essential part of the Jewish tradition. Commentary serves to keep the precepts of the Torah alive in people's minds and hearts, and also to keep them relevant through rein-terpretation. Following this introduction, the facilitator should explain the process by which the vision statement was written, and underline that, since this is to be a living document, it is now up to the rest of the con-gregation to write their own commentary. They can do this in a variety of ways: by raising and answering a question, challenging an assertion, elab-orating upon a particular point, or providing a personal perspective on the text.

Record Keeping:

These commentaries might actually be displayed in a hallway or on a bul-letin board. Others in the congregation might be invited to add their own comments to these sheets.

8

Text Study
as a Vehicle for Change

The preceding chapters on readiness and visioning employed, for the most part, generic exercises dealing with learning and with change that might be used in any change process in any educational institution. This chapter, in contrast, focuses on a key aspect of the change process that is specifically Jewish, namely text study. Text study is both a means to an end and an end in itself. It is a useful springboard for discussing such issues as what it means to be Jewish, what the ideal synagogue would look like, and what role learning should play within the synagogue. But it is also the most authentic and important form of Jewish learning and should play a special role in a congregation of learners. This chapter explains the way text study can become an integral part of the change process. It deals with the different perspectives that contemporary American Jews bring to the study of text, and presents a typology of different kinds of learners. Examples of text study materials developed by participants in the Experiment in Congregational Education appear at the end of the chapter.

What Counts as a Jewish Text?

To begin with, we must ask the question: What is a Jewish text? What counts as a text, and what doesn't? Like all interesting Jewish questions, this one can't be answered definitively. A good place to start is with the preeminent Jewish text, the Torah, known in English as the Five Books of Moses. It is not necessary to believe that the Torah is, literally, the word of God as dictated to Moses on Mount Sinai to acknowledge that it is at the center of the Jewish tradition, the linchpin that has held the Jews together through time and space. The Torah contains the narratives, laws and genealogies that have defined Jewish existence. The additional thirty-one books of the Bible are foundational as well. For example, the Prophets shaped the Jewish notion of *tzedek,* justice; psalms form an important part of the prayer service; the scrolls of Esther and Lamentations mark historical occasions that were integrated into the cycle of holidays. Each book of the Bible has been incorporated into the Jewish tradition in ways that reverberate through the centuries.

With these books as its core, the Jewish textual tradition is built up like an archeological *tel* (mound), as layer upon layer of interpretation and elaboration have been added, first as commentary on the Bible, and later as commentary on the commentary. This tradition spans at least sixteen centuries and four continents. The corpus of texts includes the Talmud (which elaborated the code of Jewish law), and the whole genre of *midrash* (works of rabbinical interpretations), as well as individual commentaries such as those by *Rashi* (the acronym for Rabbi Shlomo Yitzchaki, who lived in eleventh-century France) and Don Isaac Abravanel (in fifteenth-century Portugal), among many others. Altogether, they are called *kitvei kodesh,* Hebrew for sacred writings.

There is little debate about the canonical status of these texts and commentaries in the Jewish tradition. But how broad is the canon? Does it extend to commentaries written today? Does it include the philosophical writings of Maimonides (twelfth-century Spain and Egypt)? What about philosophical works that date from the nineteenth and twentieth centuries? Might Hebrew poems written by Judah Halevi in eleventh-century Spain be included? What about poems on Jewish subjects written by contemporary Jewish writers?

The answer to these questions depends on the definition of the term "sacred." Those who equate "sacred" with "the literal word of God" are more restrictive in their definition. Others consider the canon to be much more expansive, including a wide variety of texts that celebrate and elaborate upon the Jewish tradition, and that teach us something about ourselves as Jews.

The Benefits of Text Study

The gist of this complicated answer is that texts, however broadly or narrowly defined, bring us into direct contact with Jews who lived centuries ago and continents away. When we study these texts we are not just hearing *about* these Jews, we are hearing *from* them. Though we can never fully understand what the words meant in their original context, studying texts brings us into dialogue with our forebears and with our contemporaries. It gives us a sense of rootedness. By reading these documents from our people's past, we ourselves become part of this long tradition. In the words of educator and writer Joel Grishaver:

> The heart of Torah learning is a kind of special dialogue. The text is read slowly, word by word. As we read, questions emerge. We struggle to solve these questions. Along the way, other voices, other Jews who have looked at these words before, join the discussion with their commentaries. They point out problems, they share their personal solutions. The conversation continues. Between students, between teachers and students, the perceptions differ, the inferred meanings conflict, and the quest continues. In the end, the learner is left staring in his/her own text; the voices and insights of many others are heard, but for each learner the passage has yielded

a personal understanding. Jewish text study is a wondrous combination of learning from others and finding out about yourself.[1]

This connection with primary sources encourages the learner to take the perspective of an insider. When one studies about Jewish life as a subject matter, it doesn't really matter if one is Jewish. Whether or not one's ancestors had the same information is not pertinent; one can be an equally good student of Chinese history as of Jewish history. It is true that one can also study Jewish texts as an outsider, in a more disinterested, academic mode. But, as noted at the end of chapter 2, the *brakha* (blessing) over studying Torah, which begins with the standard formula ("Praised are you Adonai, our God, ruler of the universe") concludes with the phrase "who commands us to engage in words of Torah." When we *engage* in the words of Torah we do more than study. These words become more than interesting pieces of information; they become touchstones, helping us to define who we are, as Jews and as human beings.

To engage in the study of a text means becoming involved in it, not only intellectually, but also emotionally. Texts stimulate us to examine our lives in light of the stories they tell and the legal and philosophical principles they embody. Those who study text regularly often remark on the power of this particular form of learning. As one of the respondents in Diane Schuster's study of novice text study students said, "I love to find the meaning, it makes me so much closer to it. It's like—there's some pride in where you've come from. In that freedom of discovering yourself."[2]

This special power derives from the fact that the learner is discovering core Jewish values on his or her own. Studying a text is comparable to making a garment by hand, or cooking a meal from scratch. Handmade clothing may lack the uniform finish of store-bought, and a meal cooked at home may lack the sophistication of one cooked in a restaurant. But these deficiencies are more than compensated for by the sense of wonder and pride that comes from having watched the pieces of clothing come together, the sauce thicken, the bread rise. Likewise, the values embedded in a text might be explicated concisely and brilliantly in a lecture or sermon, but nothing can compare with the pleasure that comes from struggling with a text and uncovering a variety of interpretations on one's own. Though the "packaged" explanation might be more aptly put, it lacks the sense of personal investment and the "homegrown" insight. Comparing her experience with text study to a more conventional adult learning program, one of the respondents in the Schuster study said:

> The other program is wonderful, but you're lectured to and there's very little time for question and answer. Text study is a learning process that is done by the individual and the group. It's group learning, it's sharing of thoughts, it's exploring. I thought of it as our opening box after box after box, all gift wrapped. And it was a wonderful surprise at the end, not necessarily the right answer, but you certainly were given a lot to think about.[3]

Researchers who study cognition have found that facts embedded in vivid stories are most likely to be recalled. Similarly, values and practices embedded in texts resonate more strongly, particularly when one has wrestled with the text. The impetus to repair one's relationship with a sibling is less likely to come from an exhortation than from a discussion of, say, the complicated relationship between Joseph and his brothers, and the comparison that can be made between one's own situation and theirs. Researchers who study moral development argue that values taught singly and out of context are inert and useless in practice, because critical ethical decisions involve conflicts between values.[4] Texts are full of this kind of conflict.[5]

When the process of grappling with the text is done in a group setting, a wonderful sense of community is created. Two additional quotes from the Schuster study make this point vividly:

> I liked the opportunity to talk with other people—the communal aspect of studying together. In the small groups, we would read together and talk. And it was nice to sit back, take

a breath, hear others interpret, to think about how all the pieces fit together. It worked well.[6]

When you bring a group of people together, and it's led properly, and the questions are there, and you have a great facilitator, and everybody starts talking and airing their feelings, already you have a new bond. And then you go a step further and you start to delve into some history and some text and you explore that together, and there's another bond. And pretty soon all the bonds, the chain starts to link together, and then you can build a beautiful fence.[7]

When one studies Torah with commentaries that range across time and space, one's community expands to include all those who have studied before, from ancient rabbis to contemporary poets and theologians.

Finally, many find in the study of texts a pathway or sense of connection to God. In the Jewish tradition, study and prayer are intertwined; Jewish learning is a form of praying, a vehicle for communicating with and feeling the presence of God. This is a doubly difficult concept for contemporary American Jews. We live in a world that values only those facts that can be verified through sense perception; it is difficult to fathom a God that can't be physically perceived. Moreover, as products of schools in which learning is equated with subject matter mastery, acquired by hard work and tested by rigorous exams, we find it difficult to imagine a spiritual dimension to the process of learning. Nonetheless, even novices have felt the religious dimension of text study. In the words of one of Schuster's respondents:

Looking at those things intellectually it's neat and tidy, and it's satisfying in that sense. But I look at it from another point of view, more in terms of my own spirituality. It's not that that enriched my spirituality, per se, or did anything that made me feel closer to God; but it gave me another tool for the next time I'm in the synagogue to feel a deeper feeling about my religion, my roots, my own personal closeness to God.[8]

Talmud scholar Devorah Weisberg offers a talmudic parable to illustrate the way in which study brings her closer to God:

Rabbah bar Nahmani was studying Torah and became aware that a dispute was taking place in the heavenly academy. God was arguing one side and all the other participants were arguing the other. It was agreed that Rabbah bar Nahmani should decide, since his expertise in the matter exceeded that of the disputants. Rabbah bar Nahmani ruled in favor of the position espoused by God. Only then was the opinion of the creator accepted; God could not prevail over the heavenly academy without human assistance!

For me this story transmits several messages. Torah is not studied for purely practical reasons; God and the heavenly hosts surely have no fear of the type of ritual impurity with which the dispute dealt. Rather, . . . the study of Torah . . . is so valuable that it is an appropriate occupation even for God. Furthermore, humans play the central role in the study and interpretation of Torah; even God, who is the source and giver of Torah, requires human aid to understand the text. . . . When I study, I feel that I am an active participant in . . . an ongoing search for God's will and our place in the universe.[9]

Text Study as a Point of Entry to Jewish Life

Up to this point I have tried to make a case for the inherent virtues of text study, namely that it offers learners a new perspective on their lives, creates community, and enables them to become closer to God. Now I want to make a further claim, which is that text study is an excellent point of entry into a more active Jewish life for most members of congregations—adults who have little Jewish knowledge and for whom Jewish practices and rituals are mostly foreign. This claim is counterintuitive because of the prevailing assumption that text study is only for more advanced learners. For example, curricula and courses whose purpose is to promote Jewish literacy among adults often focus exclusively on teaching basic facts and competencies, such as the ability to recite certain prayers, or knowledge of historical events and personages.[10] Without dismissing the usefulness of this sort of cultural literacy, I would argue that text study is the most appropriate place to motivate and inspire adults who are marginally affiliated.

An overwhelming majority of synagogue members are college-educated, relatively affluent adults who are able to balance a variety of demanding family and work commitments. Many acquired the skills of close reading and critical thinking in college or graduate school. The life experience they have accumulated has given them ample opportunity to reflect on the "big questions" related to ethics and religion. However, since their Jewish education is likely to have ended in adolescence, they have not been exposed to the wealth of Jewish tradition that deals with these concerns in challenging, nuanced ways. In fact, their prior Jewish education more likely focused on "basic literacy," leaving them with the impression that Judaism consists primarily of rituals, Hebrew prayers, and Bible stories. What these highly competent and intelligent adults need is not more basic information. Rather, they need to see how Jewish scholars through the ages have grappled with the same questions they are asking themselves. And they need to see that they themselves can become part of this "grand conversation."

The Jewish textual tradition is built around the notion of the *machloket*—the debate or controversy. Every text can be (and, most likely, has been) interpreted in a variety of ways. To quote the scholar David Hartman:

> The test of excellence of the Torah scholar was the ability to read and analyze a talmudic text, to explain and defend both sides of a disagreement by offering imaginative and compelling reasons for both positions. The student's interest in and competence at reproducing both argument and counter-argument convincingly were rooted in a genuine appreciation of the moral and intellectual complexity of the subject matter.[11]

The beauty of text study is that it connects the learner to the primary source—the narrative or law as stated in its original context—and to layer upon layer of interpretation. At times the interpretation contradicts the simple meaning of the text, and often two interpretations will contradict each other. The tradition considers it important to preserve the entire, multi-faceted record.

Unfortunately, when Jewish texts are taught, too often it is in a didactic way, where one interpretation is considered as definitive. The *midrashic* and talmudic tradition, which continues today through contemporary commentaries and responsa, is, in fact, much more open-ended. "[W]hile the law may be decided according to the views of one teacher, . . . alternative views are not discarded as if falsified but are retained and studied and may even become law at some later date."[12]

Exposure to a broad range of commentaries, from ancient to contemporary, invites learners to contribute their own interpretations. Soon they discover that their own knowledge, whether derived from life experience or their studies, can illuminate aspects of the text in interesting ways. Rather than simply learning about Rashi or Rabbi Akiva, they are empowered to enter into a dialogue with these historical figures and many others.

Matching the Challenge to the Learner

It's easy to imagine a reader's incredulity. The congregant who has never studied text before may be murmuring, "How could I possibly study text? Isn't that something one needs years of rabbinical school to do?" For their part, a rabbi or educator reflecting on his or her last experience teaching text may be thinking, "I *tried* getting people to offer their own interpretations, but they were all silent, waiting to hear my opinion."

In fact, many learners are intimidated by the thought of studying texts and are, at the outset, so intent upon hearing the "expert's" opinion that they are unable to find their own voice. And, in truth, not all teachers present the text in the open way described by Hartman, and not all empower their students to enter into interpretive debates. But these problems are not insurmountable if text learning is approached as a developmental process.

The work of Carol Belenky and her colleagues is extremely helpful in gauging the appropriate level for different kinds of learners. Their book, *Women's Ways of Knowing,* reports on a study of 135 women that they interviewed at great length (some of them over time) about themselves, their relationships to family and friends, their education, and, most importantly, their ideas about learning, knowledge, and truth. Based on these interviews, the researchers proposed a developmental schema of five "positions of knowing," which I have summarized in Table 1 (see page 179). While their study focused entirely on women, they believe, as do I, "that similar categories can be found in men's thinking."[13]

Though the authors of the study found these "positions of knowing" to be global stages that color every aspect of their respondents' thought, the study also provides insight into the thinking of adults who are at different stages of knowing in different areas of their lives. A person may be one type of knower in his or her profession, a second type when dealing with his or her children, and yet a third type when it comes to Jewish living and learning. Belenky's schema can be useful to educators who seek to align the learner's attitude toward Judaic study with his or her attitude toward other areas of interest.

Belenky's schema is hierarchical, with the first position—silent knowing—being at the lowest end of the scale.

Silent knowers are like the *sh'eno yodea lishol* (the child who doesn't know enough to ask) of the Passover *Hagadah*—they don't know what they don't know, and they don't know how to begin. Silent knowers are easy to recognize—they are the ones who groan or leave the room when texts are passed out, or who sit through study sessions with a blank or uncomfortable expression. The origins of this discomfort may vary from person to person; one source is the disparity between their considerable secular knowledge and the paucity of their Judaic knowledge. For whatever reason, the silence usually masks fear or defensiveness, as illustrated in the following quotes from Diane Schuster's research:

Five Positions of Knowing[14]

Silent Knowers

- don't know they have the right to know
- don't know how to begin to acquire the knowledge
- may even shy away from knowing

Received Knowers

- see knowledge as coming from outside authorities
- are dependent on others when forming opinions

example: being afraid to offer an opinion until they hear what the instructor has to say; copying notes verbatim, but being unable to re-state ideas in their own words

strength: openness to learning

weakness: dependence on an outside source for both learning and forming opinions

Subjective Knowers

- rely on personal experience as a basis for knowledge

example: reading the a text solely through one's own experiences, and being resistant to interpretations that run counter to one's own

strength: the development of a personal voice and viewpoint

weakness: a possible rigidity and inability to learn from others

Procedural Knowers

- are trying to gain expertise
- are interested in developing tools for knowing

example: focusing on the Hebrew in the text, or on commentaries

strength: learning how to access and assess the diverse opinions of experts

weakness: a danger of losing sight of the forest when focusing only on the trees

Constructed Knowers

- want to have ownership of the material by analyzing different perspectives and by teaching others

example: giving a *d'var torah* on a topic that is personally significant but draws on a range of outside sources; creating a *Haggadah* for the family seder, drawing on a variety of different sources

> I felt total fear. This is uncharted territory. I felt like I was in school again, like a little kid. You know? You don't want to look stupid.

> I felt inadequate and kind of inept, kind of not knowing what to do with it. It felt out of context to me. So I struggled with the first time that we did it, and I had that déjà vu experience of "Uh oh. This is gonna be an alienating thing in which I feel like I don't know, I don't have enough history."[15]

A step up from silent knowing is *received knowing,* a position in which people are interested in learning, but assume that one can only learn from a teacher. Feeling too ignorant to learn on their own, received knowers perceive themselves as empty vessels, waiting to be filled by experts. Their accomplishments in other areas do not, in their eyes, transfer to the Jewish realm. Anyone who has taught adults will recognize these knowers; they are the ones who sit quietly taking notes, who might ask many questions, but rarely voice an opinion. This passivity is disconcerting to teachers who would like their students actively engaged in textual interpretation. Even more disconcerting is the fact that when given contradictory information from two different experts, received knowers may be unable or unwilling to acknowledge, or even recognize, the contradiction.

Not every learner gets beyond the stage of received knowing. But with the help of a teacher who encourages students to voice their own opinions and ask their own questions, adult learners proceed to the next stage, which is *subjective knowing,* knowing that is rooted in one's personal experience and in one's own interpretation of events. Subjective knowers believe that their experience is the most important basis for knowledge; they listen to and trust their own voice over that of teachers or books. This inward turn has both positive and negative consequences for the learner and the teacher. Learning to reflect on one's own experience and applying the lessons of experience to new situations is a critical skill for adults; it is an important stepping-stone toward empowerment and independent thought. Moreover, subjective knowers add a certain intensity and excitement to any class because they personalize their learning and because their enthusiasm is infectious. However, subjective knowers are sometimes so mired in their own experiences that they can't acknowledge the legitimacy of other views. Writing about a small subset of the subjective knowers in their study, Belenky and her colleagues state:

> They were stubbornly committed to their view of things and unwilling to expose themselves to alternative conceptions. Although they might have described themselves as generous and caring, they could be, in fact, impatient and dismissive of other people's interpretations.[16]

For those who don't get stuck in its most extreme form, subjective knowing eventually leads to the next position, in which learners again become concerned with acquiring external knowledge, but in ways that are much more active than those of the received knower. Belenky and her colleagues term this position *procedural knowing* because respondents at this stage are so focused on acquiring skills. "Aware that some events were open to more than one interpretation and that some interpretations made better sense than others, they were careful not to jump to conclusions ."[17] The name "procedural knowing" comes from the attention these knowers pay to the procedures by which they assess the quality of an idea or the ethics of an action—close observation and questioning (in personal situations), and following scholarly research protocols (in academia). In the realm of text study, procedural knowers often focus on learning Hebrew or reading Rashi script; sometimes they will read voraciously in a particular area. As one of Schuster's respondents put it: "I need more basic understanding. Take me back to the beginning, do it carefully, and spell it out slowly. My first goal really is to learn Hebrew."[18]

The last and highest position in Belenky's schema is *constructed knowing*. Constructed knowers are able to combine their subjective insights with the knowledge they've acquired and the procedures they have mastered. They have confidence in their ability to learn. They expect to encounter a variety of approaches and a variety of interpretations, and enjoy the process of sifting through and evaluating information for themselves. They may welcome the opportunity to transmit their newly found understanding to others. Constructed knowers in the area of text study are those who relish the prospect of finding a variety of commentaries on a verse or an issue. They may need help in learning to access a variety of sources, but they don't want to be spoon-fed.

Although I have seen adults go through these stages in the precise order Belenky and her colleagues describe in their study, I have also seen people leapfrog and skip intermediate stages, some even going straight from silent to constructed knowing. They were able to do this, I believe, because they were constructed knowers in other areas of their lives. Once they got past their initial resistance or block, they were able to marshal their considerable conceptual skill in the service of a new subject matter. Diane Schuster cites the example of the middle-aged academic who, after the death of his father, realized that it would be his responsibility to lead the family seder (Passover celebration). Though he had very little prior knowledge of Judaica, he used his prodigious research skills to learn about the seder's history and traditions, and ended up compiling a new *Hagadah* (prayer book for the seder) for his family.[19]

Implications for the Teaching of Text

Belenky's typology offers some important insights for everyone concerned with the teaching of Jewish texts to adults:

1. The ultimate goal is for learners to become constructed knowers. Belenky's research challenges us to think critically about our goals as teachers of adults. It is part of a larger tradition in psychology that holds that content alone is not sufficient, and that even skills, though critical, are only a part of the picture.[20] If we want to develop a cadre of adult Jewish learners who are sophisticated and self-motivated, our teaching must go beyond transmitting information and the building of skills to include empowering students to learn on their own. It is possible that some learners will be unable to reach this goal, especially if they are not constructed knowers in the rest of their lives. Nonetheless, the prevailing assumption should be that constructed knowing is the most desirable stage. When taken seriously, this goal has profound implications for the way text study in a congregation should be designed, and the way teachers should teach, as will be spelled out below.

2. The goal of constructed knowing is rarely attained in one gigantic leap. Most learners require scaffolding as they go from silent or received knowing through subjective and procedural knowing. If text teachers are aware of Belenky's schema, they can use it to tailor their teaching. Fortunately, some of the best techniques are equally appropriate for several different kinds of knowers, as will be discussed below.

3. The learning environment must be welcoming, and the learning materials accessible. All learners do best when they feel comfortable; this is particularly critical for silent knowers who are easily intimidated. Chairs should be placed in a circle or around a table. In a group of strangers, short introductions and perhaps even an ice-breaker are important. For beginners, a short text in a good colloquial translation is essential. The way in which texts appear on the page makes a big difference too: large type, plenty of white space, and a glossary for Hebrew terms make the material "user friendly."

4. The main focus of text teaching should be interpretation, rather than information. Discussion is a more appropriate method than lecture. Participants should be encouraged to ask questions about the text, and to begin to answer them by drawing on their own knowledge, and utilizing traditional commentaries to spur their thinking. The merits of different interpretations should be compared because some answers may be more warranted by the text than others. It should be clear, however, that there is no such thing as a definitive interpretation; the range of traditional commentaries that are selected should reinforce this point. Although received knowers in particular may be reluctant to venture their opinion, waiting for the teacher to offer the "right answer," the teacher should resist playing the role of expert. One way to do this is by posing one or two open-ended questions and asking students to discuss these in *hevrutah* (with a study partner). Not only is this a traditional method of Jewish study, but it is also an excellent way of encouraging people who may be terrified of speaking up in a large group.

In the past two decades a number of innovative techniques have been developed that encourage learners of all ages to bring their imagination and their life experience to the interpretation of texts. Bibliodrama, for example, invites participants to take the role of a biblical character, answering questions about their words and actions, and exploring the feelings that may underlie the very sparse narrative style of the Torah.[21] Hand-made *midrash* is a technique in which participants create a visual image of a particular text.[22] The Institute of Contemporary *Midrash* offers workshops in these techniques and publishes original *midrashim* (interpretations), short stories, poems, and plays by contemporary readers. These techniques encourage silent and received knowers to begin developing their own, independent reactions to a text. Subjective knowers enjoy these techniques as well. Because the ultimate goal is to get beyond subjective knowing, these techniques should be augmented by an additional step—the study of a small number of traditional commentaries that themselves offer varying interpretations. Seeing their own opinions reflected in traditional commentaries will strengthen participants' sense of confidence in themselves as interpreters; at the same time, divergent interpretations will broaden their appreciation of the richness of the text.

How much background information does a student need to benefit from the study of text? Some rabbis and educators assume that a great deal of background is necessary and take care to supply this information at the outset, often by means of a brisk lecture packed with names and dates. Unfortunately, learners new to text study may be overwhelmed, and even silenced, by a flood of new information. One can gain a great deal from text study even without knowing the genealogies of biblical figures or the cultural context of the ancient near east. It is more important for the beginner to find his or her own voice. Once that voice is found, and once the learner gains confidence, s/he will begin looking for additional information, entering into the position Belenky and her colleagues call procedural knowing.

5. Opportunities need to be created for intensive, ongoing study that builds the interpretive skills of the learners. The techniques discussed above, suitable to silent, received, and subjective knowers alike, can all be incorporated in a variety of ways into study sessions that range from a fifteen-minute text study at the beginning of a committee meeting to a two-hour workshop. But procedural and constructed knowers require more in-depth study and challenges of the kind that can only be offered in ongoing classes or more intensive workshops. An ongoing text class can be very simply structured: Learners read the text and, working individually or in small groups, raise as many questions as possible. They then mine a broad array of resources to find a wide spectrum of responses. The facilitator of such a study session does not need any particular technique, nor need have mastered the material. What the facilitator does need is a great library, a knowledge of the sources, and the ability to refrain from offering his or her own interpretations too soon.

6. Opportunities should be created for procedural and constructed knowers to teach and mentor others. A congregation of learners is, by definition, a congregation in which people teach one another. No matter how many rabbis or educators a congregation has, they alone will never be able to provide high-quality learning experiences for all congregants. This seeming limitation is actually a great opportunity because, for many people, procedural and constructed knowing leads to the desire to share knowledge with others. Some of these knowers will welcome the opportunity to contribute to the community by teaching or mentoring. They also make the best role models for adults who are just getting started, living proof that one need not have gone to graduate school in Judaic studies to be a student of text. The best use of the professionals' time is in teaching the procedural and constructed knowers, and creating multiple outlets for these knowers to share their knowledge: leading text study sessions at services and congregational meetings, mentoring new students, and offering courses of their own. Of course, in doing so, these knowers will need to remember that they are dealing with silent, received, and subjective knowers; they may need to be taught the techniques that were so successful in getting *themselves* involved at the outset. In this way the cycle of learning begins anew.

Texts as a Springboard for the Change Process

Understanding the preeminence of text study in congregational learning, and using Belenky's typology of knowers as a means for explaining how different attitudes of different learners can be seen as different stages in a developmental process, we see that text study can serve as a critical component of the change process and as a means to an end, in addition to being an end in itself.

Text study can make an important contribution to the process of change as it unfolds. It offers participants a glimpse of the future they are creating together, and it serves as a reminder of the ultimate goal—the creation of a congregation of learners. When a different text is studied at every meeting, members of the task force can experience first hand a type of learning that is likely to be new to them—an encounter with primary Jewish sources that is both serious and enjoyable. They can experience for themselves the ways in which text study creates community, fostering conversations that can be both deeply significant and playful (and sometimes both at the same time), raising issues of personal concern, while allowing people to reveal only as much about themselves as they feel comfortable doing.

Anyone who has studied text in this way over a period of time has probably had experiences in which entering into the text seemed to transport the participants to an entirely different place—beyond their immediate, more mundane concerns into a realm of ultimate meaning that some might call sacred. Rabbi Richard Block recounts the story of a meeting of seventh graders, their parents, and their teachers, convened for the purpose of discussing a troubling discipline problem that had arisen. Knowing that the atmosphere in the room would be charged, the rabbi and educators chose to begin the meeting with the discussion of a text from the Talmud. The text did not deal directly with the misbehavior of students, or the applicability of rules and punishments, but it raised issues regarding the kind of respect that all human beings have a right to expect.

After twenty minutes of text study in *hevrutah,* one could feel the tension ebbing and a calm entering the room. The subsequent discussion of the problem at hand was quiet and reasoned. Participants were, Rabbi Block reports, much more open than they would have been had they not begun with the text study. Having gotten in touch with the most important issue—the respect of one human being for another—they were able to rise above petty recrimination and create a joint plan of action.[23]

A similar story is told by one of the respondents in the Schuster study. Having experienced the leavening effect of text study as part of her synagogue's task force, she decided to try it out in the synagogue committee that she chaired. What led her to this experiment was her concern that members of the committee were divided on a certain issue and, rather than airing their differences openly, were lobbying behind the scenes. The chair knew that it would be tricky to raise this issue directly. Instead, she brought a number of texts on *shmirat halashon* (literally, guarding of one's tongue) to the group. She felt that the insights people gained from their discussion encouraged people to be more open and less conniving.[24]

Quotes from other people Schuster interviewed reflect a similar awareness of the value of text study:

> Maybe we should start studying some text before we start our meetings. Because it really does remind you that you're not at just yet another meeting, but that you're at something with Jewish significance.

> All these meetings. You just go from one to the next, and sometimes you don't even remember that it's really a meeting with the end being trying to make the Jewish content in the synagogue a better place. It's just kind of running yet another business. So, if you bring [texts] in, then it does change every-thing.[25]

Ideally, text study should be included in every meeting of the task force. Sometimes the text relates to an issue being discussed. For example, in the first readiness session, talmudic texts dealing with the destruction of the Temple and the founding of the yeshivah (talmudic academy) at Yavneh, in 70 C.E., can be studied as a springboard for a discussion of how difficult change is and what might be done to help people assimilate it into their lives. Similarly, texts on Moses' ambivalence about being called upon as a leader might serve as a springboard for a discussion among newly appointed leaders to explore their own concerns. These text study guides appear at the end of this chapter.

At other times the texts studied can relate to *parashat hashavuah* (the weekly Torah portion), an upcoming holiday, or simply an area of particular interest to the facilitator. These text study sessions can range in length from twenty minutes to an hour and a half. Their placement in the meeting varies—text study might take place at the beginning, the end, or anywhere in the middle. The responsibility to teach or facilitate these sessions should rotate among various members of the task force. Rather than doing most of the teaching themselves, the rabbi or educator should work with these congregants to discuss the topic and select the materials, and to plan the questions for discussion. Though sometimes frontal presentations are appropriate, most of the time should be devoted to discussion in pairs or small groups.

Some leadership teams have also committed themselves to studying every time they meet. Roslyn Roucher, an educator who served as the coordinator at Congregation Sinai in Milwaukee, described this experience in vivid terms:

> The meeting is set to begin at 2:00. We've been meeting together regularly and we've developed a routine. I'm the first to arrive, rushing from dropping my daughter off at day care. Jane has just come from working out and is still sweating. Birgit, the synagogue educator, is dressed for work and carries her Palm Pilot and a stack of folders. Sheryl and Laurie walk in together, discussing Sheryl's work and the upcoming bat mitzvah of Laurie's daughter. Caroline and her four-year-old daughter Emmie are loaded down with food and toys to keep Emmie busy during the meeting. Mimi runs in from work, worried about leaving early to pick her son up from school. Madeleine has just returned from visiting her father, and she updates us on his recovery from a sudden illness. David, the rabbi, walks in, lunch in hand, and sits down. We devote a few minutes to talking about David's sandwich and the typical Wisconsin weather. I call the meeting to order and we begin in the usual way, with text study.

We turn our attention to Sheryl, who introduces her chosen text study subject and then asks us to recite the blessing for study. Our voices fill the room. We know the blessing by heart. We've been saying it together for over two years. By saying the blessing we ready ourselves to enter into the holy space and time of study. All is left behind—the sweat, the traffic, work, schedules. "We put all the rest off to the side and become a group. Studying together puts us on common ground again," says Sheryl, commenting on the power of beginning every meeting with text study.

The leadership team of Congregation Sinai of Milwaukee is made up of three professionals—the rabbi, the educator, and the coordinator—and six synagogue lay leaders, three of whom have been part of the leadership team since its formation. The team meets regularly, and almost every single meeting has started with text study. A different member leads study at each meeting, according to a loose and flexible rotation. The subjects of our study vary widely, with study of the weekly Torah portion the most frequent topic. We have also studied traditional commentaries, modern Hebrew poetry, Jewish art, ethical texts, sources relating to Jewish practice, portions of the Prophets and Writings, and a variety of other subjects. The text study leader chooses a topic of her choice, although at different points the choice of subject has been guided by other factors; we often use the study time to "practice" or familiarize ourselves with study we will lead for other members of the congregation or to study texts related to the change process, such as texts about leadership.

The strong commitment of our team to study has been ongoing. Even during periods when we have been most pressured to produce and plan, we have devoted time to regular text study. Text study anchors us, sets the tone for our meetings, shapes the nature of our working relationship, fosters intimacy, serves as an equalizer between the lay leaders and the professionals, and reaches each individual on the team in both personal and professional ways. The educator describes beautifully the impact of study on the functioning of our team: "We are learning about each other when we study text and during our study we've had moments of vulnerability and made it through successfully. In our work as a team we have always helped each other out, and I have to think that text study is part of that—a comfort level has come out of our study."

A comment made by a lay leader on the team describes another way that study has affected our work as a group: "Text study impacts our work because it helps us work together better. It helps us to challenge each other and gives us a civil way to disagree. If we've studied together and are comfortable expressing differing opinions on a text, it is easier to express our differing opinions later in the meeting—we know each other better and have already practiced disagreeing!" While we may not always agree when we study, members of the team are exceptionally tolerant of each other's viewpoints and levels of knowledge. That tolerance spills over when we divvy up responsibilities, discuss a program, and even when we schedule meetings.

Our study time is an example of shared leadership at its best. The text study led by lay leaders is considered equally as important as that led by the Jewish professionals—and has turned out to be just as compelling as well. According to one team member, "the power of this experience has been the opportunity for us to do it together—to get the knowledge and the experience of the professionals and to understand that the least knowledgeable has something to teach to the most. It has provided us with a ready way to learn about each other and brings us together around a value." This proves true during the study time itself and during the preparation for study. Often, lay leaders will consult with the rabbi, educator, or coordinator for resources and guidance in preparing to lead text study. These sessions allow us to work together more intimately outside of our meetings. The opportunity for the professionals to work one-on-one with an adult congregant who is truly interested in learning text is the kind of guiding and teaching that makes our jobs rewarding. In addition, the lay leaders gain important skills that further their development as students and teachers of text.

However, this model of shared leadership for text study can be challenging as well. For a lay leader, leading text study for the professionals, particularly the rabbi, is often anxiety-producing. For the professionals it is an exercise in *tsimtsum,* holding back. As the rabbi describes it, "My challenge is to make the 800-pound gorilla in the room as invisible as possible." Yet even with these feelings and maybe even because we have to work to overcome them, we have come to view our group as a "safe" place in which to explore ourselves as Jews, as leaders, and as teachers.

Our regular text study has had a huge impact on each individual on our team as well. For each of us, particularly those who have not had much experience studying Jewish texts, the opportunity to study has been enriching, challenging, intellectually stimulating, religiously significant, and enjoyable. We have been convinced of the power of text study; we are evidence that text study really can be transformative.

But the above describes only part of why we have maintained our commitment to text study. We study on principle, as one member said: "We understand and buy the notion that Jewish learning is at the core of synagogue transformation." Therefore, we model this understanding. We set out to show how important the "content" (Jewish learning) is relative to the process of change. We studied even when we didn't want to, even when we did not have the time. While some in the group would bristle at the notion that we study because it is a mitzvah, a commandment, we really have taken on study as if we are commanded—as an obligation not necessarily for us as individuals but for the group. Most important, though, is that we study because we have come to treasure the time we spend studying together. The time we study is the reward we get for all of the long hours we devote to the process.

Change
in the Jewish Tradition[26]

This text study was created for use in the readiness process, but can also be used at any point to discuss the process of change. It provides a context for thinking about our resistance to change, and how this resistance might be overcome. It consists of five parts, and, if used in its entirety, can take up to ninety minutes. If time is short, one might want to skip part 2, and use only one or two of the texts in part 4.

Part One:

Read the following two texts from the Talmud:

> The Land of Israel is the navel of the world, being situated at its center; Jerusalem is at the center of the Land of Israel; the Temple, at the center of Jerusalem; the Temple Hall at the center of the Temple; the Ark, at the center of the Temple Hall. And in front of the Temple Hall is the foundation stone upon which the world was founded.
>
> Babylonian Talmud, *Sukkot* 51a

What can we learn from this text about the role of the Temple in the lives of the people?

> Rabah bar Hana said: It is a distance of ten parasangs [approximately thirty miles] from Jerusalem to Jericho. The turning of the

door hinges in the Temple Hall traveled all the way to Jericho, so that the goat in Jericho used to sneeze because of the fragrance of the incense, and the women of Jericho had no need to perfume themselves because of that fragrance. Neither did a bride in Jerusalem.

Babylonian Talmud, Yoma 39b

How is the second text different from the first? What additional things can we learn from the second text?

Part Two:

Psalm 137 was written in response to the destruction of the First Temple. It describes in vivid terms how people felt about the change in their lives when the Temple was destroyed.

By the rivers of Babylon, there we sat, sat and wept, as we thought of Zion.
There on the poplars were hung up our lyres,
for our captors asked us there for songs, our tormentors, for amusement, "Sing us one of the songs of Zion."
How can we sing a song of the Lord on alien soil?
If I forget you, O Jerusalem, let my right hand wither;
let my tongue stick to my palate if I cease to think of you, if I do not keep Jerusalem in memory even at my happiest hour.
Remember, O Lord, against the Edomites the day of Jerusalem's fall; how they cried, "Strip her, strip her of her very foundations!"
Fair Babylon, you predator, a blessing on him who repays you in kind what you have inflicted on us;
a blessing on him who seizes your babies and dashes them against the rocks!

Psalm 137

With the Second Temple destroyed, what questions do you think were on people's minds?

Part Three:

As you read the following talmudic text, try to figure out why Raban Yochanan acted the way he did. What problems was he trying to solve? On what assumptions did he base his solution?

> When Vespasian came to destroy Jerusalem . . . Raban Yochanan ben Zakai sent for his disciples, R. Eliezer and R. Joshua, and said to them, "My sons, arise and carry me forth from here. Make a coffin for me and I will lie in it." They did so, and R. Eliezer took hold of it at the head and R. Joshua at the foot, and they carried him until sunset when they arrived at the gates of Jerusalem.
>
> The gatekeepers asked, "What is this?" They replied, "A dead man; do you not know that a corpse may not be kept overnight in Jerusalem?" They said, "If it is a corpse, carry it out."
>
> They carried it out, and bore it until sunset when they arrived before Vespasian. . . .

Raban Yochanan then predicts that Vespasian will be appointed the next emperor of Rome. Shortly after that, the news arrives. In gratitude and amazement, Vespasian asks: "What shall I give you?" Yochanan replies:

> "I ask for nothing but Yavneh, whither I may go and teach my disciples, where I can institute a house of prayer, and observe all the commandments prescribed in the Torah." He said to him, "Go and do all that you wish to perform."
>
> excerpted from the Talmud, *Avot D'Rabi Natan* 4:5

Why did Raban Yochanan request an academy in Yavneh?
What assumptions was he making about the future of the Jewish people?

A HISTORICAL NOTE:

Although the text leads one to believe the synagogue replaced the Temple after its destruction, the two institutions had actually coexisted for many years. Two talmudic texts report the number of synagogues in Jerusalem at the time of the destruction of the Temple: According to *Ketubot* 105b there were 394; and according to the Jerusalem Talmud, *Megilah* 3:1 there were 480.

What additional insight does this historical note add to our understanding of what happened?

Part Four:

After the destruction of the Temple the people had many concerns. Which concerns do these texts address?

> God says, "Who has ever come into a synagogue and has not found My glory there?" "And not only that," said R. Aibu, "but if you are in a synagogue God stands by you."
>
> Deuteronomy *Rabah, Ki Tavo* 7:2

> "My love is like a gazelle" (Song of Songs 2:9). As the gazelle leaps from place to place and from fence to fence, and from tree to tree, so God jumps and leaps from synagogue to synagogue to bless the children of Israel.
>
> Numbers *Rabah, Naso* 11:2

> Abraham said to God, "If the Israelites sin before You, You might do with them as with the generations of the flood and the Tower of Babel."
> God replied, "No."
> Abraham said, "How can I know this?"
> Then God said, "Take a heifer three years old . . ." (Genesis 15:9) [i.e., sacrifices will appease Me].
> Abraham said, "That is all very well for the time when the Temple exists, but when it does not, then what will become of them?"
> God said, "I have appointed for them the chapters about the sacrifices. Whenever they read them, I will reckon it to them as if they had brought the offerings before Me, and I will forgive them their sins."
>
> Babylonian Talmud, *Megilot* 31b

God foresaw that the Temple would be destroyed, and God said, "While the Temple exists and you bring sacrifices, the Temple atones for you. When the Temple is not there, what shall atone for you? Busy yourselves with the words of the Law, for they are equivalent to sacrifices, and they will atone for you."

Midrash Tanchuma Achare Mot 35a

What concerns of the people, do these texts attempt to answer?

What can we learn from these texts about the process of making change in general, and about synagogue change in particular?

Glossary

Midrash is the general term for a genre of rabbinic literature that interprets Biblical texts. *Midrash Tanchuma* is one of the many collections of these *midrashim* (the Hebrew plural for *midrash*), as are Numbers *Rabah* and Deuteronomy *Rabah*. These classical *midrashim* were composed between 400 and 1550 C.E., but the tradition of writing *midrash* continues to this day.

Talmud is a written compilation of the "Oral Law," in which the rabbis explained the laws of the Torah and applied them to their own situation. Two different versions of the Talmud were produced, one in Babylonia and one in Palestine. The Talmud consists of two parts, the *Mishnah* (edited around 200 C.E.) and the *Gemara* (edited around 500 C.E.). It is divided into sixty-three tractates (volumes), of which *Sukot, Yoma, Megilot* and *Achare Mot* are four (*Avot D'Rabi Natan* is considered extra-canonical, and appended to the tractate *N'zikin*). The pagination in the Talmud has an *alef* and *bet* side for each page; thus the citation 31b is page 31, side *bet*.

When Does Speech Become Harmful?

The texts in this section are particularly appropriate as an introduction to the third readiness exercise, in which the state of learning in the congregation is discussed. It sensitizes the learners to the ways in which speech can be harmful, and asks them to come up with appropriate guidelines for discussions that include evaluative components.

Part One: The Value of Guarding One's Tongue

The Jewish tradition contains many texts dealing with the value of *shmirat halashon* (guarding one's tongue). Based on the texts below, why is controlling one's speech considered to be such an important value?

> Do not go about as a talebearer among your people.
>
> Leviticus 19:16

> Who is the person who is eager for life, who desires years of goodness? Control your tongue from evil and your lips from speaking deceit.
>
> Psalm 34:13–14

> "Death and life are in the power of the tongue" (Proverbs 18:21). A person's tongue is more powerful than his sword. A sword can

only kill someone who is nearby: a tongue can cause the death of someone who is far away.

Talmud, *Arakhin* 15b

Part Two: Complex Issues Related to Ethical Speech

What do the following texts add to our understanding of the concept of guarding or controlling one's tongue?

Rabah said: "Whatever is said in the presence of the person concerned is not considered *lashon hara* (harmful speech)."

Abaye countered: "All the more so; it is imprudence as well as *lashon hara.*"

Rabah replied: "I hold with Rabbi Yosi, who asserted, 'I never said anything about a person that would make me look back to see if that person were standing behind me.'"

Talmud, *Arakhin* 15b–16a

Jewish Law compares spreading humiliating or harmful information to shedding blood. . . . [But] one specific case in which you are permitted to transmit "negative truths" is when you are asked for a business reference. As the Chafetz Chayim (1838–1933), the Eastern European sage who was Judaism's preeminent authority on the laws of permitted and forbidden speech, teaches: "If a person wants to take someone into his affairs—for example, to hire him in his business, or go into partnership with him, . . . it is permitted for him to go around and ask and inquire from others, . . . so as to prevent possible loss to himself. And it is permissible for others to reveal even very derogatory information, since the intent is not to harm the prospective employee, but to tell the truth in order to save one's fellow human being from potential harm." [Chafetz Chayim, *Shmirat Halashon / Guarding One's Tongue* 4:11]

Similarly, Jewish law insists that you speak frankly when someone requests your opinion about a prospective employee whom you know to be honest or incompetent.

Joseph Telushkin, *Words That Hurt, Words That Heal,* pp. 46–47

Members of boards of directors and school faculties often have to render decisions that will be met with disapproval by those affected. It is forbidden for anyone attending such a meeting to disclose the names of people who spoke or voted against a person's interests. Even without mentioning any names, you are forbidden to say, "I myself was on your side. But what could I do? I was outvoted by the other members." This prohibition against divulging information applies even if the proceedings were not classified as secret.

Zelig Pliskin, *Guard Your Tongue*, p.38

The change process on which we have embarked presents us with an opportunity to take a very close look at who we are and how we do things, hence with an opportunity for "loose speech." These texts challenge us to reflect and evaluate in ways that neither harm nor humiliate others.

Based on your discussion of these texts, and your own personal ethics, what "ethical speech" guidelines should we set for ourselves?

The Motivations of Adult Learners

The famous story of Hillel and the three proselytes provides a wonderful opportunity to reflect on what motivates adults to learn, and the ways in which the teacher might respond.

● **Read the following texts from the Talmud, tractate** *Shabbat* **31b with your partner:**

> A certain heathen came before Shamai and asked him, "How many *Torot* do you have?" "Two," he replied, "the written Torah and the oral Torah." Said the heathen, "I believe you with regard to the written one, but I do not believe you concerning the oral one. I want you to make me a proselyte on condition that you teach me the written Torah." Shamai rebuked him and threw him out in a rage. He came before Hillel who converted him. . . .
>
> [Another Gentile came before Shamai.] He said to him, "Make me a proselyte on the condition that you teach me the entire Torah while I am standing on one foot." He drove him away with the builder's measuring stick which was in his hand. He came before Hillel, who converted him. Hillel said to him, "That which is hateful to you do not do unto your fellow. This is the entire Torah; the rest is commentary—go learn it. . . ."
>
> On another occasion, a heathen was walking behind a schoolhouse and heard the voice of the teacher saying, "And these are the garments which they shall make [for the high priest]" (Exodus 28:4). Said the heathen to himself, "I will go and become

a proselyte in order that they should make me a High Priest."
He came before Shamai and said to him, "Make me a proselyte
on condition that you make me a High Priest." He drove him away
with the measuring stick which was in his hand.

He came before Hillel, who converted him. Hillel said to him,
"Is a king ever appointed who does not know the strategies of
kingship? Go now and study the strategies of kingship (in your
case, the priesthood)."

The Talmud then explains at length that during the course of his studies
the proselyte discovers that no one who is not of the priestly lineage, not
even a king, may become a High Priest.

He came before Hillel and said to him: "O gentle Hillel, may blessings rest upon your head for bringing me under the wings of the
divine presence."

After some time, the three of them met in one place. They said,
"The impatience of Shamai sought to drive us from the world;
the gentleness of Hillel brought us under the wings of the divine
presence."

Let's assume, for the moment, that the proselytes of Hillel's era can be
compared to the Jewish adult learners of today. And let's further assume
that the proselytes can be seen as paradigms for three different types of
adult learners.

- What do the three proselytes have in common? What are the
  differences between them?

- How do you understand the different approaches taken by Hillel
  and Shamai? What reasons would Shamai give for his actions?
  What reasons would Hillel give for his?

- What insights can we get from this text about the issues and
  challenges of adult Jewish learning?

The Place of Torah in Our Lives

This text study, created by Roy Young of Temple Emanuel in Beverly Hills, provides an opportunity to think more deeply about our relationship to the Torah.

- **Among the many *midrashim* about the giving of the Torah are the following two:**

> Rabbi [Yehudah Hanasi] said: When [the people] Israel stood at Mount Sinai, they were unanimous in accepting joyfully the rule of heaven, as it is written: "All the people answered as one, saying, 'All that the Lord has spoken we will do!'"(Exodus 19:8). What is more, they vouched for one another's [commitment to fulfill the commandments].
>
> *Midrash Tanchuma, Yitro*

> Another interpretation of "Moses led the people toward God, out of the camp, and they took their places beneath the mountain" (Exodus 19:17):
>   This teaches that the Holy One, blessed be He, held the mountain over their heads like a barrel, saying, "If you take the Torah upon yourselves, it will go well [with you], but if not, this shall be your burial place" (Shabbat 88a). Thereupon they all burst out crying and poured out their hearts in penitence, saying, "All that the Lord has spoken, we will do and we will hear!"
>
> *Mekhilta deRabi Shimon Bar Yohai*[27]

The existence of these two legends about the giving of the Torah suggests that we need to receive Torah both voluntarily and involuntarily.

- In what ways do we accept the Torah involuntarily?

- In what ways do we accept it voluntarily?

- What are the implications of this idea for the planning of future learning initiatives in our congregation?

Glossary

Midrash is the general term for a genre of rabbinic literature that interprets biblical texts. *Midrash Tanchuma* is an eighth century *midrash* on the Torah. *Mekhilta deRabi Shim'on Bar Yohai,* a legal *midrash* on the book of Exodus, was written during the first two centuries of the common era, but redacted after the fourth century.

The Ambivalence of Leaders

The following texts provide an opportunity for new congregational leaders to explore their thoughts and feelings about undertaking a new assignment. They were used at an orientation meeting for new leaders in the
exploration phase, but might also be used during the readiness phase.

- **When God calls Moses to lead the Israelites out of Egypt, Moses
  voices five different concerns:**

> "Who am I that I should go to Pharaoh and free the Israelites from
> Egypt?"
>
> Exodus 3:11

> "When I come to the Israelites and say to them 'The God of your
> fathers has sent me to you,' and they ask me, 'What is God's
> name?' What shall I say to them?"
>
> Exodus 3:13

> "What if they do not believe me and do not listen to me, but say:
> 'The Lord did not appear to you'?"
>
> Exodus 4:1

> "Please, O Lord, I have never been a man of words, either in times
> past or now that You have spoken to Your servant; I am slow of
> speech and slow of tongue."
>
> Exodus 4:10

"Please, O Lord, make someone else your agent."

Exodus 4:13

In your own words, what are Moses' concerns?

Today, many of us have been called to accept a new level of leadership at our congregation. Which, if any, of Moses' concerns do you, personally, identify with?

9

Experimentation

During the very first break in the very first visioning session at one congregation, a retired corporate executive cornered me at the coffee urn and demanded, "So when are we going to get going?" Since being invited to join the task force, he had been formulating his own vision of Jewish learning and planning a variety of programs in his imagination. He had little tolerance for exercises and was frustrated by the fact that other members of the task force were not as decisive as he. This self-described "doer" stood in sharp contrast to several others on the task force who could have participated in visioning activities endlessly, without feeling a need to arrive at a conclusion or take any action whatsoever.

Most task force members will fall between the two extremes: They may enjoy the discussions in the visioning phase, and feel that they have benefited from them, yet they will also be looking for results, concrete expressions of the vision in action. Thus, even before the vision statement has been committed to paper, the task force may decide to experiment with new programs that will concretize and clarify its evolving vision. Members of the task force are likely to have come up with a variety of programmatic ideas, and will be eager to share them with others. Some of their suggestions will be truly original, while others will be borrowed from other congregations; some will be modifications of existing programs, while others will call for an entirely new approach; some will be ambitious, and some modest; some will be too wacky, some too banal, and some entirely appropriate. The outpouring of these new ideas will be both exciting and problematic. If implemented too quickly, these early brainstorms might bring the task force process to a premature conclusion, without participants having thought through the goals of congregational education and the variety of ways they can be attained. Rushing to adopt new programs is akin to impulse buying on the shopping channel without thinking about the need for the products or having done any comparison shopping.

On the other hand this type of brainstorming demonstrates the task force members' engagement and enthusiasm, and it should be welcomed. Additionally, for some of these task force members, and for most of the congregation, the concept of a congregation of learners will remain vague until it is embodied in programmatic terms. Thus one must strike a balance, welcoming the input of task force members, but restraining their impulse to embrace the first ideas that captivate them. Experimentation is a productive way of harnessing the energy of those who may be impatient with process and anxious to see products, but it must be done in a thoughtful, deliberative way.

Having reached some preliminary consensus on its vision, the task force might consider harvesting some "low hanging fruit"—the fruits that are most accessible, and, by analogy, the changes easiest to implement. In a synagogue they might include new programs that are relatively simple and inexpensive, as well as modest changes to existing programs. In choosing which programs to plan, the task force might consider a concept that derives from the Jewish tradition—the notion of foreshadowing the messianic age. Traditionally Shabbat has been referred to as *me'ain olam haba,* a taste of the world to come. The peace we experience on Shabbat gives us a concrete sense of how wonderful the world will be after the Messiah comes. Likewise, the experiments that are undertaken can give congregants a sense of what it would be like to become a congregation of learners. The new and different learning experiences, and people's positive responses to them, are the seeds from which a new culture will eventually grow.

Experimentation carries with it an additional benefit. If publicized appropriately, it broadcasts a message to the congregation that learning is a high priority and that changes are afoot in the conceptualization of learning.

But it is important to remember that experimentation will yield these results only under three conditions: 1) when those who experiment are both encouraged to dream and given permission to fail; 2) when the results of the experiment are evaluated and fed back into the visioning process; and 3) when the "low hanging fruit" are acknowledged for what they are— preliminary steps on a long and complicated journey. I will return to these points at the end of this chapter.

What Experiments Are Worth Doing?

A good scientific experiment is one that is based on sound premises, adheres to rigorous standards, and employs well-calibrated instruments. Experiments in congregational education, on the other hand, are not subject to standardized criteria. Each congregation begins from a different baseline, and has different resources and constraints. One congregation, for example, may have a long-standing lecture series that is very well attended; less intellectual and more experiential experiments might be more appropriate there. Another congregation might have rich and varied offerings in the arts, but a weak Hebrew program. Some congregations can rely on their professional staff, while others need congregants to implement new programming. Some congregations will find the money to support new ideas easily, while others will have a harder time. No set standard can apply to congregations that are so varied.

That is not to say that there are no criteria for evaluating proposed experiments. The following are some questions to consider:

1. Does this experiment exemplify values that have come up repeatedly during the visioning phase? Certain themes are likely to emerge over and over again during the visioning phase. They might include, for example, the value of intergenerational learning, the need for learners to be active rather than passive, and a desire for emotional, as well as intellectual, engagement. Devising experiments that exemplify these values will validate their importance, and require task force members to examine their practical implications. It will also sensitize people to the fact that values are open to a variety of interpretations, each interpretation resulting in a different programmatic outcome.

2. Is this experiment something members of the task force are genuinely excited about? As those who have studied social psychology can attest, a group of people can sometimes be moved to action against their better judgment. It is unlikely that any task force members will engage in demagoguery; nonetheless, we have all seen instances of a group carried away by the spirit of the moment, committing itself to a project for which there is little enthusiasm once the moment has passed. Alternatively, the group may be reluctant to disagree publicly with an individual (or subgroup) who champions a particular cause, and may feel compelled to endorse it. To allow for true consensus, the task force should consider any proposals very carefully over the course of several meetings. Genuine enthusiasm is more than a matter of majority vote; without it, the experiment may never get off the ground.

3. Will this experiment give people new learning experiences or expose them to new ideas? Since an important goal is laying the groundwork for becoming a congregation of learners, every proposed experiment should be evaluated by the following criteria: Does it have the potential to turn participants on to learning? Can it be so enjoyable and rewarding that they will be eager for more? Will it give them a glimpse of future learning possibilities?

4. Will this experiment capture people's attention? Will it make congregants sit up and take notice? As marketers know, the "buzz" that surrounds a product or event is often more important than the thing itself. No matter how small the event or how low the attendance, the publicity before the program and the "buzz" about it afterwards will reach a much larger group. Most synagogues do a lackluster job of promoting themselves and their programs; compared to the glitzy commercials, ads, and billboards that surround us, the typical synagogue flyer or invitation barely gets noticed. During this phase, the task force has an opportunity to experiment with new modes of communication and publicity. The promotional materials themselves can constitute an experiment, as will be described below. But in many instances the task force will discover that person-to-person communication, telephone, or e-mail is the most effective way to reach people.

5. Can the congregation mount a high-quality product without expending undue effort? Of all the criteria, this one is the most crucial. Low hanging fruit are meant only as appetizers, inklings of the changes to come. They cannot take so much effort that task force members are diverted from their main activity, which is the deliberation of the task force. At the same time, these experiments must be of very high quality. This argues for selectivity, attempting a small number of exemplary experiments that will support, but not overwhelm, the task force process.

A Menu of Low Hanging Fruit

Not every experiment will meet every one of these criteria; it is likely, for example, that an easily mounted event of very high quality will be one that is geared to a select number of people, and may not lend itself to publicity. Similarly, a glitzy promotional piece may well grab people's attention, but may not offer them a powerful learning experience. Each task force will have to decide for itself which criteria are most important as it selects its areas for experimentation.

With this in mind, the following types of experiments should be considered:

Repackaging Old (but Good) Programs

Many congregational schools have ongoing family education programs, including classes for parents and Sundays set aside as celebrations of learning. Without much effort some of these programs might be offered to the entire congregation and renamed and reconsidered as "congregational education" days or classes. While the programs may have to be retooled a bit to accommodate empty nesters and/or young adults without children, the real challenge will lie in persuading these other congregants to attend. Even if only a few adults without children attend at the outset, the publicity could send a clear message about the importance of intergenerational learning. Over time, if the programs are sufficiently stimulating and enjoyable, more people will participate.

Instead of offering atomized programs, all offerings would come under the general rubric of "congregation of learners." For example, an educational event of the sisterhood might be renamed "a congregational learning event sponsored by the sisterhood." The regular schedule of adult-education classes might be publicized as "part of our effort to become a congregation of learners." Even a program that was in the planning stages before the convening of the task force could be claimed as "the first fruit of our new learning initiative." Assuming the programs being reoriented and repackaged exemplify some of the values identified in the visioning process, this is a good way to begin. For very little time and money, some people can be exposed to new experiences, and others can be made aware that an effort is underway to promote learning.

Adding a Learning Dimension to Existing Programs

One step up from repackaging that requires more resources is incorporating learning into the full range of congregational activities. For example, learning might become part of worship through a discussion about prayer before the service begins or Torah study in *hevrutah* (study partners) before or after the Torah reading. Mitzvah Day might begin with a text study related to *tikun olam* (the repair of the world). Committee meetings might include fifteen to twenty minutes of learning related to the matter at hand. The possibilities are endless, so it is important to evaluate them according to the criteria proposed above. How many congregants would participate? Would the experience whet people's appetites for more learning? Which values underlie this activity, and are these the values that should be emphasized? Who would be responsible for this effort? Does that person or group have sufficient time? Would they be given sufficient support?

Task force members at Westchester Reform Temple, having identified interactive learning as a high priority, came up with an ingenious add-on to a very popular program, the scholar-in-residence series. Weeks in advance, congregants received in the mail two short articles by the visiting scholar, along with an invitation to several different discussion groups, both before and after the lectures. Though not all who attended the lecture read the articles or participated in a discussion group, those who did were much more engaged in the topic of the lecture. Moreover, news of the small groups traveled quickly through the congregation, and a similar effort the next year attracted even more people. The cost was relatively low—photocopying and mailing, plus a preparatory session for the volunteer discussion leaders—and the word-of-mouth publicity was invaluable.

Every year the religious school at Temple Shalom of Newton distributed a photocopied calendar listing the dates of holidays and religious school events. After meeting for over a year, the task force decided to make the calendar into both a vehicle and an advertisement for learning. They followed the prototype of the typical twenty-four-page wall calendar, but instead of a picture for each month, they featured a quote from a Jewish text, surrounded by commentaries written by members of the synagogue community. These quotes were taken from study sessions that had been conducted the previous year, so the work involved was not overwhelming. The selection was done by a small committee; a member of the task force contributed the design and layout. The increased cost of production (photocopying on slightly nicer paper stock) and distribution (slightly higher postage for the regular Fall membership packet) were modest. The attractive design caught everyone's attention; people hung the calendar proudly on their refrigerators. Although reading the commentaries while putting away the groceries was probably not a profound experience, people were struck by the significance of the texts and the insightful commentary of their fellow congregants. Above all, the calendar proclaimed the message that the congregation values texts and lively discussion about them.

A number of congregations produced and distributed a variety of tapes—one had the kiddush and blessings for Friday night, another the Shabbat morning liturgy, and a third had songs and blessings for the Passover seder. The singing was done by the cantor and the tapes were reproduced commercially and sold at cost. The tapes sold out repeatedly.

New Programs

Some congregations have been more ambitious, devising altogether new programs to promote learning. For example, Temple Emanuel of Beverly Hills created a four-session *Havdalah* program called "Stop and Smell the Spices." Each session focused on one of the four *brakhot* in the *Havdalah* service: light, spices, wine, and the separation between *kodesh* (the holy) and *chol* (the secular). Each began with singing and ended with a snack and *Havdalah*. In between, participants could choose one of four or five learning opportunities related to the day's theme: acting out a story, text study, a crafts project, Jewish meditation, etc. At every program a small group of participants worked on the creation of an interpretive *Havdalah* service. Though the program required a great deal of effort to plan and to publicize, the numerous benefits made this effort worthwhile: It brought together multiple constituencies of the congregation, including day school parents and children, religious school parents and children, senior citizens, teenagers, and young adults. By the third session, people who had never met before were greeting each other warmly. The energy it took to recruit these groups taught the planning committee (made up of six congregants and two staff members) a great deal about scheduling and publicity. The range of activities gathered under the rubric of learning sent a message that learning has many meanings. The fact that more than half of the activities were led by congregants gave participants an appreciation of their fellow members' talents. And the composition of the planning committee, half of which were members of the adult-education committee and the other half were members of the task force, set a precedent for further cooperation among heretofore separate entities.

Another ambitious experiment, undertaken at The Temple in Atlanta, was the creation of a four-page insert on learning that appeared regularly in the bulletin. Written and illustrated by members of the task force, this insert was so appealing in its layout, and contained so many engaging items that it was widely read. Though the time involved in writing and editing was considerable, and the production costs relatively high, this project attracted a great deal of attention and sent a clear message that learning was for the whole congregation.

Each of these programs qualifies as a low hanging fruit, but no congregation could possibly offer all of them. The choice of which experiments to pursue will hinge on many factors: the interests and talents of task force members; the perceived needs of the congregation; and the availability of both human and financial resources. In deciding where to begin, the task force might look to the gap between the values identified in the visioning process and the congregation's current values. If only a small percentage of adults are engaged in Jewish learning, and if lifelong learning is one of the values that has come up repeatedly, adult learning might be a natural place to start. If one of the ideals articulated by the task force is for everyone to become a teacher but the congregation leaves all the teaching to professionals, experiments might be geared toward highlighting the teaching skills of congregants. If the existing learning opportunities fit well with the values of the task force but congregants are not aware of what is being offered, publicity would be an important place to begin. If, on the other hand, a particular type of learning valued by the task force has never been offered, new programming would be advised.

Some Final Thoughts on Experimentation

1. Select the Planning Group with Care.

Though the task force should participate in deciding upon the areas for experimentation, a group that large cannot actually plan specific programs. That task should be delegated to a committee drawn from members of the task force, and include an appropriate staff member. If possible, the committee should also include representatives of committees that oversee this type of programming. Other members of the congregation with relevant expertise (such as song leading, arts and crafts, design, or public relations) may be invited as well.

2. Experiments Don't Always Succeed.

Implicit in the term experimentation is the possibility of failure. Not every program dreamed up by the task force will attract hundreds of eager participants and send them home transformed. Not every piece of publicity will be effective, nor will every piece be acclaimed. A spirit of adventure should characterize this phase; planners should be encouraged to set their sights high, while being assured (honestly) that falling short of their goals is okay too. In the world of science, experiments that always yield predicted results are viewed with suspicion; if there were no uncertainty it wouldn't be genuine science. This should be the mindset for synagogue experimentation as well, where, in fact, few programs are total failures. A program that draws twenty instead of 100 can still provide a high-quality experience for that group. One boring or unfocused text study session will not turn people off permanently. Congregants are generous and forgiving when a fellow congregant goes out on a limb.

On the other hand, the task force should limit experimentation to situations in which learning from one's mistakes outweighs the potential damage to the task force or congregation's reputation. The Kol Nidre service is probably not an appropriate time for an experiment where learning is led by novice congregant-teachers. It may not be appropriate to include a flyer with commentaries on *tsedakah* in the invitation to the year's major fund-raiser. But these are extreme examples. In most cases the stakes are not so high, and the repercussions not so drastic. It may be difficult for board or staff members to practice restraint and give the task force responsibility for planning a program or producing a widely disseminated document. But congregants will not be invested in this new initiative if they are not full partners in the process of decision-making.

3. Evaluation Is Critical.

To their detriment, synagogues rarely build evaluation into their programming. The sponsors of a program may think that their own impressions or the comments of a few participants are a sufficient measure of its success; or they may not value the opinion of participants; or they may simply feel too overwhelmed to deal with evaluation. The experiments of the task force offer a wonderful opportunity to introduce evaluation as a "new way of doing business around here." A written questionnaire is a relatively simple method for soliciting the feedback of participants. The questionnaire should consist of only a few multiple choice questions, with room for additional comments; if possible, time should be allotted within the program for filling out the questionnaire. If time permits and the group is not too large, each participant can be asked to share one comment with the entire group. A discussion of this sort allows people to hear each other's comments; they are often surprised to find that their opinions are not shared by all.

Whether or not it is feasible to survey participants, a second type of evaluation should be conducted: a frank sharing of feedback by its planners and by several designated observers who are asked, in advance, to watch the participants' reactions. Evaluation discussions can teach everyone a great deal, but they require effort and commitment. Observers may hesitate to make critical comments; alternatively, the criticism may be so harsh that the program's planners and facilitators feel under attack. The guidelines for these sessions should be set forth at the outset. Observers should be encouraged to offer descriptions, rather than judgment. The positive aspects of the event should be discussed, along with the negative, which should be limited to a few salient points. It may be useful to have these evaluation discussions facilitated by a congregant with professional supervisory skills. Though the initial discussions may be awkward, this type of evaluation will prove to be invaluable if done consistently. Over time, participants will improve their ability to give feedback, and to receive it. They will undoubtedly find that these sessions raise important issues that can be fed back into the visioning process.

4. Experimentation Is Only the First Step.

Though some of the task force's experiments will fail, others will succeed beyond all expectation: Participants will be wildly enthusiastic, begging for more of the same; task force members will gain greater clarity about what it means to become a congregation of learners; the synagogue's board will be confirmed in its commitment to learning. Though these responses are most welcome, they pose a potential pitfall. The task force may feel compelled to repeat these programs, making them an ongoing part of the congregation's offerings. If sufficient staff and/or volunteers are available this may not be problematic, but because synagogues are notoriously understaffed, it is important for the task force to agree ahead of time on the limits that may need to be imposed. In addition, there is an even greater danger that the energy of the task force may be consumed by maintaining these programs. It would be unfortunate if the group charged with rethinking and reconfiguring learning were to get derailed by its own experiments, however successful these prove to be.

10

Outreach to the Congregation: Planning and Facilitating Community Conversations

Imagine that a task force has been meeting for three to six months, and that its members have found their discussions about Jewish learning both enjoyable and productive. They have compiled a set of sentences and paragraphs that express their collective vision and a smaller group is meeting to weave these fragments into a formal vision statement. Experimental learning programs are underway, and the response to them has been gratifying. A few members of the task force have dropped out along the way, but the remaining members are really into Jewish learning, enjoying the text study at the meetings and beginning to become more active learners themselves. They are excited to be the vanguard of a new learning initiative at the congregation. In short, the task force is feeling good about what it has accomplished so far.

Of course, the goal for the entire planning process goes far beyond satisfying this small group. Having reached this comfortable plateau, the task force must now reach out to the rest of the congregation, spreading its enthusiasm for learning to the others. It is difficult to pinpoint exactly when this type of outreach should be undertaken. It can't begin until task force members have become articulate and energetic advocates, but it should be well underway before the group has become too insular and too enamored of its own vision to hear dissenting voices or accept new ideas. Therefore, once there is a sense that the task force has begun to gel and a coherent shared vision has emerged, the time to begin outreach has arrived.

How should this emergent vision of learning be shared? Typically, synagogues communicate with their members through sermons, announcements from the *bimah* (pulpit), and articles in the synagogue bulletin. But these are uni-directional modalities whose purpose is to inform, rather than to open up a dialogue. Now the task force needs ways for congregants to become engaged in discussing the vision, thinking about its applicability, and giving feedback to its authors. To encourage this type of exchange, discussions can be held at "back-to-school night," at sisterhood and men's club events, and at committee meetings. One task force held a "town meeting" and 200 people showed up. Experiments themselves are a form of communication, especially if feedback mechanisms are built into them.

One form of outreach that has been particularly effective because it engages people most actively is what we have come to call "community conversations." These are small parlor meetings or focus groups held in people's homes, where participants are invited to reflect on their own Jewish learning experiences and imagine what congregational learning might become. While mounting a series of community conversations can be very labor-intensive, every congregation that has tried them has found them to be well worth the effort. Synagogues rarely give members opportunities to meet in small groups for purposes other than fund-raising; for many participants, the community conversation will be the first time anyone in the synagogue has solicited their opinion on a substantive matter of synagogue policy. Participants are generally grateful for the opportunity to meet informally with other congregants and to envision the future of the congregation.

Informal though they might be, the community conversations require careful planning. Clarity about goals, a plan that allows for focused but unhurried conversation, and good facilitation and notetaking are key to maximizing the benefits of this outreach effort. In this chapter I will discuss each of these.

The Goals of Community Conversations

The community conversations can be designed to fulfill six different goals. The first three involve selling congregants on the idea of Jewish learning; the next three relate to improving the planning process and its outcomes.

Promoting Jewish Learning

1. Raising people's consciousness about the importance of Jewish learning. For most members of most congregations, being Jewish is a very part-time activity. Only on major holidays or in connection with life-cycle events do average, marginally affiliated American Jews devote much time to thinking about or doing anything Jewish. They are either preoccupied with other concerns or ambivalent about Judaism. The community conversations provide an opportunity for congregants to devote an hour and a half to one Jewish activity—Jewish learning. It is unlikely that those who feel totally indifferent or negative will bother to attend the meetings; those who do participate are likely to be open to thinking about learning and the role it can play in their lives. The community conversations can serve as a consciousness-raising device, putting people in touch with positive past experiences, rekindling old interests, and creating anticipation for the future. Of course, it is likely that these discussions will also remind people of their negative Jewish learning experiences, and there is always a danger that these meetings may turn into gripe sessions. But negative stories could be used to reflect on the positive changes the synagogue might make in the learning experiences they, or their children, can have in years to come. A good facilitator will be able to draw people out while keeping the tone of the conversation positive; preparation for the facilitators will be discussed below.

2. Giving people a short, but stimulating experience with Jewish learning. The community conversations might be designed to give participants a powerful, shared learning experience. Studying together, the participants might experience firsthand how enjoyable and involving it can be to learn in a group. The sample facilitator guides, which appear on pages 227–229, include two examples of short learning experiences that were used in two congregations. In contrast, other congregations decided to focus on the other goals because the time allotted was not sufficient for a satisfying learning experience.

3. Generating enthusiasm about a new learning initiative. Though sermons and bulletin articles may have heralded the formation of the task force, most congregants are likely to have only a vague recollection that such an initiative is underway. In the beginning, the task force should maintain a low profile because it will not have much to report. However, once a vision is articulated and experimentation has begun, the community conversations are an excellent way to raise the congregation's awareness of the task force's work.

Improving the Planning Process

4. Getting feedback on the vision statement. If a draft of the vision statement has been completed by the time the community conversations are underway, time might be devoted to discussing it.

5. Identifying additional congregants interested in joining the task force. Participants in the community conversations may well have ideas and talents that could be of use in the later stages of the task force process, such as analyzing the responses and/or planning long-term initiatives. One of the purposes of the community conversations should be to find these people, and recruit them.

6. Gathering information about people's interests and learning styles. Task force members will have already discovered the variety of learning interests and learning styles that exist in their group. But the task force's predilections may or may not reflect those of the congregation as a whole; the community conversations are an opportunity to determine the extent to which the task force is representative of a larger constituency. Bearing in mind that congregants who attend the community conversations are likely to be more interested in learning than those who do not, there is still a great deal of valuable information to be collected about the opportunities congregants might welcome, and the ways in which they might be packaged and promoted.

By now, anyone who has ever planned a meeting will be shaking his or her head in dismay: Six goals for a time slot of two hours or less? Impossible. The planners of the community conversations will indeed have to be selective, thinking carefully about which goals are most critical, which are of secondary importance, and which can be given up altogether. For example, if goal #2 (giving participants a learning experience) is important, it may be necessary to shorten the period of time allotted to goal #6 (gathering information about interests and needs). Or, if the task force does not yet have a satisfactory draft of its vision statement, time would be available for some of the other goals to be pursued more fully.

Regardless of the particular goals that are chosen, the community conversations are sure to have two ancillary but important byproducts:

- *Giving congregants an opportunity to meet one another.* The larger the congregation, the more likely that congregants will have only a passing acquaintance with one another, or none at all. The community conversations can be a first step in breaking down this anonymity and creating opportunities for the meaningful encounters that lead to genuine community.

- *Demonstrating that the leadership is responsive to the concerns of its members.* Many congregants perceive their synagogue as a service organization, and themselves as consumers whose only options are to purchase or not purchase the services offered. The community conversations can afford participants a different perspective, in which congregants and the synagogue are partners in addressing needs and desires, and in creating the future.

A Step-by-Step Guide to Conducting Community Conversations

1. Designate a committee to oversee the community conversations.

Though the major policy decisions regarding the community conversations should be made by the task force, a smaller committee will be required to plan the particulars and ensure that the process runs smoothly. This committee should be separate from the leadership team, though there might be one or two overlapping members. While most members of the committee will be drawn from the task force, this may be an appropriate time to recruit a few new participants who have particular expertise in conducting focus groups, facilitating discussions, or analyzing data.

Members of the staff should not sit on this committee and, in fact, should not be present at the community conversations. Even when relationships between congregants and the staff are excellent, the presence of staff might inhibit congregants and prevent them from being fully candid lest they offend the clergy or other staff members.

2. Prioritize the goals.

Again, it is impossible to meet all of the goals in a single community conversation. The subcommittee, upon consultation with the task force and leadership team, will have to decide which goals are most important.

3. Carefully determine the composition and size of the groups.

Once the goals have been decided, the committee should consider whether it wants to invite homogenous or heterogeneous groups. In other words, should the participants in a single community conversation be drawn from one particular constituency (such as religious school parents or regular participants in worship) or should they represent the spectrum of members? To some extent, this depends on which goals have the highest priority. If, for example, the goal of introducing members to one another is paramount, heterogeneous groupings will be called for. If, on the other hand, the committee hopes to elicit specific suggestions for new learning initiatives, it might be helpful for participants with similar needs and experiences to brainstorm together. There are also some practical considerations. When congregants are identified randomly (as would be the case with heterogeneous groupings) a higher percentage of inactive members end up on the list of invitees; these inactive members are more likely to decline, so getting them to attend will require extra effort. On the other hand, when the groupings are homogenous, it will be easier to get people to attend, but care must be taken to represent the full diversity of each constituency, to assure that the invitees are not all members of the same in-group.

How many people should be invited to each community conversation? Fewer than seven participants might be awkward, while more than fifteen might make it difficult for everyone to speak. However, not every invitee will attend and some may cancel at the last minute. If homogenous groups are desired, the number of RSVPs should be monitored carefully and, if necessary, additional invitations issued. If heterogeneous groups are desired, people can be given the choice of several different dates to increase the likelihood that they will be able to attend.

4. Determine logistical details.

Among the decisions to be made are: What are the procedures for issuing the invitations? What will be the setting? How many conversations will be held? Will observers be present?

With regard to the invitations, a letter signed by the rabbi and/or task force chair can be followed up with phone calls by committee members. The committee members should be prepared to make repeated calls. They should not feel insulted by lack of response to the letter, nor by invitees' failure to return phone calls. The typical congregant is overcommitted and pressured, but if members of the committee persist gracefully, they will be able to recruit many of the congregants they desire.

If at all possible, the community conversations should be held in people's homes, where the atmosphere will be more personal and more welcoming than in the synagogue. Of course, the living room furniture may have to be rearranged to allow participants to sit in a large circle or square.

How many community conversations should be held altogether? This, again, depends on the goals. If the primary goal is to obtain information, relatively few need to be held. On the other hand, if the goal is to create opportunities for community building and a sense of inclusion, the more the better. The size of the congregation is an important factor as well, as is the person-power available for making phone calls, facilitating, and note taking. In those synagogues where community conversations have been held, the number of conversations ranged between ten and twenty-five.

Finally, with regard to observers, at least at the beginning, it would be a good idea for two types of observers to be present: someone to give feedback to the facilitator, and a member of the task force to fill out the notes with some commentary. Again, the observers should *not* include members of the professional staff.

A final logistical detail: It would be advisable to implement a procedure for sending thank-you notes to participants and keeping them informed about the planning process.

5. Prepare a facilitators' guide.

Those responsible for the guide should ask themselves the following questions:

- How will participants be welcomed?
- What basic information on participants is being sought, and how will that information be collected?

- How will the work of the task force be explained?

- How will the goals of the community conversation be explained?

- What ground rules for discussion will be set?

- What will participants be told about the time frame of the session?

- Are the questions worded clearly?

- Is there a smooth transition from one question to another?

The first two or three conversations should be considered pilots. If possible, the facilitators, notetakers, and observers should meet to review and finalize the guide after the pilots have taken place. If this is too difficult to arrange, one person might solicit the others' feedback and make the revisions suggested by the group.

The following sample facilitator guides from three congregations suggest a range of possibilities. Depending on your goals, you might choose to adopt one of these, create an eclectic combination, or devise your own outline from scratch.

Outline for Community Conversations at Westchester Reform Temple, Scarsdale, New York

1. Welcome; introductions; explanation of the purpose of this meeting. (15 min.)

2. Describe one positive experience of Jewish learning (broadly conceived—not just classroom learning) you have had, either as a child or as an adult. (30 min.)

3. Please look over draft of our vision statement. Do you have any reactions, positive or negative? (15 min.)

4. Write on index cards your responses to the following question: What positive Jewish learning experiences would you expect from an ideal congregation? (5 min.)

5. Choose one of your responses to share with the group (these are listed on a flip chart). Open conversation in reaction to these ideas. (from 20–40 minutes, depending on people's energy)

Outline for Community Conversations at Temple Emanu-El, San Diego

1. Welcome and introductions. (10 min.)

2. "Brainwriting" (making notes to yourself) on previous experiences with Jewish learning. (5 min.)

3. Brief discussion and sharing of experiences. (15 min.)

4. "Brainwriting" on pleasant learning experiences of any kind. (5 min.)

5. Brief discussion and sharing of experiences. (15 min.)

6. "Brainwriting" or thinking concerning how we can translate pleasant learning experiences into a vision for Jewish learning in our synagogue. (10 min.)

7. Recording of ideas. (20 min.)

8. Discussion and clarification of ideas.

9. Prioritizing ideas using stickers on flip charts. (10 min.)

10. Wrap-up and review of results. (10 min.)

Outline for Community Conversations at Temple Shalom of Newton in Massachusetts

1. Welcome and introductions. (10 min.)

2. Give an adjective to describe the congregation. (10 min.)

3. Describe a memorable Jewish learning experience you have had. (15 min.)

4. People given a stack of cards, with words such as "mitzvah," "relationship with God," "values," "identity." They are asked to sort the cards into three piles:

a) something that is working well—you feel positive about it;

b) something that is not working so well that you have serious concerns about it;

c) something you don't have a strong feeling about either way. People can move cards around, EXCEPT that once a card ends up in the "concerns" pile, it can't be removed. There are also blank cards for people to fill in with their own words. (15 min.)

5. Discussion of why certain cards were placed in a certain pile. (20 min.)

6. "Dream a little" about what Jewish learning could look like at the congregation. "Pretend you have a magic wand and you wave it over the synagogue. What would Jewish learning look like after you waved the magic wand?" As people answer, probe with the following questions:

• Where does learning take place?

• When does it happen?

• Who is learning?

• Who is teaching? (20 min.)

6. Recruit and orient facilitators and notetakers.

Every congregation has members who are skilled at facilitation; they may be teachers, social workers, psychologists, marketing consultants, or simply people who have a knack for conducting meetings with grace. The number of facilitators needed will depend upon how many conversations each can facilitate, and how many conversations are planned. The facilitators should be brought together to review and revise the facilitators' guide and prepare for their meetings. They can brainstorm how to break the ice, introduce participants to one another, and deal with any potential problems (such as a person trying to dominate the conversation or negative comments that arise). In addition, a group of notetakers should be recruited. All the answers do not need to be recorded, but it is important to have a record of people's ideas. If the facilitators' guide calls for group reactions to the ideas that are generated, it would be important to record them on a large flip chart so they can be referred to during the conversation.[1]

7. Remain flexible as the conversations are conducted.

Ideally, the community conversations should be scheduled in clusters, allowing time for evaluating and revising the protocol between each cluster. The first few conversations should be seen as pilots, with the expectation that the guide will be revised after they have taken place. After the second cluster, minor changes might be made. After the third cluster, the task force might meet for preliminary data reduction, as will be described in the next step. Having had an opportunity to view the results up close, the task force and/or the community conversations' committee might wish to change the protocol even further.

Along the way, a number of more specialized conversations might be held—one with members of the Board of Directors, one with each of the committees related to learning (such as the religious school committee or the adult-education committee), one with members of the staff who do not sit on the task force, and one or more with teachers in the congregation's schools. In each case, the protocol might be varied to draw on the expertise of the participants.

The time devoted to community conversations will vary, depending upon the availability of facilitators and other members of the committee. One congregation held twenty community conversations in three months, while another conducted the same number over the course of a year; most congregations fell somewhere in between the two.

8. Reduce and summarize the data and discuss your conclusions.

After each community conversation, the notes should be typed up, question by question. Ideally these notes should be accompanied by commentary, because the notes are summaries of the remarks that don't necessarily capture the effect behind the statement. Immediately after the conversation, or within the next day or two, the facilitator, note taker, and observers should record their own reactions to the participants' responses, noting the comments that struck them as particularly significant.

When all the conversations have been completed, an overwhelming amount of data will have been collected. Since the participants are self-selected and the procedures for recording their answers are not rigorous, the data need not be quantified nor treated with the rigor of a scientific sample; but the data will need to be reduced and summarized to be of use. Who should be involved in this task? Once again, there are a number of possible answers. The most efficient is to enlist the efforts of individuals with a social science background and experience with data reduction. On the other hand, there is great value to giving task force members an opportunity to "muck around" in the data, to get a flavor of the responses rather than simply receive a general summary. A good middle ground would be for members of the task force to work for several hours on data reduction, and then give the remainder of the task over to a smaller committee of "experts" to complete. Most congregations have used a technique with their task force called "affinity grouping."

Instructions for Affinity Grouping Exercise with Members of the Task Force

- Type up the responses to each of the important questions (you may decide to exclude the warm-up questions) on separate sheets of paper, with space between each answer and the next.

- Divide the task force into groups of three or four. Give each group several sets of answers to one of the questions. Depending upon how many answers there are, this might be the data from three to seven separate conversations. In all, there shouldn't be more than sixty to seventy discrete responses or the task will be too overwhelming.

- Have the group cut up the sheets so that every answer is on a different slip of paper. Put the slips of paper on a large table, or tape them to the wall.

- Working silently, have members of the group move the slips of paper around, clustering them into categories. It will take a while for people to move the pieces back and forth, but eventually the categories will "stand still." (It is important to do this silently so that individuals don't influence each other.) Once consensus has been reached on the groupings, tape down the slips of paper by category.

- Discuss each category, and write one or two sentences that summarize the gist of this category.

This procedure should take from an hour to an hour and a half. It is unlikely that one meeting of the task force will be sufficient to summarize all the data. You may want to schedule this type of task force meeting after the first three to five community conversations, which will allow you to assess the facilitators' guide and suggest changes. If the task force seems energized by the affinity group exercise, you may want to schedule a second session when the remainder of the community conversations are complete. Otherwise, you may decide to appoint a smaller group to deal with the remaining data.

Once the community conversations' notes have been reduced and summarized, the task force should meet to begin to interpret them. If possible, they should receive the summary of the data in advance and be asked to think about what the data reveal about:

- the interests, needs, and relevant characteristics of the learners,

- the optimal conditions for learning,

- the characteristics of teachers and discussion leaders,

- the subject matters that seem most appealing or appropriate,

- other aspects of the congregation.

The entire group should be asked to consider:

- What are the most important points that were made, and why?

- Which aspects of synagogue life in general and of Jewish learning in particular should be the focus of further investigation?

The conclusions reached at the end of this session will determine the areas for further exploration and long-term planning, which will be taken up in the next phase. Chapter 11 will be devoted to this topic.

9. Report the results to the congregation.

Even before the summary and analysis are completed, members of the leadership team should begin to think about the dissemination of the results. Different types of reporting will be appropriate for different constituencies. The task force will require the most detailed summary; the board may or may not need as much detail, but should certainly be informed of the general outcomes. With regard to other congregants, the following questions should be considered: Should a short written report be sent to community conversation participants? Should one be made available to the entire membership? What sorts of oral reports can be given that will publicize the initiative as it gathers momentum?

The report that follows, which was distributed to the board and the task force of Congregation Sinai in Milwaukee, is a good example for two reasons. First, it lays out very clearly the goals of the community conversations, their method, and a detailed description of the analysis of the results. Second, it gives clear and unvarnished descriptions of both the positive and the negative comments made by participants. Readers who did not attend a community conversation had an opportunity to understand the effort they entailed, and to appreciate the weight of the findings. The report was written by Marleen Pugach and Roslyn Roucher.

• • •

Excerpts from the
Community Conversation Report,
Congregation Sinai, Milwaukee

OVERVIEW

The Community Conversations (CC) phase of the Experiment in Congregational Education (ECE) took place between June 1998 and December 1998. During the CCs small groups of Sinai congregants engaged in thoughtful, guided discussions about Jewish education and Jewish life. This phase of the ECE project was preceded by an eighteen-month visioning process with a group of 25 congregants (the Task Force) who were engaged in an in-depth process of understanding the congregation's past and present. This was followed by a forward-looking process of dreaming about a future in which the congregation would strive to become a Congregation of Learners and a Learning Congregation.

GOALS

The goals of the Community Conversations were:

1. To introduce congregants to the ECE process.

2. To facilitate a text study experience, provide a taste of what the ECE could offer to congregants.

3. To solicit input from congregants about their hopes and dreams for Sinai's future, particularly in terms of Jewish education.

4. To allow congregants to talk about their own past experiences in Jewish education.

5. To bring together congregants of different backgrounds.

A total of fourteen Community Conversations were held. Over 120 congregants participated in these CCs. CCs were held in members' homes and at the temple. Each CC lasted 1½ hours. The number of participants at each CC ranged from 5–18. Some CCs were composed of a random sampling of congregants and others were with existing temple groups, for example, the Jewish Women's Spirituality Group *(Brit Nashim)* and the Schmoozers' Havurah. One CC was held for 9th- and 10th-grade students.

PROTOCOL

The CC program included the following elements: Congregants introduced themselves and were asked to share one thought, feeling, or stereotype from their own experience that they had about Jewish education. The goal of this section was to allow participants to describe their current feelings about Jewish education. In addition, many participants shared a great deal about their Jewish upbringing, family life, etc. Next, participants broke into small groups of 2–4 and related their most positive learning experiences and what made them positive. The goal of this exercise was to find out what makes a learning experience positive for people so that this information could be used in our future planning.

What followed next changed from CC to CC, but was a flip-flop of either text study or dreaming about the potential for Jewish education at Congregation Sinai. The text study section was designed to allow people to study with and learn from each other with the help of a knowledgeable and trained text study facilitator. In addition, the text studied was chosen because of its accessibility and relevance. The subject of the text study was *Shmirat Halashon,* or the Ethics of Speech. During the dreaming section, participants were asked to write down their "dreams"—their ideas for what they would like to see happen at Sinai, with no budgetary or resource/facilities restrictions to constrain their dreams, one idea per Post-it note. The results of the dreaming section became the content of the Data Analysis from the CCs and the Working Groups were determined from these data as well as from the input of the Leadership Team (which includes the professional staff of the congregation.)

OBSERVATIONS

1. The invitation process and attendance issues were a constant challenge for the Community Conversations. A major effort was made to encourage attendance at the CCs: A special, printed invitation was designed and sent to each congregant, congregants were given opportunities to attend a variety of CCs, and new CC dates were added to accommodate schedules. In addition, when it became clear that certain elements of the congregational membership were not adequately represented at the CCs, additional CCs were added for these groups, most importantly, parents of religious school-age children. Although ultimately 120 people attended CCs, it was a long and sometimes arduous process to reach this level of attendance.

2. Although the initial question asked of CC participants was to give one thought, stereotype, or feeling they had about Jewish education, in almost every CC people described the nature of their Jewish upbringing in great detail. These descriptions were very interesting and revealed a lot about the members of Sinai. It seemed important for people to have this opportunity to discuss their Jewish past. In some cases, more time was spent on this section than was allocated, and over the course of the CCs this question was adapted to encourage more brief and direct sharing.

3. The text study section, for the most part, was a positive experience for participants. For some, it was the first time they had studied text in a hands-on way—that is, actually working with a variety of texts from classical Jewish literature and applying it to our modern lives through an interactive discussion with fellow congregants. For others, they had never known that Judaism had such extensive texts on subjects that touch people in their daily lives. The text study was adapted many times throughout the CCs. By the final CCs, the text study seemed to meet its goals of allowing people to interact with each other and with the text and to engage in a meaningful text study experience that followed a different model than that of frontal teaching by an expert.

DATA

Four sets of data were collected at the CCs: 1) A list of participants' thoughts, feelings, and stereotypes of Jewish education; 2) a list of participants' positive learning experiences and what made them positive; 3) a list of the dreams and ideas participants gave about their hopes and dreams for education—broadly defined—at Congregation Sinai; and 4) the notes and observations made by the note takers at the CCs. The following is a summary of the elements of a positive learning experience—in other words, what made a particular learning experience positive for people. These data will be used in the Working Groups in determining what models of learning might be included in the implementation plans.

The data analysis presented in this report focuses on the dreaming section.

DATA ANALYSIS METHOD

The analysis of data for the dreaming section of the Community Conversations included every response recorded by all participants at every one of the fourteen Community Conversations. The purpose of the analysis was to group like responses and discover the patterns they represented. From these patterns, the ECE Leadership Team could identify which areas were of greatest interest/concern to the congregants as focal points for the next stage of ECE work.

For each CC, a typed version taken from the handwritten Post-it notes containing all of the dreaming statements was made in preparation for a large group data analysis meeting that was held on January 10, 1999. A total of approximately 600 individual statements representing congregants' dreams (see description of CC agenda) was made during these CCs. These typewritten versions were then color-coded to correspond with each of the fourteen CCs that took place.

All CC participants were invited to come to the data analysis meeting. At that meeting, which was attended by members of the ECE Leadership Team, members of the ECE Task Force, and nine voluntary participants from the CCs, the typewritten versions of the data were cut up so that each individual response was on a separate slip of paper (the CCs from which the individual responses came could be identified via the color coding). Participants broke up into five small groups of 5–7 and each small group was given a random stack of individual responses from various CCs to sort. The purpose of this round of sorting was to get an initial sense of what categories of dreams these data might represent. No preset category names were provided to the groups; instead, we wanted the categories to come out of the small group discussions of the data themselves. The goal was not necessarily just to count the number of responses that fit into each of the categories, but rather to get a good sense of the intent of the responses and what the larger issues were that these responses represented.

After this initial round of sorting we posted all the category names each group came up with for their data set and had a whole group discussion about how these initial categories were being defined by each group. As anticipated, there was a great deal of overlap in many of these first passes at categorizing, and some categories had many, many responses. If we all agreed on the general definition of a certain category, we put all of those statements together. Not all categories were collapsible at this point.

Following the discussion, each small group took a few sets of responses—now with tentative category names—and analyzed them again to see if they indeed represented a consistent concept or idea. This was a highly spirited part of the data analysis session and it was not unusual to see someone holding up a slip of paper and searching for a group at another table that had a category better suited to a particular individual response, or "dream." Group members reworked the data until they felt comfortable with the categories they were seeing and defining. Some were the same category names that they began with, other names changed upon further analysis of the responses, and still other responses were regrouped into new categories. At the end of this round of data analysis we had a tentative set of six large categories with several subsets of related responses in them and six categories with small numbers of responses in them.

The categories broke out as follows:

Large Categories:	Smaller Categories:
1. Adult Learning	1. Children
2. Nontraditional Learning	2. Social Action
3. Teens	3. Interfaith
4. Community	4. Home
5. Worship/Shabbat	5. Israel
6. Staff and Teaching	6. Financial Issues

Following the data analysis meeting the ECE Leadership Team revisited these categories and all the responses in them and targeted three areas from the categories that would constitute the focus of the next phase of the project, the creation of working groups. These three issues include: 1) Adult Learning (including Nontraditional Learning), 2) Teens, and 3) Community.

Although all of the resulting categories from the data analysis activity are important, these three were targeted for the following reasons:

1. Adult learning and providing varied structures within which adults can engage in learning generated the greatest numbers of responses from all of the CCs and represented several subgroups of issues. Significant opportunities for adult learning already exist within the congregation and are well received. The specific dreams raised in the CCs provide a window on making adult education opportunities even stronger. They include a wider range of content, different modes of learning/delivery, and ideas for publicizing and scheduling adult learning opportunities.

2. Several different issues around solidifying the community feeling at Sinai were also raised in the CCs. Again, these issues were raised in the spirit of improving the already existing community rather than to suggest that community does not already exist in the congregation. Some of the community issues and dreams seemed to be things that might easily be accomplished—for

example, ideas for improving written communications—while others, for example, facilities, represent long-range plans and have many wide-reaching implications, not the least of which are financial.

3. The ECE Leadership Team targeted teen issues as the third focus for an initial working group. One of the CCs was held with eighth- and ninth-grade students who attend Mini-U education program, so their concerns and dreams were included in the consideration of this targeted area. Although the issue of teen programming was not raised as often as adult learning or community as a category, it appeared to represent a very important issue that, once addressed, might bring immediate results. Further, teen programming has a far-reaching impact in terms of the long-term connection our adolescents might have with Judaism. Finally, teen programming is a central issue for the Reform Movement at present, and it appears that it is also an issue locally for us at Sinai.

Clearly there are other significant areas that were raised during the Community Conversations in addition to these three. One such issue would be conceptualizing whom we would like to see as teachers in our congregation. Other issues, such as Shabbat, are connected both to building community in the larger sense and specifically to ritual and worship. These clearly represent other important issues for the congregation that are on the back burner, so to speak, and it will be important to address them in the near future.

Based on the responses in each of the three targeted categories, the ECE Leadership Team will guide the Working Groups in defining the specific charge for each Working Group. The role of these Working Groups is to intersect with the existing organizational and governance structures within the congregation and connect the dreams and ideas from the CCs into the work of these existing groups. For example, the chair of Sinai's Adult Education Committee will be the Chair of the Adult Learning Working Group as a way of bridging the input from the CCs with the existing plans of the Adult Education Committee. Likewise, our educator, Birgit

Anderson, would be a major participant in the Working Group on teen issues. Subsequent to the CCs and the data analysis work, the role of ECE is to create and sustain ongoing dialogue and action that will keep the goal of learning as a central focus within the Sinai community. Consistent with the idea of informed choice as a value in Reform Judaism, the ECE can serve a role in helping to make sure that access to Jewish learning is available as a basis for informed choice.

• • •

As indicated in the report, congregants who attended the community conversations offered a host of ideas for improving existing learning opportunities and creating new ones. They made suggestions regarding other aspects of congregational life as well, such as increasing congregants' involvement in prayer services and making both newcomers and old-timers feel more welcome. Members of the task force worked together to compile and categorize all of these comments, identifying twelve separate areas of concern. To pare these twelve down to a manageable number, the leadership team took stock of the short-term needs of the congregation, as well as the constraints on the time of both the professional staff and the lay leadership. They chose three areas for further exploration—adult learning, teens, and community building. Other congregational teams, taking into account the responses of their own congregants and their own special circumstances, may arrive at similar topics or somewhat different ones, such as prayer, Shabbat, Hebrew, intergenerational learning, text study, and outreach to new members. What to do once the areas for further exploration have been identified is the subject of the next chapter.

11

Exploration

The selection of a small number of themes (ideally between three and five) for further exploration should be based on the findings of the community conversations, filtered through and informed by the vision articulated by the task force. Since the primary focus of the entire process has been on learning, it is to be expected that the majority of the themes will be learning-related. But to the extent that issues such as community-building, prayer, or *tikun olam* were discussed, one or more of these themes may also be selected. Just how many areas of exploration should be chosen depends upon the frequency with which certain topics were mentioned, the priorities of the staff and the leadership team, and the availability of a new pool of congregants to join one of the exploration groups.

Who Participates in the Exploration?

The group designated to explore a particular theme can be formed in either of two ways. An ad hoc working group can be convened and asked to focus on this topic. Alternately, if the theme falls within the purview of one of the synagogue's standing committees, the committee can be asked to undertake the exploration. For example, the theme of youth could be assigned to the youth committee, that of prayer to the ritual committee, and so on. As always, there are pros and cons to each of these alternatives. Synagogue committees are usually responsible for either setting policy or maintaining programs; while the work to be done during this exploratory phase might include both of these, they would be set in a much wider context—the discussion of some fundamental issues in this area and the planning of a series of short- and long-term initiatives.

A new working group will be unfettered by the limiting assumptions of the past and will contribute new energy and new ideas. On the other hand, many of its members may be unaware of the synagogue's past efforts, and may needlessly repeat past mistakes. The standing committee may be less inclined to take on the larger task of rethinking their themes and reconfiguring their programs; they may be happy running the programs as they are. Yet they might feel slighted by the creation of a new entity. Ultimately the choice of whether to work within the committee system or to create ad hoc working groups will depend on how active the committees have been, and how forward-thinking and flexible their members are. A moribund committee, or one that is dominated by controlling and unimaginative insiders, is not an appropriate group to carry out an exploration.

On the other hand, a powerful committee can undermine the work of what it considers to be an "upstart" group whose presence they resent. The most effective solution is probably to create some amalgam of the standing committee and the free-standing group, either by bringing in newcomers to the existing committee, or inviting key committee members to join the new working group.

Coming after the long, intensive effort expended on the community conversations, the beginning of the exploration phase is a natural juncture for a change in leadership. Some members of the task force may wish to join one of the exploration groups; others might want to resign from the task force entirely. Similarly, some members of the leadership team might be ready to move on to other positions of responsibility within the synagogue, or to different types of volunteer work. This creates another opportunity to promote members of the task force to the leadership team and to reach out to the congregation and involve new people in the exploration groups. It is important to remember, however, that the new participants will be at a very different place from veterans of the process. These new members should be oriented in a variety of ways—through written materials, one-on-one discussions, and an orientation session that launches the exploratory phase. A model for such an orientation session appears on page 252.

What Happens during the Exploration Phase?

The exploratory phase combines inquiry, experimentation, and planning. "Inquiry" means asking difficult questions and weighing a range of possible answers. For example, a group whose theme is youth might consider the following questions at the outset:

- What are the goals of teen learning? What is the relative importance of the following goals?
  - to keep teens connected to Jewish life
  - to keep teens connected to the synagogue
  - to teach teens additional Jewish content
  - to connect teens to their Jewish peers
  - to offer teens a safe Jewish environment for hanging out and seeking support
  - to teach teens about Jewish approaches to some of their dilemmas
  - to prepare teens to render service to the community
  - to inspire teens to work in the synagogue in a meaningful capacity
- Given the time pressures on adolescents in terms of their academic work and extracurricular activities, how much time should we expect teenagers to devote to Jewish living and learning?

- Given our goals, who are the most appropriate teachers? How do we recruit and/or train them?

To answer these questions, members of the group would read articles, reports, or excerpts from books related to both adolescence and Jewish education. They might invite speakers to address them. They would seek to identify exemplary youth programs, gather information on them, and determine their strengths and limitations. After fleshing out some promising models, they might convene several focus groups of adolescent congregants and their parents.

The Temple in Atlanta developed a generic inquiry guide for each of their exploration groups; this was modified further by Congregation Beth Torah in Kansas City (see pp. 246–247).

At some point in the process of inquiry, members of the group will have a sense that they have raised the key issues and investigated the major initiatives. This is a sign that it is time to move from inquiry into experimentation. The experiments sponsored by the exploration group can build on the earlier ones and incorporate suggestions that were made in the community conversations. Based on the research they have conducted, they should lay out a range of initiatives that might further their goals. In evaluating the alternatives, a force-field analysis might be a useful tool. For each option under consideration, the group would list the factors that would enable this option to succeed in one column, and the factors that might inhibit its success in another. They would assess as best they could the strength of these factors. For example, imagine that one of the alternatives under consideration is the creation of an alternative track to the religious school, which parents and children would attend together. The following is what one congregation's force-field diagram might look like:

The choice between various options will depend on balancing realities (such as: how much will it cost, and can we raise the money?) and values (is this worth a major fund-raising effort?). As the different options are weighed, it may turn out that certain pieces of information are missing

Research Guide of Congregation Beth Torah of Kansas City

1. What is the focus of this action group?

   - What does it mean in general?

   - What message did the congregation deliver through the community conversations?

   - How do we as a group want to define the focus for this investigation?

2. What is happening at our synagogue in regard to this focus?

   - What programs have been held within the past two years that "address" this focus or theme?

   - What traditions (if any) does our congregation have in regard to this focus?

   - What attitudes do our members have regarding this focus?

3. What is happening at other congregations (Jewish and other) in regard to this focus?

   - What programs have they done that could be connected to this focus?

   - What has contributed to the success or failure of those programs?

   - What attitude do the other congregations seem to have (i.e.,

---

policies, written material, frequency of related programming) with regard to this focus?

4. What does the Reform Movement say about this focus? What propositions have been discussed at UAHC Biennials? What have the HUC, UAHC, CCAR, NATE, or program directors of other congregations written about this focus?

- Are there articles in *Reform Judaism* or other magazines about our focus?

5. What does the Jewish tradition say about this focus?

- Traditional texts like the Torah and Talmud?
- Modern Jewish philosophers?

6. What secular solutions/information are pertinent to this topic?

- Do corporations or businesses deal with similar topics? How?
- Do schools/universities deal with similar topics? How?

Option:
Parent-Child Learning Havurot

ENABLING FACTORS

- Interest expressed at the community conversations

- Good feedback from Congregation X, which has been doing this for 3 years

- An active core group of first-grade parents, who have studied with the rabbi on a weekly basis

- A grant from the X foundation to cover our costs for the first 2 years might be available

INHIBITING FACTORS

- Many parents still assume that their role is simply to drop off their children

- Such a program would require a part-time coordinator and X new teachers

- Potential participants might be discouraged if an additional fee were charged

Questions:

1. Assuming we had the funds to pay them, could we find the right staff for this program?

2. Should we add an additional grade each year? If not, how would the graduates of this program be integrated with students who have been through religious school?

3. What will the effects of the program be on the religious school families who do not choose to enroll?

(such as whether appropriate staff members could be found, or whether materials are already available). Once this information is obtained, it is likely that a consensus will emerge as to the best option(s) to pursue. The group might agree on short-, medium-, and long-term strategies. It might divide into three sub-groups: the first to oversee implementation of short-term projects, the second to plan in detail middle-range ones, and the third to assess the feasibility of the more ambitious long-term plan.

Though the creation of innovative programs is essential, preparing congregants to participate is equally important. Thus the final responsibility of the group is communication and marketing: informing congregants of the new opportunities and persuading them to give these programs a try. The challenge is to go beyond the fliers, brochures, bulletin notices, and announcements from the *bimah* to find a more direct and personal way to grab people's attention and pique their interest.

Maximizing the Power of the Exploration Phase

By the time the exploration phase is reached (somewhere between one and two years after readiness was begun), some members of the task force may have become bored, some may feel burnt out, and most will be itching for action. They may become so impatient with inquiry that they begin lobbying for the creation and/or replication of certain programs, without considering either the full range of options or the full impact of their choice. The pressure to rush to program should be resisted politely but firmly. It would be better to allow impatient task force members to resign (with thanks and recognition for their efforts) than to lose this opportunity for setting a successful future course.

A great deal hangs in the balance—not only the quality of future programs, but also the precedent that is set for how changes are made in the years to come. A decision-making process that is thorough and deliberate will increase the chances that the resultant programs appeal to a broad spectrum of potential learners. If the exploration groups succeed, they will set a high standard for future change efforts, creating an expectation in the congregation that change is predicated on thoughtful planning. By modeling this type of planning, the exploration groups (be they standing committees, ad hoc task forces, or some combination of the two) can become incubators for future congregational leadership.

What follows are some suggestions for launching the exploratory groups in a way that will increase their chances for success:

1. Select the participants carefully.

The leadership of each group should consist of a chair (or two co-chairs), a liaison from the leadership team, and a liaison from the professional staff. It is important to include in the group several members of the board of directors, who can provide a reality check in terms of finances and governance, and who can serve as advocates within the board when the plan is complete. It is important to include members of the relevant standing committees. You may wish to refer back to chapter 6 for the qualities these leaders should have, and the constituencies that should be represented.

2. Each group should be given a "charter" that includes:

- a statement of the theme (including relevant comments that were made at the community conversations);

- a suggestion for possible meeting topics, including relevant exercises and text study resources. If it seems appropriate, a tentative timeline might also be given;

- a clear sense of whom the group is accountable to (the task force? the leadership team? the board of directors? the chairs of standing committees?), and what they are accountable for;

- a mechanism for communication among the various exploration groups (whose themes are likely to be somewhat overlapping) and between the groups and the leadership team.

3. A joint orientation session should be held for all the exploration groups.

Rabbi Sam Joseph created the outline for an orientation program on page 252. Its two chief goals are: 1) to orient new members of the working groups to the planning process and its key concepts, and 2) to give the groups their "charter."

4. The exploration should be both challenging and nurturing.

Participation in this group should involve much more than attending meetings. Members can be asked to read articles and excerpts from books related to their theme, visit synagogues with innovative programs, do research on the Internet to identify exemplary programs throughout North America, and interview the staff and lay leaders involved with those programs. At the same time, members of the exploration group should feel that they are gaining a great deal from their participation: an exposure to new ideas, an opportunity to discuss important Jewish issues, and a close collegial relationship with fellow committee members. It is the responsibility of the leadership team to make sure that this balance between challenging and nurturing is maintained.

Should There Be a Formal End to the Exploration Phase?

As with most of the questions posed in this book, the answer is, *it depends*. Closure provides a sense of emotional satisfaction after such a long, drawn-out procedure. Participants in the exploration phase (and indeed, in the entire process) will feel justifiable satisfaction if they can conclude with the results of their efforts written up in the form of a report approved by the board of directors. They will feel proud to end their work by being honored by the congregation. On the other hand, if the exploration phase is truly successful, its participants will realize that they are on a never-ending

Outline for an Orientation for Working Groups

1. Text Study. This should be done in small groups led by members of the task force.

2. An Exercise to Get People Thinking about Learning in the Congregation. See the exercises in chapter 7 for possible samples.

3. Two Short Vision Presentations. Two people (perhaps a lay person and a staff person) should offer their own vision of what learning in the congregation might become when the working groups have done their job.

4. Presentation of a Summary of the Data Gathered from Community Conversations. This can be short; the point is to establish that the topics of the working groups came from the CCs.

5. Meet by Working Groups. This preliminary discussion should focus on the different ways in which the group's theme can be articulated. The goal is to arrive at a common definition of the theme and a list of related sub-themes.

6. General Discussion of Each Group's "Charter."

ONE FINAL SUGGESTION:

Consider whether this might be the appropriate forum to honor members of the task force.

---

journey. Though they already will have implemented some changes, and recommended even larger ones, a great deal of work remains. The programs they have developed need to be evaluated and fine-tuned. The long-range plan they have proposed will need advocates and an implementation team to become a reality. And, as often happens, some new issues or ambitious ideas may have bubbled up toward the very end of the process, and these might merit an exploration of their own.

Ideally, a core of those who were part of each exploration group will be willing to take on these responsibilities. Ideally, the key staff and a critical mass of task force and leadership team members will apply the lessons they have learned from the process and their newly acquired leadership skills to other realms of synagogue life. Ideally, these leaders will feel that they have gained so much from the process that they will be willing to continue.

The challenge at the end of the exploration period is to maximize both of these goods—to provide closure and a sense of appreciation for a job well done, on one hand, and to remain mindful of the work that lies ahead, on the other. The final chapter offers some suggestions as to how these sometimes contradictory impulses can be balanced.

The following excerpts from the report of one exploration group exemplifies the way achievements can be reviewed at the same time that future direction is given. The Adult Learning Task Force at Congregation Beth Am in Los Altos Hills, CA, staffed by educators Lisa Langer and Rabbi Josh Zweiback, met for a period of fifteen months. This report, edited by Langer and Zweiback, distilled the group's deliberations and decisions, conveying both the concrete recommendations and the enduring issues.

• • •

Report of the Adult Learning Task Force
at Congregation Beth Am

Congregation Beth Am is a large, vibrant, Reform congregation that has spent a number of years focusing an enormous amount of time, energy and resources on educational transformation. After developing a variety of family learning programs and revitalizing a number of youth education experiences—the time came to concentrate on lifelong learning for adults.

For many years Beth Am, with the leadership of a small yet active Adult Education Committee, has supported a diverse and extensive program of meaningful adult Jewish learning opportunities for our congregants and other members of our community. However, our commitment to being a learning congregation compels us constantly to re-examine our program by asking ourselves the following questions:

1. Are we doing all we can to provide opportunities for any and all congregants who want to learn?

2. Are we being sensitive to the different needs and learning styles of all of our congregants?

3. Are we identifying and overcoming obstacles to engaging in study that inhibit lifelong learning?

4. Have some of our programs outlived their usefulness?

5. How should we experiment with new learning paradigms (e.g., individualized study and on-line learning) that may offer unique opportunities to expand and enrich our programs?

6. What is the best possible way to utilize our new Adult Learning Coordinator to improve and extend our program?

7. How can we finance our growing program in a responsible fashion?

8. Ultimately, are we as a congregation enabling our congregants to become knowledgeable, participating, Reform Jews?

The Adult Learning Task Force (ALTF) was created to explore these and related issues. As we shared our hopes, experiences and questions over the year, we began to develop a somewhat clearer (but by no means perfectly clear) vision of what lifelong adult Jewish learning should look like at Congregation Beth Am. This process included a substantial amount of research, study, and brainstorming.

We believe that we could be doing more or should be doing some things differently. There is within the task force a shared perception that a core group of congregants comprises the majority of those who take advantage of our programming. Such a group certainly represents only a minority of our membership. Thus, there are a great number of people whose needs and interests we must understand and address. But in addition to evaluating our programs and formulating strategies that will bring new learners into our community, we have also spent considerable time reflecting upon what adult Jewish learning is, who adult Jewish learners are, why learners choose to participate, and how we can best create learning experiences that are meaningful and authentically Jewish.

Through a process involving both professional and lay leaders, our congregation has created a "Lifelong Jewish Learning Map." . . . The map represents our communal ideal of what a knowledgeable Reform Jew could know, do, and value at various stages in her/his life. In the spirit of Reform Judaism, we hope this map will serve as a guide, helping individuals make choices from among the many learning opportunities that will emerge. We hope to enable every adult learner to establish and achieve personal education goals within the context of a learning congregation. . . .

RECOMMENDATIONS:
How Can We Implement the Lifelong Jewish Learning Map?

1. Develop an "educational intake" form that will help us to assess the learner's current level of Jewish knowledge, preferred learning style, educational interests and goals.

2. Offer adult learning opportunities at various levels, introductory through advanced. Articulate clear expectations regarding both the learners' incoming knowledge and the hoped for outcome at the conclusion of the course of study. This will help beginners feel less intimidated and assure advanced learners that their continuing Jewish growth is important to the community.

3. Offer both independent and group study opportunities in a variety of forms—with professional guidance—that address a spectrum of previous knowledge, background and interests.

4. Build our Hevrutah-Study Partnerships program that allows learners to explore any subject area of the map at any time on any level.

5. Experiment! Offer a variety of levels and types of learning opportunities that reflect the content of the Lifelong Jewish Learning Map.

6. Each year, focus on 2–3 content areas of the Lifelong Jewish Learning Map.

7. Create opportunities for participants to put their learning into action. . . .

RECOMMENDATIONS:

1. Learning opportunities should be scheduled at times of maximum convenience for our various learning communities.

2. Offer variety and creativity in scheduling. While ideally lifelong learning would include ongoing learning experiences that build upon one another, we also must be practical and flexible when scheduling. Examples of creative scheduling include:
   • Structure classes so that occasional absences will not be obstacles to learning.
   • Offer double sessions of some of our classes on different nights of the week or times of the day.

- Vary the timeframe of courses: weekly, monthly, year-long, six months, three sessions, weekend, day-long intensive, brief and extended travel courses, etc.
- Provide on-line learning opportunities so that congregants have the option to 'plug-in' whenever and wherever they may be.

3. As a desire for more time with our families is often in conflict with our desire to engage in lifelong Jewish learning, we should continue to explore ways in which the entire family can participate together in aspects of our educational program.

4. At the same time, care must be taken not to over-program. We have limited resources that must be wisely allocated. . . .

Our Lifelong Jewish Learning Map will be published and distributed in the next few months. Initial reactions to the map in a presentation that we made about it at our adult learning retreat were mixed. Some congregants felt that our goals were too lofty—"people won't do what you are suggesting," said one. Others in the group, however, responded by saying that their families were already doing some of what the Map suggests. One congregant argued that without addressing the issue of motivation, our work on content is meaningless. Clearly, we need to do a better job of publicizing our new *keruv* (drawing near) efforts! The facilitator of this session did point out that a group of lay leaders was working on that issue currently.

Clearly, we have much work to do. We feel, though, that the work of the task force will guide us and help us in our efforts. It has helped us prioritize our current goals and better structure our time. By focusing on *keruv*, by using the map as a guiding tool, and by continually opening ourselves to experimentation, we hope to build a stronger, deeper, and broader community of lifelong Jewish learners.

Having labored for months, or even years, members of an exploration group are likely to be weary at the conclusion of the process. They may be hesitant to devote additional time and energy to writing up a report, wishing to do no more than pass along their recommendations to the board. Despite this natural and fully understandable resistance, it is important for the group to persevere and to produce a document that reviews the process, explains the issues that were debated, enumerates the principles that informed the conclusions, and justifies the conclusions themselves. Such a report will help any congregant, and any new staff member, understand in a deep sense the intent and significance of the new initiatives. In time, as the memory of their deliberations fades, the report will serve a useful purpose even for the original members of the exploration group, enabling them to reconnect with the vision and the passion that fueled their work.

12

The *Mishkan:*
A Source of Inspiration
for the Long Journey

Every tradition has at its center a "master narrative," whose frequent retelling serves to etch in people's memories core values and key historical events. The Jewish master narrative—the story of the Exodus—tells of the Jewish people's transformation from slavery to freedom. Each time we tell the story (at length at the Passover seder and, in more abbreviated fashion, in daily prayer and holiday celebrations) we are reminded of our origins as the Children of Israel, of the bitterness of slavery, and of God's power to redeem the oppressed. Our narrative reaches its climax at the parting of the Red Sea and the miraculous way the Israelites were saved, and many versions of the story end there. But the biblical story continues, recounting the forty years of wandering in the wilderness, before the promised land is reached. This part of the Jewish master narrative is told less frequently, and with considerably less gusto; but it has as much, and perhaps more, power to inspire contemporary American Jews.

Though the former slaves were physically free, they were hardly free spiritually. They had barely reached the Red Sea when they began complaining, pining for the comforts of old, forgetting the pain and indignity of slavery. Though God provided for their hunger, thirst, and physical safety, their faith wavered. When Moses absented himself to receive the Torah at Mount Sinai, the Israelites demanded that Aaron build a golden calf. Later, their spies toured the Land of Israel and reported that they would never be able to defeat its giant inhabitants. God concluded that the generation of slavery would be unable to undertake the responsibilities of freedom in their own land. To paraphrase an old commercial, "God could take the people out of Egypt, but God couldn't take Egypt out of the people." The former slaves were condemned to wander in the wilderness for forty years, until a new generation replaced them.

Perhaps this second half of the Exodus narrative is told less frequently because it focuses more on the failings of human beings than on the wonders of God. But it captures enduring truths, among them the fact that psychological change may be more difficult than physical change. To quote one management consultant, "The outlook, attitudes, values, self-images, ways of thinking that had been functional in the past have to 'die' before people are ready for life in the present."[1]

The master narrative of the Israelites' wanderings in the wilderness contains important lessons for a congregation embarking on change. It teaches us that it takes time to make the psychological transition from one state to another. No sooner do we encounter freedom than we begin to romanticize a life of more limited choice. Our faith in our leaders falters to the point that we need constant proof of their capabilities. If we could only have more patience with the vicissitudes of the journey, more trust in our leaders, and a greater commitment to our vision, we might arrive at our destination more quickly.

Congregational leaders launching an effort to create a congregation of learners are likely to encounter many of the problems that beset Moses and the Children of Israel. For all their complaints about "the way things are," congregants who are relatively uninvolved in synagogue life may be surprisingly wedded to conventional customs and institutions. A congregant who attends prayer services only on the High Holidays may expect the service to be the same year in and year out, and become incensed when changes are made. Others may feel like the religious school parent who said, "Part of being Jewish is hating religious school; I hated it, and I expect my son to hate it too." Some congregants will be skeptical, and even feel threatened by the synagogue's attempt to become a congregation of learners. Is the new vision an attempt to dictate new terms for membership in the synagogue? Does it imply that those who are not learners are incomplete, or even bad, Jews? Is there really a promised land, and can it be as rewarding as the vision suggests?

What Can We Carry to Sustain Us?

In the last third of the book of Exodus, God comes up with a plan for bolstering the spirits of the Israelites, enabling them to feel the presence of God in their lives. God instructs Moses and the Israelites to build a *mishkan,* a temporary, portable tabernacle. Commentators have stressed that the *mishkan* was built as a concession to human frailty. God, who dwells everywhere, does not require a special sanctuary. The people, on the other hand, needed physical evidence that God was in their midst.

If the wanderings of the Israelites in the wilderness can be seen as paradigmatic of a congregation's journey toward more intense and more fulfilling learning, what would be the equivalent of the *mishkan*? What might a synagogue carry with it (physically or metaphorically) on its journey that would remind members of their common vision and of the holiness of their task?

Several possible answers suggest themselves. First, the congregation's vision should be embodied as concretely as possible in both words and images. Once consensus is reached on the vision statement, it should be publicized widely. It can become the subject of sermons and study sessions, displayed in the hallways, and reproduced in brochures and other promotional materials. A member of the congregation who is artistically inclined might be asked to design a logo that captures the essence of the vision. Congregations have displayed their logos on mugs, tote bags, and bumper stickers, and distributed them to parents on the opening day of school, to committee members on Volunteer Appreciation Day, and so on.

A second way to inspire people on their journey is by telling stories of learning "heroes." Just as businesses display prominently the picture of the "employee of the month," the synagogue might display the picture and story of the "learner of the month." Synagogue bulletins often feature donors and active volunteers; what if the bulletin were to begin profiling exemplary learners?

A third way would be for the bulletin to include a discussion guide to the weekly Torah portion, the Hebrew word of the week, or other features related to learning. One congregation created an attractive and glossy insert to the bulletin that explained its learning initiative. Another congregation dedicated the inside pages of every bulletin to stories, puzzles, questions, and answers on different themes.

Finally, "low hanging fruit"—the experimental programs that are the vanguard of the change effort—are excellent ways of capturing and sustaining interest. Every time a successful educational program is offered, its publicity materials should indicate that this is part of the congregation's ongoing effort to become a congregation of learners.

Benchmarks of Success

The leaders of the change effort, the members of the task force, and the leadership team may face difficulties of their own as the journey proceeds. They may feel burnt out and underappreciated, frustrated with the lack of response from uninvolved members. "We've been talking about a vision of learning for two (or three, or four) years, and they *still* don't get it!" It would be easy for these leaders to feel the impatience, and even the anger, that Moses displayed when the Israelites complained, yet again, about the lack of water.

These active and involved volunteers require sustenance of their own. They need to be reminded, periodically, of the value of the ultimate goal. And they need to feel genuinely appreciated for their efforts. This type of appreciation goes beyond the once-a-year awards luncheon or the special dinner at which certificates are given. It requires day-to-day recognition and gratitude, shown in small ways—the smile of a staff member, or the comments of the congregation's president.

Along with these intangible measures, what will sustain the task force and leadership team the most is tangible evidence of their success. This can be accomplished through a simple monitoring process. As early as the readiness phase, the task force can begin gathering baseline data about the state of learning in the congregation. They can collect additional data every six months. Over time, this will enable them to discern which efforts have been most successful. This type of data collection need not be scientifically rigorous; the purpose is not to publish a definitive study, but to get a sense of the results. It is likely that some of the answers sought will defy precise measurement, and estimates will have to suffice. For example, it may be too cumbersome to count precisely the number of participants at a large program, but counting the number of cars in the parking lot or cups of coffee consumed might yield an approximate number. This type of data gathering is fine, if used consistently. If, to take another example, the number of books borrowed from the synagogue library increases over time, that is one measure of an increased interest in learning.

The following is a list of questions that congregations have asked themselves in an effort to track their success:

1. What new learning programs have been created/implemented during the past six months?

2. How many people participated in each of the following learning activities? (list activities) What evidence do you have for this?

3. What new learning dimensions or components were added on to existing programs during the past six months? Are any planned for the future?

4. Is study included in committee and board meetings? (list the committee, date, and type of study)

5. Have any new constituencies for learning been identified? Who are they? What plans are being made to serve them?

6. Are more people involved in planning the learning component of various programs? Who are these people, and how did they get involved?

7. Is a new cadre of teachers or study facilitators being developed? How? Who are these new teachers?

8. What new teaching or learning resources have been developed?

9. What evidence is there for a growing awareness in the congregation-at-large that learning is a priority?

Visible signs of success along any of these dimensions will provide the best inspiration and sustenance.

Giving Freely Is Its Own Reward

Nearly a third of the Book of Exodus (chapters 25–40) is taken up with a description of the building of the *mishkan*. These chapters contain long lists of the materials that were collected, the dimensions of the structure and its furnishings, and God's instructions to the builder. Most remarkable about the process is that the precious metals, fine woods, and other rare materials that were used were all contributed *voluntarily*. One might imagine that the *mishkan* would be financed by a form of taxation, but the Bible makes it clear that this was not the case. The text uses the same phrase four times to describe this free-will offering: "every person whose heart so moves him" the text says, brought gifts for the building of the *mishkan*.

In its own way, the building of the *mishkan* is as miraculous as the parting of the Red Sea. The same people who were grumbling constantly a few chapters back (and would continue to grumble as their journey wore on) here are seized by a generosity of spirit. What moved them to contribute so freely to this effort? *How* this happened remains one of the enduring mysteries of this story; *that* it happened can serve as an inspiration to all who work to build and rebuild their own synagogues. Much has been said in this book about congregants who are only marginally involved or who have complaints about the synagogue (though they might not be as vocal as the Israelites were). In response, some synagogue leaders berate these members for their apathy and attempt to set higher standards for the membership. The building of the *mishkan* offers a different perspective. It reminds us that even those who are most peripheral and most recalcitrant are capable of great generosity, generosity that leads to their involvement. Again and again, in my work with congregations, I have seen members who were originally inactive come forth and give freely of their time, energy, and talent. In the process they felt more connected to the synagogue and began to participate more actively.

A final point of inspiration may be drawn from the *mishkan*. At least one commentator, Mordechai Yosef Leiner of Izbica, remarked on the teamwork that it took to build it, and the humility of the builders. He wrote:

> In the building of the Tabernacle, all Israel were joined in their hearts; no one felt superior to his fellow. At first, each skilled individual did his own part of the construction, and it seemed to each one that his own work was extraordinary. Afterward, they saw how their several contributions to the "service" of the tabernacle were integrated—all the boards, the sockets, the curtains, and loops fit together as if one person had done it all. Then they realized how each of them had depended on the other. Then they understood that what they had accomplished was not by virtue of their own skill alone, but that the Holy One had guided the hands of everyone who had worked on the Tabernacle. They had merely joined in completing its master building plans, so that "It came to pass that the Tabernacle was one." (Exodus 36:13) Moreover, the one who made the holy ark itself was unable to feel superior to the one who had made only the courtyard tent pegs.[2]

I have seen similar teamwork time and again among members of a congregation. Everyone contributed what they were able to, and more, not because of any honor or reward they would receive, but because of the pleasure and satisfaction of working with their fellow congregants on a task that was sacred to them all. I suppose their generosity of spirit should not surprise us. They are, after all, the descendants of the Israelites who built the *mishkan*.

13

Becoming a Learning Congregation

The journey toward being a congregation of learners will be long and complicated. As with any journey, it will have its ups and downs, times when the travelers forge ahead at full speed, and times when they hesitate to take the next step. But as the exploration phase moves forward, momentum will pick up and the ultimate destination will come sharply into focus. New formats for Jewish learning will be created and increasing numbers of congregants will be drawn to them. The pool of teachers and mentors will expand as veteran learners assume new roles and responsibilities. Even those who are least involved will be exposed to some memorable learning experiences, whether at a new member brunch, a meeting of religious school parents, a Shabbat service, or a holiday celebration. Walking through the hallways and perusing the bulletin, congregants will be bombarded with the message that learning is important, and that a wide variety of opportunities are open to them. The cumulative effect of these changes will be the beginning of a cultural shift in which learning is seen as an essential part of being Jewish and being a member of the congregation.

If the process outlined in this book is followed, a second cultural shift should also occur—a shift in the congregation's ability to be self-reflective and self-critical. It will no longer be a "given" that the vision belongs to the rabbi, or that certain programs and procedures are set in stone. Lay and professional leaders will have seen, first hand, the benefits of shared leadership. The professionals will feel less isolated and beleaguered, while the lay leaders will be more invested and better informed. Together they will have reaped the rewards of soliciting the feedback of congregants. Having researched a variety of new programs and deliberated on the pros and cons of each, they will be more open to experimentation. In short, having invested its collective intelligence in the process of becoming a congregation of learners, the synagogue will find itself becoming a learning congregation.

The term *learning congregation* derives from a concept that has become popular in the business world, the *learning organization.* Peter Senge, the organizational theorist most responsible for introducing this term into our vocabulary, defines learning organizations as:

> organizations where people continually expand their capacity to create the results they truly desire, where new and expansive patterns of thinking are nurtured, where collective aspiration is set free, and where people are continually learning how to learn together.[1]

It is not sufficient, Senge argues, for organizations to be reactive, dealing with problems as they arise; the world changes too rapidly. The truly successful organization not only articulates its vision, but also monitors its progress toward that vision and is on the lookout for ways in which the vision is incomplete and in need of revision. This requires a continuous cycle of learning and action as the organization learns to scan and interpret its environment, explore a range of possibilities, take action, assess the outcome, and, without missing a beat, begin the cycle anew.

Successful synagogues require a comparable capacity—to think clearly about their goals, conduct rigorous and scrupulous self-assessments, and brainstorm creative initiatives. Making the connection between Jews and the Jewish tradition is a perennial challenge. While some synagogues have hit on what seems a magic formula, there is no guarantee that their programs can be transplanted to other congregations. Nor can these synagogues rest on their laurels; it seems unlikely that the magic will endure indefinitely. To truly serve its current members and appeal to its future ones, every synagogue needs to become a learning congregation.

It sounds like a daunting challenge, and it is. But two factors make it slightly less daunting. First, as the theory and practice of the learning organization reach further into the workplace, congregants will become increasingly comfortable with this way of operating. Second, people will discover how deeply satisfying it is to work with a group that is continually learning to do its job better. As Senge puts it:

> Learning organizations are possible because, deep down, we are all learners. . . . [N]ot only is it in our nature to learn but we love to learn. Most of us at one time or another have been part of a great "team," a group of people who functioned together in an extraordinary way—who trusted one another, who complemented each other's strengths and compensated for each others' limitations, who had common goals that were larger than individual goals, and who produced extraordinary results. I have met many people who have experienced this sort of profound teamwork—in sports, or in the performing arts, or in business. Many say that they have spent much of their life looking for that experience again. What they experienced was a learning organization. The team that became great didn't start off great—it *learned* how to produce extraordinary results.[2]

After working together to become a congregation of learners, the leadership team and the task force will experience what being part of an extraordinary team, and accomplishing extraordinary things is all about. That experience, like the experience of Jewish learning, will be its own reward.

The Jewish Connection

Earlier in this book I noted that the concept of *lifelong learning,* which was first coined in the 1970s, is closely connected to the Jewish concept of *torah lishmah,* which is centuries old. The type of learning exemplified in the learning organization also has a traditional Jewish analog, the talmudic debate. The Talmud, a written record of legal debates that took place in Israel and Babylonia between the first and sixth centuries, is known for its nonlinear style, in which law and narrative are interwoven, and one tangent is built upon the other. The laws of the Talmud are embedded in this very complex and sometimes opaque context.

For example, tractate *Pesachim* 114a records a debate between *Bet* (literally *the House of,* meaning, the followers of) Hillel and their rivals, *Bet* Shamai, concerning the proper order of the *brakhot* (blessings) in the kiddush at the Passover seder: Which should come first, the *brakha* over the wine, or the *brakha* over the holiday? Halfway through the discussion, the text states clearly that the law follows Bet Hillel. But that doesn't end the discussion, which concerns itself with the reasoning behind the decision: Was the decision based on the fact that Bet Hillel cite two reasons, while Bet Shamai cite only one? Is it because a *bat kol* (a heavenly voice) was heard, declaring Bet Hillel to be correct? This leads to another issue: Is it permissible for a *bat kol* to be used to settle a debate? Clearly, the rabbis' interests go far beyond the order of the two *brakhot.* For them the debate has a spiritual dimension; the dialogue itself is holy.

If one simply wanted to know the outcome of this debate one could bypass the Talmud entirely and simply look in the Passover Hagadah. In fact, all the laws of the Talmud are recorded elsewhere in more straightforward books of codes. But one doesn't study Talmud to learn about the end result; one studies it to enter into the debate and into the spirit that animates the law. In the modern period, as many Jews became less concerned with many of the specific laws, the context in which they were embedded, the legends, biblical citations, and arguments assumed greater importance. This rich and evocative context is what enabled Judaism to maintain its flexibility over the centuries, adapting to new settings and new circumstances, while remaining faithful to the essential values.

The study of Talmud helps Jews maintain a balance between the eternal values of the tradition and the temporal exigencies of their environment. Similarly, the skills and expectations of the learning organization can help congregations maintain their own sense of balance between past and present. The content of its programs are important in the here and now, but only an understanding of the context that led to their creation will keep the programs fresh and relevant.

A synagogue can (and many do) run on automatic pilot, scheduling the same events in the same manner year in and year out. Such a synagogue may attract members who are looking for the typical menu of services. It may even have a core of active and devoted members who like things just the way they are. But if it continues to operate in this fashion, this synagogue will lose touch with both the tradition and the contemporary realities. If it doesn't engage in self-reflection, it won't be able to separate the successful from the unsuccessful or the ancillary from the essential. If it doesn't experiment and learn from its experiments, it will be unable to imagine, and invent, a better future.

A famous talmudic debate in tractate *Kidushin* 40b concerns the relative merits of study and action:

> Rabbi Tarfon and the Elders were once reclining in the upper story of Nitzah's house, in Lydda, when this question was raised: "Is study greater, or practice?" Rabbi Tarfon answered, saying: "Practice is greater." Rabbi Akiva answered, saying: "Study is greater, for it leads to practice." They all answered and said: "Study is greater, for it leads to practice."

Though framed as a debate, the point of the discussion seems to be that study and action are complementary. Study without action is incomplete; action without study is mindless.

One can imagine a similar debate taking place between the advocates of a congregation of learners, and those of a learning congregation. Asking which is more important is another way of asking which goal should take priority. Inspired by the foregoing talmudic debate, I would argue that the two cannot be separated so easily. A congregation of learners that is not, at the same time, a learning congregation, will not retain the vitality of its learning for very long. A learning congregation that is not, at the same time, a congregation of learners will have difficulty remaining rooted in the Jewish tradition. Jewish learning is both a process and a product.

NOTES

CHAPTER 1

1. Bernard Lazerwitz et al., *Jewish Choices: American Jewish Denominationalism* (Albany: SUNY Press, 1998), p. 125.
2. It is estimated that only 2 percent of American Jews aged 16–19 participated in an "educational trip" to Israel; see Jack Wertheimer, "Jewish Education in the United States" (1999) in *The American Jewish Yearbook* (Philadelphia: Jewish Publication Society), p. 94. Approximately 40 percent of students enrolled in a Jewish school are enrolled in a day school; see David Shluker, "The Impact of Jewish Day Schools: A Briefing Paper" (JESNA, July 1998). Though estimates of JCC membership vary, it does not exceed 20 percent; see Wertheimer, p. 84.
3. Data from the 1990 National Jewish Population Study show that although 66 percent claim to have been members of a synagogue at some point, only 45 percent were members at the time the survey was conducted; see Lazerwitz et al., *Jewish Choices*, p. 125.
4. Wade Clark Roof, *A Generation of Seekers* (San Francisco: HarperCollins, 1994), pp. 4–5.
5. Donald E. Miller, *Reinventing American Protestantism* (Berkeley: University of California Press, 1997), pp. 184–85.
6. These projects have been described by Lisa Malik, in "Synagogue Change in America: A Map of Synagogue Change Initiatives" (New York: Mandel Foundation, December 1998).
7. C. Ellis Nelson, *Congregations: Their Power to Form and Transform* (Atlanta: John Knox, 1988), p. 7.

CHAPTER 2

1. See Samuel Heilman, *Synagogue Life* (Chicago: University of Chicago Press, 1973).
2. Stuart Schoenfeld, "Folk Judaism, Elite Judaism and the Role of the Bar Mitzvah in the Development of the Synagogue and Jewish School in America," *Contemporary Jewry* 9 (1988): pp. 67–85.
3. Robert Wuthnow, *Sharing the Journey: Support Groups and America's New Quest for Community* (New York: The Free Press, 1994), p. 65.
4. The following quotations are taken from Schuster's study, "Perceptions of ECE Text Study" (unpublished report commissioned by the Experiment in Congregational Education, 1997).
5. For ethnographies see Joseph Reimer, *Succeeding at Jewish Education* (Philadelphia: Jewish Publication Society, 1998); David Schoem, *Ethnic Survival in America: An Ethnography of a Jewish Afternoon School* (Atlanta: Scholar's Press, 1989); and Samuel Heilman, "Inside the Jewish School," in *What We Know About Jewish Education,* ed. by Stuart Kelman (Los Angeles: Torah Aura Productions, 1992). See also Barry Holtz, *Best Practices Project: The Supplementary School* (Cleveland: Council for Initiatives in Jewish Education, 1993).

CHAPTER 3

1. For example, though interesting learning opportunities are available at a number of Orthodox congregations, I was unable to persuade leaders of these congregations, or even people knowledgeable about their programs, to contribute to this volume.
2. Harold Schulweis, *For Those Who Can't Believe* (New York: HarperCollins, 1994), p. 3.
3. Readers interested in learning more about this congregation will want to refer to Rabbi Schwarz's book, *Finding a Spiritual Home: How a New Generation of Jews Can Transform the American Synagogue* (San Francisco: Jossey Bass, 2000), an account of four exemplary congregations.
4. Interview with Rabbi Harold Schulweis, June 14, 1999.
5. Saul Wachs, "The Prayer of Empathy," *United Synagogue Review,* Spring 1995, p. 25.

CHAPTER 4

1. A fascinating account of a voluntary program that was extremely successful but became controversial when it was made into a requirement may be found in chapter 6 of Joseph Reimer's *Succeeding in Jewish Education* (Philadelphia: Jewish Publication Society, 1997).
2. Senge, Peter et al., *The Dance of Change: The Challenges to Sustaining Momentum in Learning Organizations* (New York: Anchor Doubleday, 1999), p. 33.
3. Some congregations, disliking the elitist connotation of this term, have preferred to call it a steering committee or a core planning group.
4. Edgar Schein, *Organizational Culture and Leadership,* 2nd edition (San Francisco: Jossey Bass, 1992), pp. 334–35.
5. Ibid., p. 342.

CHAPTER 5

1. For a fascinating study of a rabbi's largely unsuccessful attempts to reinvigorate his congregation singlehandedly see Paul Wilkes, *And They Shall Be My People: An American Rabbi and His Congregation* (New York: Atlantic Monthly Press, 1994).
2. Weinberg, Robert, "Corporate Culture," in *The New Frontier in Bank Strategy: Managing People for Results in Turbulent Times* (Homewood, Ill.: Dow Jones-Irwin, 1990).

CHAPTER 6

1. Peter Senge et al., *The Dance of Change* (New York: Doubleday, 1999), p. 39.
2. Laura Samuels and Isa Aron, "Shared Leadership in a Congregational Change Effort," *Jewish Education* 65 (Summer, 1999): pp. 25–41.
3. Eugene Borowitz, "Tsimtsum: A Mystic Model for Contemporary Leadership." Originally published in 1974; reprinted in *What We Know About Jewish Education,* edited by S. Kelman (Los Angeles: Torah Aura Productions, 1992).
4. Jon R. Katzenbach and Douglas K. Smith, "The Discipline of Teams" in *Harvard Business Review,* March–April, 1993, pp. 11–12.

5. For more on responsibility charting, see R. Beckhard and R. T. Harris, *Organizational Transitions* (Reading, Mass.: Addison-Wesley, 1987).
6. B.W. Tuckman and M.A.C. Jensen, "Stages of Small Group Development Revisited," *Group and Organizational Studies* 2 (1977): pp. 419–427.
7. After three years, most advisers reduced the number of days spent with the congregation.
8. Chris Argyris, *Increasing Leadership Effectiveness* (New York: Wiley-Interscience, 1976).
9. Senge et al., *The Dance of Change,* p. 321.
10. Samuels and Aron, "Shared Leadership," p. 32.

CHAPTER 7
1. Burt Nanus, *Visionary Leadership* (San Francisco: Jossey Bass, 1992).
2. See Ronald Heifetz, *Leadership Without Easy Answers* (Cambridge, Mass.: Belknap Press, 1994); Wilfred Drath, "Approaching the Future of Leadership Development," in *The Center for Creative Leadership Handbook of Leadership Development,* ed. by Cynthia McCauley, et al. (Jossey Bass, 1999); and Wilfred Drath and Charles Palus, *Making Common Sense: Leadership as Meaning-making in a Community of Practice* (Greensboro, N.C.: Center for Creative Leadership, 1994).
3. In keeping with the spirit of the change process, Temple Emanu-El considers this statement to be in draft form.
4. This idea originated with Linda Thal, who used it at Leo Baeck Temple in Los Angeles. See Linda Thal, "Reimagining Congregational Education: A Case Study" in *A Congregation of Learners,* ed. by Isa Aron, Sara Lee, and Seymour Rossel (New York: UAHC Press, 1995).

CHAPTER 8
1. Joel Grishaver, *Learning Torah* (New York: UAHC Press, 1990), p. 11.
2. Diane Schuster, "Perceptions of ECE Text Study" (Unpublished report commissioned by the Experiment in Congregational Education, 1997), p. 11.
3. Ibid., p. 15.
4. Joseph Reimer, D. Paolitto, and R. Hersh, *Promoting Moral Growth* (New York: Longman, 1979).
5. Michael Rosenak, *Teaching Jewish Values: A Conceptual Guide* (Jerusalem: Melton Centre for Jewish Education, 1986).
6. Schuster, "Perceptions . . . ," pp. 15–16.
7. Ibid., pp. 20–21.
8. Ibid., p. 20.
9. Dvorah Weisberg, "The Study of Torah as a Religious Act," in *Four Centuries of Jewish Women,* ed. by Ellen Umansky and Diane Ashton, pp. 276–77.
10. See, for example, Rela Geffen Monson, "Response to 'Will More and More Be Known by Fewer and Fewer,'" in *Imagining the Jewish Future,* ed. by David Teutsch (Albany: SUNY Press, 1992), pp. 113–116.
11. David Hartman, *A Heart of Many Rooms: Celebrating the Many Voices Within Judaism* (Woodstock, Vt.: Jewish Lights, 1999), p. 23.

12. Ibid., p.21.
13. Mary Belenky et al., *Women's Ways of Knowing* (New York: Basic Books, 1986), p. 15.
14. Adapted from an outline created by Diane Schuster.
15. Schuster, "Perceptions . . . ," pp. 5–6.
16. Belenky, et al., pp. 83–4.
17. Ibid., p. 84.
18. Schuster, "Perceptions . . . ," p. 18.
19. Diane Schuster, personal communication.
20. See, for example, Robert Kegan, *The Evolving Self* (Cambridge: Harvard University Press, 1982); William Perry, *Forms of Intellectual and Ethical Development in the College Years* (New York: Holt, Rinehart and Winston, 1970); and Jack Mezirow, *Transformative Dimensions of Adult Learning* (San Francisco: Jossey Bass, 1991).
21. Peter Pitzele, *Scripture Windows: Towards a Practice of Bibliodrama* (Los Angeles: Torah Aura, 1998).
22. Jo Milgrom, *Hand-made Midrash* (Philadelphia: Jewish Publication Society, 1992).
23. Rabbi Block told this story in a lecture at HUC-JIR, Los Angeles, in the Fall of 1998.
24. Schuster, "Perceptions . . . ," p. 22.
25. Ibid., p. 23.
26. Thanks to Rabbi Sheldon Marder for assembling these texts.
27. Reprinted in S. Y. Agnon, *Present at Sinai* (Philadelphia: Jewish Publication Society, 1994), pp. 149–150.

CHAPTER 10

1. A series of books that may be helpful to both facilitators and note takers is *The Focus Group Kit* by Richard Krueger, David Morgan, and colleagues (Thousand Oaks, Calif.: Sage Publications, 1998). The six short volumes in this series cover all the logistics of conducting focus groups, from creating the facilitation guide to the analysis of the data.

CHAPTER 12

1. William Bridges, *Managing Transitions* (Reading, Mass.: Addison-Wesley, 1991), p. 37.
2. Lawrence Kushner and Kerry Olitzky, *Sparks Beneath the Surface: A Spiritual Commentary on the Torah* (Northvale, N.J.: Jason Aronson, 1993), pp. 109–110.

CHAPTER 13

1. Peter Senge, *The Fifth Discipline: The Art and Practice of the Learning Organization* (New York: Doubleday, 1990), p. 3.
2. Ibid., p. 4.

About JEWISH LIGHTS Publishing

People of all faiths and backgrounds yearn for books that attract, engage, educate and spiritually inspire.

Our principal goal is to stimulate thought and help all people learn about who the Jewish People are, where they come from, and what the future can be made to hold. While people of our diverse Jewish heritage are the primary audience, our books speak to people in the Christian world as well and will broaden their understanding of Judaism and the roots of their own faith.

We bring to you authors who are at the forefront of spiritual thought and experience. While each has something different to say, they all say it in a voice that you can hear.

Our books are designed to welcome you and then to engage, stimulate and inspire. We judge our success not only by whether or not our books are beautiful and commercially successful, but by whether or not they make a difference in your life.

We at Jewish Lights take great care to produce beautiful books that present meaningful spiritual content in a form that reflects the art of making high quality books. Therefore, we want to acknowledge those who contributed to the production of this book.

Stuart M. Matlins, Publisher

PRODUCTION
Marian B. Wallace & Bridgett Taylor

EDITORIAL
Sandra Korinchak, Emily Wichland,
Martha McKinney & Amanda Dupuis

COVER DESIGN
Lisa Buckley, San Francisco, California

TEXT DESIGN
Chelsea Cloeter, Chelsea Designs, Scotia, New York

COVER & TEXT PRINTING AND BINDING
Versa Press, East Peoria, Illinois

Spirituality

The Women's Torah Commentary: *New Insights from Women Rabbis on the 54 Weekly Torah Portions* Ed. by *Rabbi Elyse Goldstein*

For the first time, women rabbis provide a commentary on the entire Torah. More than 25 years after the first woman was ordained a rabbi in America, women have an impressive group of spiritual role models that they never had before. Here, in a week-by-week format, these inspiring teachers bring their rich perspectives to bear on the biblical text. A perfect gift for others, or for yourself. 6 x 9, 496 pp, HC, ISBN 1-58023-076-8 **$34.95**

Bringing the Psalms to Life
How to Understand and Use the Book of Psalms by *Rabbi Daniel F. Polish*

Here, the most beloved—and least understood—of the books in the Bible comes alive. This simultaneously insightful and practical guide shows how the psalms address a myriad of spiritual issues in our lives: feeling abandoned, overcoming illness, dealing with anger, and more. 6 x 9, 208 pp, HC, ISBN 1-58023-077-6 **$21.95**

Stepping Stones to Jewish Spiritual Living: *Walking the Path Morning, Noon, and Night* by *Rabbi James L. Mirel* & *Karen Bonnell Werth*

Transforms our daily routine into sacred acts of mindfulness. Chapters are arranged according to the cycle of each day. "A wonderful, practical, and inspiring guidebook to gently bring the riches of Jewish practice into our busy, everyday lives. Highly recommended." —*Rabbi David A. Cooper.* 6 x 9, 240 pp, Quality PB, ISBN 1-58023-074-1 **$16.95**; HC, ISBN 1-58023-003-2 **$21.95**

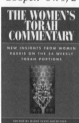 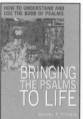  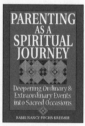 

Parenting As a Spiritual Journey:
Deepening Ordinary & Extraordinary Events into Sacred Occasions
by Rabbi Nancy Fuchs-Kreimer 6 x 9, 224 pp, Quality PB, ISBN 1-58023-016-4 **$16.95**

The Year Mom Got Religion: *One Woman's Midlife Journey into Judaism*
by Lee Meyerhoff Hendler 6 x 9, 208 pp, Quality PB, ISBN 1-58023-070-9 **$15.95**;
HC, ISBN 1-58023-000-8 **$19.95**

Moses—The Prince, the Prophet: *His Life, Legend & Message for Our Lives*
by Rabbi Levi Meier, Ph.D. 6 x 9, 224 pp, Quality PB, ISBN 1-58023-069-5 **$16.95**;
HC, ISBN 1-58023-013-X **$23.95**

Ancient Secrets: *Using the Stories of the Bible to Improve Our Everyday Lives*
by Rabbi Levi Meier, Ph.D. 5½ x 8½, 288 pp, Quality PB, ISBN 1-58023-064-4 **$16.95**

Or phone, fax or mail to: **JEWISH LIGHTS Publishing**
Sunset Farm Offices, Route 4 • P.O. Box 237 • Woodstock, Vermont 05091
Tel: (802) 457-4000 • Fax: (802) 457-4004 • www.jewishlights.com
Credit card orders: (800) 962-4544 (9AM–5PM ET Monday–Friday)
Generous discounts on quantity orders. SATISFACTION GUARANTEED. Prices subject to change.

Spirituality

My People's Prayer Book: *Traditional Prayers, Modern Commentaries*
Ed. by *Dr. Lawrence A. Hoffman*

This momentous, critically-acclaimed series is truly a people's prayer book, one that provides a diverse and exciting commentary to the traditional liturgy. It will help modern men and women find new wisdom and guidance in Jewish prayer, and bring liturgy into their lives. Each book includes Hebrew text, modern translation, and commentaries *from all perspectives* of the Jewish world. Vol. 1—*The Sh'ma and Its Blessings,* 7 x 10, 168 pp, HC, ISBN 1-879045-79-6 **$23.95**
Vol. 2—*The Amidah,* 7 x 10, 240 pp, HC, ISBN 1-879045-80-X **$23.95**
Vol. 3—*P'sukei D'zimrah* (Morning Psalms), 7 x 10, 240 pp, HC, ISBN 1-879045-81-8 **$23.95**
Vol. 4—*Seder K'riyat Hatorah* (Shabbat Torah Service), 7 x 10, 240 pp, ISBN 1-879045-82-6 **$23.95**

Voices from Genesis: *Guiding Us through the Stages of Life*
by *Dr. Norman J. Cohen*

In a brilliant blending of modern *midrash* (finding contemporary meaning from biblical texts) and the life stages of Erik Erikson's developmental psychology, the characters of Genesis come alive to give us insights for our own journeys. 6 x 9, 192 pp, HC, ISBN 1-879045-75-3 **$21.95**

  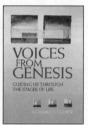 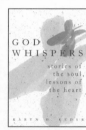 

God Whispers: *Stories of the Soul, Lessons of the Heart*
by Rabbi Karyn D. Kedar 6 x 9, 176 pp, Quality PB, ISBN 1-58023-088-1 **$15.95**; HC, ISBN 1-58023-023-7 **$19.95**

Being God's Partner: *How to Find the Hidden Link Between Spirituality and Your Work*
by Rabbi Jeffrey K. Salkin; Intro. by Norman Lear AWARD WINNER!
6 x 9, 192 pp, Quality PB, ISBN 1-879045-65-6 **$16.95**; HC, ISBN 1-879045-37-0 **$19.95**

ReVisions: *Seeing Torah through a Feminist Lens* AWARD WINNER!
by Rabbi Elyse Goldstein 5½ x 8½, 208 pp, HC, ISBN 1-58023-047-4 **$19.95**

Soul Judaism: *Dancing with God into a New Era*
by Rabbi Wayne Dosick 5½ x 8½, 304 pp, Quality PB, ISBN 1-58023-053-9 **$16.95**

Finding Joy: *A Practical Spiritual Guide to Happiness* AWARD WINNER!
by Rabbi Dannel I. Schwartz with Mark Hass
6 x 9, 192 pp, Quality PB, ISBN 1-58023-009-1 **$14.95**; HC, ISBN 1-879045-53-2 **$19.95**

The Empty Chair: *Finding Hope and Joy—*
Timeless Wisdom from a Hasidic Master, Rebbe Nachman of Breslov AWARD WINNER!
Adapted by Moshe Mykoff and the Breslov Research Institute
4 x 6, 128 pp, Deluxe PB, 2-color text, ISBN 1-879045-67-2 **$9.95**

The Gentle Weapon: *Prayers for Everyday and Not-So-Everyday Moments*
Adapted from the Wisdom of Rebbe Nachman of Breslov by Moshe Mykoff and
S. C. Mizrahi, with the Breslov Research Institute
4 x 6, 144 pp, Deluxe PB, 2-color text, ISBN 1-58023-022-9 **$9.95**

"Who Is a Jew?" *Conversations, Not Conclusions* by Meryl Hyman
6 x 9, 272 pp, Quality PB, ISBN 1-58023-052-0 **$16.95**; HC, ISBN 1-879045-76-1 **$23.95**

Spirituality & More

These Are the Words: *A Vocabulary of Jewish Spiritual Life*
by *Arthur Green*

What are the most essential ideas, concepts and terms that an educated person needs to know about Judaism? From *Adonai* (My Lord) to *zekhut* (merit), this enlightening and entertaining journey through Judaism teaches us the 149 core Hebrew words that constitute the basic vocabulary of Jewish spiritual life. 6 x 9, 304 pp, HC, ISBN 1-58023-024-5 **$21.95**

The Enneagram and Kabbalah: *Reading Your Soul*
by *Rabbi Howard A. Addison*

Combines two of the most powerful maps of consciousness known to humanity—The Tree of Life (the *Sefirot*) from the Jewish mystical tradition of *Kabbalah*, and the nine-pointed Enneagram—and shows how, together, they can provide a powerful tool for self-knowledge, critique, and transformation. 6 x 9, 176 pp, Quality PB, ISBN 1-58023-001-6 **$15.95**

Embracing the Covenant
Converts to Judaism Talk About Why & How
Ed. and with Intros. by *Rabbi Allan L. Berkowitz* and *Patti Moskovitz*

Through personal experiences of 20 converts to Judaism, this book illuminates reasons for converting, the quest for a satisfying spirituality, the appeal of the Jewish tradition and how conversion has changed lives—the convert's, and the lives of those close to them. 6 x 9, 192 pp, Quality PB, ISBN 1-879045-50-8 **$15.95**

Shared Dreams: *Martin Luther King, Jr. and the Jewish Community*
by Rabbi Marc Schneier; Preface by Martin Luther King III
6 x 9, 240 pp, HC, ISBN 1-58023-062-8 **$24.95**

Mystery Midrash: *An Anthology of Jewish Mystery & Detective Fiction*
Ed. by Lawrence W. Raphael; Preface by Joel Siegel, ABC's *Good Morning America*
6 x 9, 304 pp, Quality PB, ISBN 1-58023-055-5 **$16.95**

The Jewish Gardening Cookbook: *Growing Plants & Cooking for Holidays & Festivals*
by Michael Brown 6 x 9, 224 pp, HC, Illus., ISBN 1-58023-004-0 **$21.95**

Wandering Stars: *An Anthology of Jewish Fantasy & Science Fiction* Ed. by Jack Dann; Intro. by Isaac Asimov 6 x 9, 272 pp, Quality PB, ISBN 1-58023-005-9 **$16.95**

More Wandering Stars
An Anthology of Outstanding Stories of Jewish Fantasy and Science Fiction
Ed. by Jack Dann; Intro. by Isaac Asimov 6 x 9, 192 pp, Quality PB, ISBN 1-58023-063-6 **$16.95**

A Heart of Wisdom: *Making the Jewish Journey from Midlife through the Elder Years*
Ed. by Susan Berrin; Foreword by Harold Kushner
6 x 9, 384 pp, Quality PB, ISBN 1-58023-051-2 **$18.95**; HC, ISBN 1-879045-73-7 **$24.95**

Sacred Intentions: *Daily Inspiration to Strengthen the Spirit, Based on Jewish Wisdom*
by Rabbi Kerry M. Olitzky and Rabbi Lori Forman
4½ x 6½, 448 pp, Quality PB, ISBN 1-58023-061-X **$15.95**

Spirituality—The Kushner Series

Honey from the Rock, Special Anniversary Edition
An Introduction to Jewish Mysticism
by *Lawrence Kushner*

An insightful and absorbing introduction to the ten gates of Jewish mysticism and how it applies to daily life. "The easiest introduction to Jewish mysticism you can read."
6 x 9, 176 pp, Quality PB, ISBN 1-58023-073-3 **$15.95**

Eyes Remade for Wonder
The Way of Jewish Mysticism and Sacred Living
A Lawrence Kushner Reader

Intro. by *Thomas Moore*

Whether you are new to Kushner or a devoted fan, you'll find inspiration here. With samplings from each of Kushner's works, and a generous amount of new material, this book is to be read and reread, each time discovering deeper layers of meaning in our lives.
6 x 9, 240 pp, Quality PB, ISBN 1-58023-042-3 **$16.95**; HC, ISBN 1-58023-014-8 **$23.95**

Invisible Lines of Connection
Sacred Stories of the Ordinary
by *Lawrence Kushner* **AWARD WINNER!**

Through his everyday encounters with family, friends, colleagues and strangers, Kushner takes us deeply into our lives, finding flashes of spiritual insight in the process.
6 x 9, 160 pp, Quality PB, ISBN 1-879045-98-2 **$15.95**; HC, ISBN 1-879045-52-4 **$21.95**

The Book of Letters
A Mystical Hebrew Alphabet **AWARD WINNER!**
by Lawrence Kushner
Popular HC Edition, 6 x 9, 80 pp, 2-color text, ISBN 1-879045-00-1 **$24.95**; *Deluxe Gift Edition,* 9 x 12, 80 pp, HC, 2-color text, ornamentation, slipcase, ISBN 1-879045-01-X **$79.95**; *Collector's Limited Edition,* 9 x 12, 80 pp, HC, gold-embossed pages, hand-assembled slipcase. With silkscreened print. Limited to 500 signed and numbered copies, ISBN 1-879045-04-4 **$349.00**

The Book of Words
Talking Spiritual Life, Living Spiritual Talk **AWARD WINNER!**
by Lawrence Kushner   6 x 9, 160 pp, Quality PB, 2-color text, ISBN 1-58023-020-2 **$16.95**; 152 pp, HC, ISBN 1-879045-35-4 **$21.95**

God Was in This Place & I, i Did Not Know
Finding Self, Spirituality & Ultimate Meaning
by Lawrence Kushner   6 x 9, 192 pp, Quality PB, ISBN 1-879045-33-8 **$16.95**

The River of Light: *Jewish Mystical Awareness*
by Lawrence Kushner   6 x 9, 192 pp, Quality PB, ISBN 1-879045-03-6 **$14.95**

Life Cycle & Holidays

How to Be a Perfect Stranger, In 2 Volumes
A Guide to Etiquette in Other People's Religious Ceremonies
Ed. by *Stuart M. Matlins* & *Arthur J. Magida* AWARD WINNER!

What will happen? What do I do? What do I wear? What do I say? What should I avoid doing, wearing, saying? What are their basic beliefs? Should I bring a gift? In question-and-answer format, *How to Be a Perfect Stranger* explains the rituals and celebrations of America's major religions/denominations, helping an interested guest to feel comfortable, participate to the fullest extent possible, and avoid violating anyone's religious principles. It is not a guide to theology, nor is it presented from the perspective of any particular faith.

Vol. 1: *America's Largest Faiths,* 6 x 9, 432 pp, HC, ISBN 1-879045-39-7 **$24.95**
Vol. 2: *Other Faiths in America,* 6 x 9, 416 pp, HC, ISBN 1-879045-63-X **$24.95**

Putting God on the Guest List, 2nd Ed.
How to Reclaim the Spiritual Meaning of Your Child's Bar or Bat Mitzvah
by *Rabbi Jeffrey K. Salkin* AWARD WINNER!

The expanded, updated, revised edition of today's most influential book (over 60,000 copies in print) about finding core spiritual values in American Jewry's most misunderstood ceremony.
6 x 9, 224 pp, Quality PB, ISBN 1-879045-59-1 **$16.95**; HC, ISBN 1-879045-58-3 **$24.95**

For Kids—Putting God on Your Guest List
How to Claim the Spiritual Meaning of Your Bar or Bat Mitzvah
by Rabbi Jeffrey K. Salkin 6 x 9, 144 pp, Quality PB, ISBN 1-58023-015-6 **$14.95**

Bar/Bat Mitzvah Basics
A Practical Family Guide to Coming of Age Together
Ed. by Cantor Helen Leneman 6 x 9, 240 pp, Quality PB, ISBN 1-879045-54-0 **$16.95**;
HC, ISBN 1-879045-51-6 **$24.95**

The New Jewish Baby Book AWARD WINNER!
Names, Ceremonies, & Customs—A Guide for Today's Families
by Anita Diamant 6 x 9, 336 pp, Quality PB, ISBN 1-879045-28-1 **$16.95**

Hanukkah: The Art of Jewish Living
by Dr. Ron Wolfson 7 x 9, 192 pp, Quality PB, Illus., ISBN 1-879045-97-4 **$16.95**

The Shabbat Seder: The Art of Jewish Living
by Dr. Ron Wolfson 7 x 9, 272 pp, Quality PB, Illus., ISBN 1-879045-90-7 **$16.95**
Also available are these helpful companions to *The Shabbat Seder*: Booklet of the Blessings and Songs, ISBN 1-879045-91-5 **$5.00**; Audiocassette of the Blessings, DN03 **$6.00**; Teacher's Guide, ISBN 1-879045-92-3 **$4.95**

The Passover Seder: The Art of Jewish Living
by Dr. Ron Wolfson 7 x 9, 352 pp, Quality PB, Illus., ISBN 1-879045-93-1 **$16.95**
Also available are these helpful companions to *The Passover Seder*: Passover Workbook, ISBN 1-879045-94-X **$6.95**; Audiocassette of the Blessings, DN04 **$6.00**; Teacher's Guide, ISBN 1-879045-95-8 **$4.95**

Life Cycle

Jewish Paths toward Healing and Wholeness
A Personal Guide to Dealing with Suffering
by *Rabbi Kerry M. Olitzky*; Foreword by *Debbie Friedman*

"Why me?" Why do we suffer? How can we heal? Grounded in the spiritual traditions of Judaism, this book provides healing rituals, psalms and prayers that help readers initiate a dialogue with God, to guide them along the complicated path of healing and wholeness.
6 x 9, 192 pp, Quality PB, ISBN 1-58023-068-7 **$15.95**

Mourning & Mitzvah: *A Guided Journal for Walking the Mourner's Path through Grief to Healing*
by *Anne Brener, L.C.S.W.*; Foreword by *Rabbi Jack Riemer*; Intro. by *Rabbi William Cutter*

For those who mourn a death, for those who would help them, for those who face a loss of any kind, Brener teaches us the power and strength available to us in the fully experienced mourning process. 7½ x 9, 288 pp, Quality PB, ISBN 1-879045-23-0 **$19.95**

Tears of Sorrow, Seeds of Hope
A Jewish Spiritual Companion for Infertility and Pregnancy Loss
by *Rabbi Nina Beth Cardin*

A spiritual companion that enables us to mourn infertility, a lost pregnancy, or a stillbirth within the prayers, rituals, and meditations of Judaism. By drawing on the texts of tradition, it creates readings and rites of mourning, and through them provides a wellspring of compassion, solace—and hope. 6 x 9, 192 pp, HC, ISBN 1-58023-017-2 **$19.95**

Lifecycles
V. 1: *Jewish Women on Life Passages & Personal Milestones* AWARD WINNER!
Ed. and with Intros. by Rabbi Debra Orenstein
V. 2: *Jewish Women on Biblical Themes in Contemporary Life* AWARD WINNER!
Ed. and with Intros. by Rabbi Debra Orenstein and Rabbi Jane Rachel Litman
V. 1: 6 x 9, 480 pp, Quality PB, ISBN 1-58023-018-0 **$19.95**; HC, ISBN 1-879045-14-1 **$24.95**
V. 2: 6 x 9, 464 pp, Quality PB, ISBN 1-58023-019-9 **$19.95**; HC, ISBN 1-879045-15-X **$24.95**

Grief in Our Seasons: *A Mourner's Kaddish Companion*
by Rabbi Kerry M. Olitzky 4½ x 6½, 448 pp, Quality PB, ISBN 1-879045-55-9 **$15.95**

A Time to Mourn, A Time to Comfort: *A Guide to Jewish Bereavement and Comfort*
by Dr. Ron Wolfson 7 x 9, 336 pp, Quality PB, ISBN 1-879045-96-6 **$16.95**

When a Grandparent Dies
A Kid's Own Remembering Workbook for Dealing with Shiva and the Year Beyond
by Nechama Liss-Levinson, Ph.D.
8 x 10, 48 pp, HC, Illus., 2-color text, ISBN 1-879045-44-3 **$15.95**

So That Your Values Live On: *Ethical Wills & How to Prepare Them*
Ed. by Rabbi Jack Riemer & Professor Nathaniel Stampfer
6 x 9, 272 pp, Quality PB, ISBN 1-879045-34-6 **$17.95**

Theology/Philosophy

Torah of the Earth: *Exploring 4,000 Years of Ecology in Jewish Thought*
In 2 Volumes Ed. by *Rabbi Arthur Waskow*

Major new resource offering us an invaluable key to understanding the intersection of ecology and Judaism. Leading scholars provide us with a guided tour of ecological thought from four major Jewish viewpoints. Vol. 1: *Biblical Israel & Rabbinic Judaism,* 6 x 9, 272 pp, Quality PB, ISBN 1-58023-086-5 **$19.95**; Vol. 2: *Zionism & Eco-Judaism,* 6 x 9, 336 pp, Quality PB, ISBN 1-58023-087-3 **$19.95**

Broken Tablets: *Restoring the Ten Commandments and Ourselves*
Ed. by *Rabbi Rachel S. Mikva;* Intro. by *Rabbi Lawrence Kushner;*
Afterword by *Rabbi Arnold Jacob Wolf* **AWARD WINNER!**

Twelve outstanding spiritual leaders each share profound and personal thoughts about these biblical commands and why they have such a special hold on us.
6 x 9, 192 pp, HC, ISBN 1-58023-066-0 **$21.95**

Evolving Halakhah: *A Progressive Approach to Traditional Jewish Law*
by *Rabbi Dr. Moshe Zemer*

Innovative and provocative, this book affirms the system of traditional Jewish law, *halakhah,* as flexible enough to accommodate the changing realities of each generation. It shows that the traditional framework for understanding the Torah's commandments can be the living heart of Jewish life for all Jews. 6 x 9, 480 pp, HC, ISBN 1-58023-002-4 **$40.00**

God & the Big Bang
Discovering Harmony Between Science & Spirituality AWARD WINNER!
by Daniel C. Matt
6 x 9, 216 pp, Quality PB, ISBN 1-879045-89-3 **$16.95**; HC, ISBN 1-879045-48-6 **$21.95**

Israel—A Spiritual Travel Guide AWARD WINNER!
A Companion for the Modern Jewish Pilgrim
by Rabbi Lawrence A. Hoffman 4¾ x 10, 256 pp, Quality PB, ISBN 1-879045-56-7 **$18.95**

Godwrestling—Round 2: *Ancient Wisdom, Future Paths* AWARD WINNER!
by Rabbi Arthur Waskow
6 x 9, 352 pp, Quality PB, ISBN 1-879045-72-9 **$18.95**; HC, ISBN 1-879045-45-1 **$23.95**

Ecology & the Jewish Spirit: *Where Nature & the Sacred Meet* Ed. and with Intros. by
Ellen Bernstein 6 x 9, 288 pp, Quality PB, ISBN 1-58023-082-2 **$16.95**;
HC, ISBN 1-879045-88-5 **$23.95**

Israel: *An Echo of Eternity* by Abraham Joshua Heschel; New Intro. by
Dr. Susannah Heschel 5½ x 8, 272 pp, Quality PB, ISBN 1-879045-70-2 **$18.95**

The Earth Is the Lord's: *The Inner World of the Jew in Eastern Europe*
by Abraham Joshua Heschel 5½ x 8, 112 pp, Quality PB, ISBN 1-879045-42-7 **$13.95**

A Passion for Truth: *Despair and Hope in Hasidism* by Abraham Joshua Heschel
5½ x 8, 352 pp, Quality PB, ISBN 1-879045-41-9 **$18.95**

Theology/Philosophy

A Heart of Many Rooms
Celebrating the Many Voices within Judaism
by *Dr. David Hartman* AWARD WINNER!

Named a *Publishers Weekly* "Best Book of the Year." Addresses the spiritual and theological questions that face all Jews and all people today. From the perspective of traditional Judaism, Hartman shows that commitment to both Jewish tradition and to pluralism can create understanding between people of different religious convictions.
6 x 9, 352 pp, HC, ISBN 1-58023-048-2 **$24.95**

A Living Covenant: *The Innovative Spirit in Traditional Judaism*
by *Dr. David Hartman* AWARD WINNER!

Winner, National Jewish Book Award. Hartman reveals a Judaism grounded in covenant—a relational framework—informed by the metaphor of marital love rather than that of parent-child dependency. 6 x 9, 368 pp, Quality PB, ISBN 1-58023-011-3 **$18.95**

The Death of Death: *Resurrection and Immortality in Jewish Thought*
by *Dr. Neil Gillman* AWARD WINNER!

Does death end life, or is it the passage from one stage of life to another? This National Jewish Book Award Finalist explores the original and compelling argument that Judaism, a religion often thought to pay little attention to the afterlife, not only offers us rich ideas on the subject—but delivers a deathblow to death itself. 6 x 9, 336 pp, Quality PB, ISBN 1-58023-081-4 **$18.95**; HC, ISBN 1-879045-61-3 **$23.95**

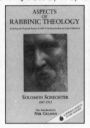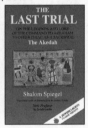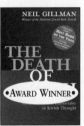

Aspects of Rabbinic Theology by Solomon Schechter; New Intro. by Dr. Neil Gillman
6 x 9, 448 pp, Quality PB, ISBN 1-879045-24-9 **$19.95**

The Last Trial: *On the Legends and Lore of the Command to Abraham to Offer Isaac as a Sacrifice* by Shalom Spiegel; New Intro. by Judah Goldin
6 x 9, 208 pp, Quality PB, ISBN 1-879045-29-X **$17.95**

Judaism and Modern Man: *An Interpretation of Jewish Religion* by Will Herberg; New Intro. by Dr. Neil Gillman 5½ x 8½, 336 pp, Quality PB, ISBN 1-879045-87-7 **$18.95**

Seeking the Path to Life AWARD WINNER!
Theological Meditations on God and the Nature of People, Love, Life and Death
by Rabbi Ira F. Stone
6 x 9, 160 pp, Quality PB, ISBN 1-879045-47-8 **$14.95**; HC, ISBN 1-879045-17-6 **$19.95**

The Spirit of Renewal: *Finding Faith after the Holocaust* AWARD WINNER!
by Rabbi Edward Feld
6 x 9, 224 pp, Quality PB, ISBN 1-879045-40-0 **$16.95**

Tormented Master: *The Life and Spiritual Quest of Rabbi Nahman of Bratslav*
by Dr. Arthur Green
6 x 9, 416 pp, Quality PB, ISBN 1-879045-11-7 **$18.95**

Your Word Is Fire: *The Hasidic Masters on Contemplative Prayer*
Ed. and Trans. with a New Introduction by Dr. Arthur Green and Dr. Barry W. Holtz
6 x 9, 160 pp, Quality PB, ISBN 1-879045-25-7 **$14.95**

Children's Spirituality

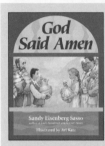

God Said Amen
by *Sandy Eisenberg Sasso*
Full-color illus. by *Avi Katz*

For ages 4 & up

MULTICULTURAL, NONDENOMINATIONAL, NONSECTARIAN

A warm and inspiring tale of two kingdoms: Midnight Kingdom is overflowing with water but has no oil to light its lamps; Desert Kingdom is blessed with oil but has no water to grow its gardens. The kingdoms' rulers ask God for help but are too stubborn to ask each other. It takes a minstrel, a pair of royal riding-birds and their young keepers, and a simple act of kindness to show that they need only reach out to each other to find God's answer to their prayers.

9 x 12, 32 pp, HC, Full-color illus., ISBN 1-58023-080-6 **$16.95**

For Heaven's Sake
by *Sandy Eisenberg Sasso*; Full-color illus. by *Kathryn Kunz Finney*

For ages 4 & up

MULTICULTURAL, NONDENOMINATIONAL, NONSECTARIAN

Everyone talked about heaven: "Thank heavens." "Heaven forbid." "For heaven's sake, Isaiah." But no one would say what heaven was or how to find it. So Isaiah decides to find out, by seeking answers from many different people. "This book is a reminder of how well Sandy Sasso knows the minds of children. But it may surprise—and delight—readers to find how well she knows us grown-ups too." —*Maria Harris*, National Consultant in Religious Education, and author of *Teaching and Religious Imagination* 9 x 12, 32 pp, HC, Full-color illus., ISBN 1-58023-054-7 **$16.95**

But God Remembered: Stories of Women from Creation to the Promised Land
by *Sandy Eisenberg Sasso*; Full-color illus. by *Bethanne Andersen*

For ages 8 & up

NONDENOMINATIONAL, NONSECTARIAN

A fascinating collection of four different stories of women only briefly mentioned in biblical tradition and religious texts. Award-winning author Sasso vibrantly brings to life courageous and strong women from ancient tradition; all teach important values through their actions and faith. "Exquisite. . . . A book of beauty, strength and spirituality." —*Association of Bible Teachers* 9 x 12, 32 pp, HC, Full-color illus., ISBN 1-879045-43-5 **$16.95**

God in Between
by *Sandy Eisenberg Sasso*; Full-color illus. by *Sally Sweetland*

For ages 4 & up

MULTICULTURAL, NONDENOMINATIONAL, NONSECTARIAN

If you wanted to find God, where would you look? A magical, mythical tale that teaches that God can be found where we are: within all of us and the relationships between us. "This happy and wondrous book takes our children on a sweet and holy journey into God's presence." —*Rabbi Wayne Dosick, Ph.D.*, author of *Golden Rules* and *Soul Judaism*
9 x 12, 32 pp, HC, Full-color illus., ISBN 1-879045-86-9 **$16.95**

Children's Spirituality

A Prayer for the Earth
The Story of Naamah, Noah's Wife
by *Sandy Eisenberg Sasso*
Full-color illus. by *Bethanne Andersen*

For ages 4 & up

NONDENOMINATIONAL, NONSECTARIAN

This new story, based on an ancient text, opens readers' religious imaginations to new ideas about the well-known story of the Flood. When God tells Noah to bring the animals of the world onto the ark, God also calls on Naamah, Noah's wife, to save each plant on Earth.

"A lovely tale. . . . Children of all ages should be drawn to this parable for our times."
—*Tomie dePaola*, artist/author of books for children
9 x 12, 32 pp, HC, Full-color illus., ISBN 1-879045-60-5 **$16.95**

The 11th Commandment: Wisdom from Our Children
by *The Children of America*

For all ages

MULTICULTURAL, NONDENOMINATIONAL, NONSECTARIAN

"If there were an Eleventh Commandment, what would it be?" Children of many religious denominations across America answer this question—in their own drawings and words. "A rare book of spiritual celebration for all people, of all ages, for all time."—*Bookviews*
8 x 10, 48 pp, HC, Full-color illus., ISBN 1-879045-46-X **$16.95**

Sharing Blessings: Children's Stories for Exploring the Spirit of the Jewish Holidays
by *Rahel Musleah* and *Rabbi Michael Klayman*
Full-color illus. by *Mary O'Keefe Young*

For ages 6 & up

What is the spiritual message of each of the Jewish holidays? How do we teach it to our children? Many books tell children about the historical significance and customs of the holidays. Now, through engaging, creative stories about one family's preparation, *Sharing Blessings* explores ways to get into the *spirit* of 13 different holidays. "Lighthearted, and yet thorough—allows all Jewish parents (even those with very little Jewish education) to introduce the spirit of our cherished holiday traditions." —*Shari Lewis*, creator and star of PBS' *Lamb Chop's Play-Along*
8½ x 11, 64 pp, HC, Full-color illus., ISBN 1-879045-71-0 **$18.95**

The Book of Miracles
A Young Person's Guide to Jewish Spiritual Awareness
by *Lawrence Kushner*

For ages 9 & up

From the miracle at the Red Sea to the miracle of waking up this morning, this intriguing book introduces kids to a way of everyday spiritual thinking to last a lifetime. Kushner, whose award-winning books have brought spirituality to life for countless adults, now shows young people how to use Judaism as a foundation on which to build their lives. "A well-written, easy to understand, very lovely guide to Jewish spirituality. I recommend it to all teens as a good read." —*Kimberly Kirberger*, co-author, *Chicken Soup for the Teenage Soul* 6 x 9, 96 pp, HC, 2-color illus., ISBN 1-879045-78-8 **$16.95**

Healing/Wellness/Recovery

Jewish Pastoral Care
A Practical Handbook from Traditional and Contemporary Sources
Ed. by *Rabbi Dayle A. Friedman*

This innovative resource builds on the classic foundations of pastoral care, enriching it with uniquely Jewish traditions and wisdom. Gives today's Jewish pastoral counselors practical guidelines based in the Jewish tradition. 6 x 9, 352 pp, HC, ISBN 1-58023-078-4 **$34.95** (Avail. Jan. 2001)

Healing of Soul, Healing of Body
Spiritual Leaders Unfold the Strength & Solace in Psalms
Ed. by *Rabbi Simkha Y. Weintraub, CSW,* for The National Center for Jewish Healing

A source of solace for those who are facing illness, as well as those who care for them. Provides a wellspring of strength with inspiring introductions and commentaries by eminent spiritual leaders reflecting all Jewish movements. 6 x 9, 128 pp, Quality PB, Illus., 2-color text, ISBN 1-879045-31-1 **$14.95**

Self, Struggle & Change: *Family Conflict Stories in Genesis and Their Healing Insights for Our Lives*
by *Dr. Norman J. Cohen*

How do I find wholeness in my life and in my family's life? Here a modern master of biblical interpretation brings us greater understanding of the ancient text and of ourselves in this intriguing re-telling of conflict between husband and wife, father and son, brothers and sisters. 6 x 9, 224 pp, Quality PB, ISBN 1-879045-66-4 **$16.95**; HC, ISBN 1-879045-19-2 **$21.95**

Twelve Jewish Steps to Recovery: *A Personal Guide to Turning from Alcoholism & Other Addictions . . . Drugs, Food, Gambling, Sex . . .* by Rabbi Kerry M. Olitzky & Stuart A. Copans, M.D. Preface by Abraham J. Twerski, M.D.; Intro. by Rabbi Sheldon Zimmerman; "Getting Help"by JACS Foundation 6 x 9, 144 pp, Quality PB, ISBN 1-879045-09-5 **$13.95**

One Hundred Blessings Every Day: *Daily Twelve Step Recovery Affirmations, Exercises for Personal Growth & Renewal Reflecting Seasons of the Jewish Year* by Rabbi Kerry M. Olitzky, with selected meditations prepared by Rabbi James Stone Goodman, Danny Siegel, and Gordon Tucker. Foreword by Rabbi Neil Gillman, The Jewish Theological Seminary of America; Afterword by Dr. Jay Holder, Director, Exodus Treatment Center 4½ x 6½, 432 pp, Quality PB, ISBN 1-879045-30-3 **$14.95**

Recovery from Codependence: *A Jewish Twelve Steps Guide to Healing Your Soul* by Rabbi Kerry M. Olitzky; Foreword by Marc Galanter, M.D., Director, Division of Alcoholism & Drug Abuse, NYU Medical Center; Afterword by Harriet Rossetto, Director, Gateways Beit T'shuvah 6 x 9, 160 pp, Quality PB, ISBN 1-879045-32-X **$13.95**; HC, ISBN 1-879045-27-3 **$21.95**

Renewed Each Day: *Daily Twelve Step Recovery Meditations Based on the Bible* by Rabbi Kerry M. Olitzky & Aaron Z. *Vol. I: Genesis & Exodus*; Intro. by Rabbi Michael A. Signer; Afterword by JACS Foundation. *Vol. II: Leviticus, Numbers and Deuteronomy*; Intro. by Sharon M. Strassfeld; Afterword by Rabbi Harold M. Schulweis
Vol. I: 6 x 9, 224 pp, Quality PB, ISBN 1-879045-12-5 **$14.95**
Vol. II: 6 x 9, 280 pp, Quality PB, ISBN 1-879045-13-3 **$14.95**

Jewish Meditation

Discovering Jewish Meditation
Instruction & Guidance for Learning an Ancient Spiritual Practice
by *Nan Fink Gefen*

Gives readers of any level of understanding the tools to learn the practice of Jewish meditation on your own, starting you on the path to a deep spiritual and personal connection to God and to greater insight about your life. 6 x 9, 208 pp, Quality PB, ISBN 1-58023-067-9 **$16.95**

Meditation from the Heart of Judaism: *Today's Teachers Share Their Practices, Techniques, and Faith*
Ed. by *Avram Davis*

A "how-to"guide for both beginning and experienced meditators, drawing on the wisdom of 22 masters of meditation who explain why and how they meditate. A detailed compendium of the experts' "best practices" offers advice and starting points. 6 x 9, 256 pp, Quality PB, ISBN 1-58023-049-0 **$16.95**; HC, ISBN 1-879045-77-X **$21.95**

The Way of Flame
A Guide to the Forgotten Mystical Tradition of Jewish Meditation
by *Avram Davis* 4½ x 8, 176 pp, Quality PB, ISBN 1-58023-060-1 **$15.95**

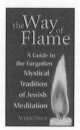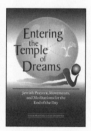

Entering the Temple of Dreams: *Jewish Prayers, Movements, and Meditations for the End of the Day* by *Tamar Frankiel* and *Judy Greenfeld*
Nighttime spirituality is much more than bedtime prayers! Here, you'll uncover deeper meaning to familiar nighttime prayers—and learn to combine the prayers with movements and meditations to enhance your physical and psychological well-being.
7 x 10, 192 pp, Illus., Quality PB, ISBN 1-58023-079-2 **$16.95**

Minding the Temple of the Soul: *Balancing Body, Mind, and Spirit through Traditional Jewish Prayer, Movement, and Meditation*
by *Tamar Frankiel* and *Judy Greenfeld*
This new spiritual approach to physical health introduces readers to a spiritual tradition that affirms the body and enables them to reconceive their bodies in a more positive light. Focuses on traditional Jewish prayers, with exercises, movements, and meditations. 7 x 10, 184 pp, Quality PB, Illus., ISBN 1-879045-64-8 **$16.95**; Audiotape of the Blessings, Movements and Meditations (60-min. cassette), JN01 **$9.95**; Videotape of the Movements and Meditations (46-min. VHS), S507 **$20.00**